AuthorHouse™
1663 Liberty Drive
Bloomington, IN 47403
www.authorhouse.com
Phone: 1-800-839-8640

© 2011 Joseph 'Reds' Perreira. All rights reserved.

No part of this book may be reproduced, stored in a retrieval system, or transmitted by any means without the written permission of the author.

First published by AuthorHouse   4/19/2011

ISBN: 978-1-4567-4168-6 (e)
ISBN: 978-1-4567-4169-3 (sc)

Printed in the United States of America

Any people depicted in stock imagery provided by Thinkstock are models, and such images are being used for illustrative purposes only. Certain stock imagery © Thinkstock.

This book is printed on acid-free paper.

Because of the dynamic nature of the Internet, any web addresses or links contained in this book may have changed since publication and may no longer be valid. The views expressed in this work are solely those of the author and do not necessarily reflect the views of the publisher, and the publisher hereby disclaims any responsibility for them.

Living My Dreams

BY

JOSEPH 'REDS' PERREIRA

with Katherine Atkinson

Foreword by Tony Cozier

Dedication

For my mother Claudia and my father John,
For my brothers and sisters and the friends who have been there for me.

JOSEPH PERREIRA
Bonne Terre
Gros Islet
St Lucia, W.I.
(758) 518-0136
E-mail: perreiraj@hotmail.com

Paperback: ISBN 978-976-8204-47-9
Copyright © 2010 by Joseph Perreira

Acknowledgements

I would like to express my sincere gratitude to the following private sector companies for making this book possible.

United Insurance Co. Ltd
Sandals Resort Hotels
LUCELEC
Ferrands Food Products Ltd
Scotiabank
FICS
Barons Foods
John Fernandes Group of Companies (Guyana)
Domino's Pizza (St Lucia)
M&C Group of Companies
1st National Bank
Prestige Autos
Joe Maxwell (SHELL)
Bay Gardens Resort
Visions St Lucia (Anthony Austin)
Stephen Paul
Glace Motors Limited
W.I.C.B.
LIME
J.E. Bergasse
LIAT

Foreword

WHEN "Reds" Perreira told me he was getting down to writing an autobiography and flattered me by asking that I would do the foreword, my first thoughts were that, while it would make fascinating reading, he would never be able to complete the story of such a full and varied life.

I should have known better; a few hundred thousand words should be a breeze for a boy from the Pomeroon in Guyana (in other words the back of beyond) who wasn't put off his dream of becoming a cricket commentator by the little matter of a serious stammer well into his teenaged years or who shook off the setback of a serious stroke when into his 50s to regain his strength and fervour and be again as active as he ever was.

These are just two instances that should make this book an inspiration to all those who seek to live their dreams, whatever their handicaps. Nor has "Reds" been simply a cricket commentator. Of course, it is the role through which he as become famous, and widely admired, wherever the game is played. But, as he relates, he has been closely involved in a variety of sports, either describing the play into the microphone, passing on knowledge as a coach, or organising tournaments from behind a desk.

He has become a true Caribbean man, covering West Indies cricket, living in his native Guyana, Barbados and, now, St Lucia and traversing the Windwards and Leewards on an almost daily basis in his years as Sports Co-ordinator of the Organisation of Eastern Caribbean States (OECS). I sense that his success in that position, along with his creation of the "Reds" Perreira Foundation in Guyana, gave him as much satisfaction as anything he has ever done – and he has done a lot. I know, as well, that he is more crestfallen than most at the rapid degeneration of West Indies cricket and the reasons for it. It has been in sharp contrast to its protracted era of excellence when he proudly reported on its triumphs from every corner of cricket's empire. Through more than 30 years, travelling the world together and following the ups and downs of West Indies teams, often as the only West Indian media men present, "Reds" has been a valued colleague and friend. We have shared many good times, if not all fit to be recorded in these pages. I never fail to marvel at his enthusiasm and his zest for life, traits that are certain to be obvious as he commits to print the story of living his dreams.

TONY COZIER
Barbados, October 2009

TABLE OF CONTENTS

1	My Pomeroon Life	5
2	Early Georgetown Years	10
3	A Caribbean Cricket Experience	15
4	Atlantic Crossing	19
5	Returning to Guyana	26
6	A Sad Return to England	29
7	Becoming a Real Broadcaster	32
8	A Fresh Start	36
9	The Broadcast Circuit	39
10	Down Under	43
11	Establishing Myself	48
12	A Cricket Revolution	50
13	Meeting the Legends	53
14	A Near Miss at Jonestown	56
15	My Involvement with Kerry Packer	59
16	Barbados	61
17	My Reputation on the Line	65
18	Last Years in Barbados	67
19	An Indian Odyssey	73
20	Moving to St Lucia	80
21	The OECS Years	86
22	A Life Changing Event	99
23	A Year in My Old Stomping Grounds	106
24	The St. Lucia Tourist Board Years	109
25	Amateur Boxing Years	116
26	World Cup Homecoming	124
27	Endings	128
28	Reflections	130

Appendices

Appendix I	The Reds Perreira Sport Foundation	133
Appendix II	For the Love of the Game: Commentators Who Made a Difference	135
Appendix III	Those Who Might Have Played	136
Appendix IV	Captain Hooper's Demise	138
Appendix V	Letters of Testimonial	139

A photograph of the author at age 10

Chapter 1

My Pomeroon Life

As I look back on my life, coming out of a very humble, rural Guyana country environment, and growing up on the bank of the Pomeroon River in the county of Essequibo, it would only be fair to say that I have been extremely fortunate. I have been able to overcome major handicaps, and what little I have been able to accomplish was very much against the odds. But I had dreams from very young of wanting to achieve, even knowing I did not really have the requirements to reach those heights I was dreaming of or thinking about.

I was born in 1939. A world away, war had started, and the cogs and wheels of conflict and industry whirred. But on a land grant on the Pomeroon River in the Essequibo, my parents, descended from Portuguese immigrants, were building a life that was far removed from all of that. The days' rhythms were dictated by the rise and set of the sun, the tides on the river and the seasons of planting and harvesting.

My father was a farmer. He had a small estate on the sweet side of the river; the salt side backed up on the Atlantic, but the sweet side savannah lands were fertile and very productive. He mainly grew coffee, oranges and avocados. My father was a serious man. He was the third generation of Portuguese immigrants who had come to Guyana to make their fortunes as indentured labourers after slavery was abolished. He was, I suppose, possessed of a single sense of purpose, which was to provide for his family above any other concern. Our land grant was called 'Now and Ever' which speaks to his commitment.

My mother was a warm counterpoint to my father's seriousness; she was affectionate and embracing. She didn't work outside of the home. I suppose when you are the wife of a farmer, there is no surprise at your having nine children. She devoted most of her life to our upbringing. When somebody was unwell she would go around with her Limacol or sugar water for energy. And later, when we lived in Georgetown, if there was an accident, she would be the first one in the street with her iodine, mercurochrome, and her bandages. My father relied on my mother very much for family matters and she would go out to look after business on his behalf. She was a very good communicator and a respected woman in her own right.

The season of my birth, I was later told, had been a particularly wet one. The rains were tremendous and the local midwife, concerned about complications, persuaded my mother to make the trek to Georgetown to deliver me. She made the twelve-hour journey by boat, train and bus to her sister's in Hadfield Street, Georgetown where I was born a few days later. That was how I came to be the only one of nine children to be born in the capital. Though I was born there, Georgetown would only be a distant reality for many years. I could not have anticipated how later it would play such an important role in my life. Until I was six years old all I was to know was country life on the Pomeroon and the river named for it which was an integral part of life growing up. When the tide was high you could almost lie in your bed and hear the river which was a different sound from when the tide was falling.

There is a kind of pureness about country life which is hard to explain to anyone who hails from the city. I grew up on the bank of a river. For the first six years of my life I knew nothing about city life; I knew nothing about street lights, about radio or airplanes and I only rarely ever saw a motor car. I was a country boy, a country bumpkin. We lived in a nicely designed wooden house on concrete stilts with Demerara windows made by indigenous carpenters. The windows and banisters were carved decoratively with the skill that was typical of country artisans. Life was simple, pure and very beautiful.

Our rural existence was one of plenty; while war measures and shortages plagued Georgetown, in the Pomeroon we were never without. We foraged for fruit which was in abundance, fished in the trenches and in the river, and cooked bread in a wood-fired oven. I remember that oven well. It was fashioned from a big coal pot and galvanised steel and we kept a wet bag over the top as a precaution against fire.

In the mornings we had a swim, cleaned ourselves using a cob of a corn and salt soap, and looked after our early morning preparation before heading off to school. Our drinking water we collected from the rains. We had a huge vat, from an old sugar plantation; it was a large metal vat over which my father had built a wooden roof, and the water poured into that. We drew from it with a bucket or drank from a goblet if we got up in the night. There was no toilet; there was an outhouse behind our home. Heaven help you if you woke up at two in the morning as a five or six year old and needed to go to the toilet. You would be looking to wake up your nearest brother or sister to follow you because it was pitch black outside and you did not relish the prospect of going out alone. We had been regaled with stories of mythical river creatures and the terrifying blood sucking higue.

But by day the river and the flood plains were our playground. I learned to swim almost as soon as I could walk. My older siblings put me on buoyant bamboo stalks to keep me afloat and I eventually learned to propel myself with strokes and kicks. In the early years life was about swimming, fishing, learning how to handle a boat, paddling on the river. I learned how to fish in the trenches and canals that ran off the Pomeroon through the estate. My older brother Desmond was a master; where I would be gratified with the modest catch of one, I would look over to see that he had landed eight. There was nothing like that to diminish my sense of accomplishment. Occasionally we would set a line heavy with expectation, to find our catch gone and a satisfied piranha on the hook. Piranhas were a constant threat but they tended to gather around the waterfront if you were careless enough to clean chicken or meat near the river. For the most part though, they avoided the paddling and boating activity.

The Gouveia's held the grant land across the river from us. It was a 200 yard crossing that took on immense proportions when we challenged each other to swim it. There was a real skill to the crossing. You had to be able to monitor the tide, catch it at its most neutral or you would find yourself well off the mark. But apart from the threat of the tides and the piranhas, what instilled a real fear in the younger of us was the huge, monstrous, metal trap, the Tarpon. The Tarpon was the steamer that plied the Pomeroon collecting produce and connecting us however vaguely, to Georgetown. I was not to appreciate that connection until much later. The Tarpon for me was the most frightening spectre, more so because it would cut its engines to coast the river and its sudden presence would be announced by an ominous wail that ricocheted across the water; we ran like hell down the main dam to the savannah lands, to re-emerge after the Tarpon had passed.

If we could not beat it, we would join it. Long summer days were spent devising every type of vessel that would float, however precariously, on the water. We would make sail boats with bamboo frames using flour bags for sails. Invariably they would not last terribly long, and often I was saddled with the task of bailing. You never set off without a calabash bowl for that very purpose and sometimes it would be your sole responsibility the whole day. Many of the games we played were about honing our skills on the water. I remember that we would deliberately sink our father's small corial, fill it with water and then test ourselves to see who could tread water, bail out the boat and then climb aboard without touching bottom.

We paddled to the first major town called Charity which was a couple of miles up river. There were a few motor cars in Charity, a large bus, cricket grounds, and a telephone in the police station that was big and voluptuous and when it rang you were totally astonished. On Saturdays we would go with my father who would have some business and we would wonder around in awe at the shops and roadside markets, the bustle in the post office. Charity was the centre of community activity and we looked forward to church every Sunday. Dressed in our best clothes, we clambered aboard my father's Hog Trough boat, and if we were lucky, we paddled with the tide, but sometimes, if the tide was against us, we'd have to leave early. We were well-dressed but wore no shoes. Those we carried, a soft shoe we called yatin made by Bata. (I suppose if the boat tipped, then you'd struggle to swim with shoes on, or perhaps my mother thought it was the best way to keep them clean). We would paddle, nicely dressed, with an eight cent piece pressed into our palms and we would look forward to being able to give that at collection. The church at Charity was a wooden Catholic church and after mass you would socialise. You would meet other people, cousins and family friends and sometimes on the way back from church you might stop in and they would serve something nice and maybe even have a little music and dancing. Though my father was often strict, it was at these occasions that he showed a little social flare and would enjoy dancing.

We danced a lot as a family. There were brothers and sisters and cousins enough to make up a good party. The music was provided by an old RCA gramophone which had these huge 78 records. Sometimes though, depending on the occasion, we would have a live contingent with mandolins and guitars. The main social thing in those days, other than parties and weddings and church events, was cricket. It's amazing how people learnt because there was no formal coaching, and no television or movies on cricket to learn from. People who had come from Georgetown, or those who had gone to visit Georgetown for a week or two, shared their skill and enthusiasm. Without any type of formal association, people would organise teams to play each other from different areas of the river.

In the Pomeroon cricket was not just a game, it was an institution. Allegiances and friendships as well as rivalries were formed around the sport; it was a mobilising force for people, a true reflection of our communities, a major social event. People came from all parts of the river, paddling, walking, getting there by outboard motor or by launch when there was a cricket match. There would be eating, drinking, laughing, and the meeting of friends.

Cricket matches normally culminated with a dance at the school hall, though as children, we mainly watched as the big people had a great time. My brothers and sisters and cousins would watch the festivities play out a rhythm on the wooden floors of the school hall, enveloped in the glow of the sole gas lamp. There was such an atmosphere of gaiety it was hard not to be enraptured by it. But where there was alcohol there was room for trouble, and at the end of the day some of the biggest fights could break out among people who over the years had been friends. Sometimes it was very funny. I remember very clearly once after a fight had broken out and chaos had taken over, the man who owned the gas lamp (he happened to be my uncle) got annoyed and packed up his gas lamp and left the astonished party in darkness. That was the end of the dance.

When the school hall was not serving as a venue for parties, it was packed full of children of all ages, the different classes divided only by chalkboard. School was a simple, humble government primary school, a walk along the river bank to Martindale, so named for my mother's father who was involved in the building of the school house. The school was presided over by Mr. Wilson who was afforded nothing but the greatest respect by the community. There was the bustle of industry with the chatter of students and pencil on slate, the strong authoritative voice of our teachers, and the choral recitations of our lessons. Though I was accustomed to the rules and strictness of my father's home I remember clearly being scolded by my aunt who taught me. The infraction escapes me now, but what remains is that sense of shock and betrayal that my own aunt should scold me. Our father expected that we should apply ourselves to our lessons; it would not do to displease him.

Though he placed great deal of emphasis on our school work we were not exempt from our share of chores around the estate. We had to feed the pigs, which in fact I liked doing. They ate with such gusto; seeing a pig eat is like watching the last supper. We fed them molasses, plantain and cassava. We had to make sure that the fowl pen was put up and that the occupants were secured, pick up firewood, and ensure there was fruit in the house. My mother had enough to do. We were interested in the reaping of cocoa because it was tasty and we took an interest in our father's coffee grinding. It would be picked and hulled and then we had to bag it and there was a great interest in the process and how the bags were stitched. He had built a coffee house for grinding using a stubborn five horsepower engine. I remember my brother Desmond sweating over it, trying for months to be able to start it. It required not just strength, but timing. There was a drying process with the cocoa with these big huge trays and sometimes you would have to push them and turn them over and make sure the sun dried them out. At night you had to make sure the mosquito nets were down and put under the mattresses, and that the lamps were lit and there was enough kerosene. By six o'clock our curtains would be down. The Pomeroon was mosquito-infested, and I hate to admit this, but we used DDT to fight off the mosquitoes. We would be in bed by eight unless there was moonlight. Then we would play games, chase each other in the fields behind the house, play catch up.

You were conscious of poisonous snakes, you heard stories about tigers, caimans and alligators, and sometimes you would have a glance of them but you grew up with no fear, you just believed that it would not happen. In a way, I suppose, we were fearless then. But even with the audacity that a childhood of relative freedom gave me, it was very early evident that I had a major stammering handicap. Around my family it was fine; my brothers and sisters understood. I was neither introverted, nor unhappy. In fact I was extremely outgoing and very happy-go-lucky, but I did have a stammering problem and that was to be a handicap that marked the first twenty odd years of my life, and which had a major effect on me. I struggled socially because I could not interact at simple parties and as I became older and we moved to Georgetown, it got worse.

Georgetown was such a distant concept growing up. We had a slight indication that there was a life beyond Charity. Charity was the road that led you towards Georgetown, a day's journey away, and when you saw that bus take off from Charity and head towards Anna Regina and eventually cross the Essequibo, you knew that there was another life somewhere. But there was never a rush. I never had any desire to go before my time. My father decided when we would go. That would be in 1945.

Chapter 2
The Early Georgetown Years

Though he was to maintain his grant in the Pomeroon for several years afterwards, my father had decided to establish a base in Georgetown. We moved by boat, a boat my father had built called "Joan Patsy" after my two sisters. Joan Patsy had two masts, a mainsail and a jib, and we had a 44 Kelvin diesel engine. The family packed all its worldly goods for a new life in Georgetown.

The journey took us sixteen hours. I remember my father had an arrangement with a taxi driver in a black Vauxhall who took us to a house at the corner of Russell and Howes Streets where we all lived until we started to depart for other parts of the world. When we arrived, I slept on old newspapers on the floor with my brothers while the women in my family slept on the mattress. The next day my father invested in bunk beds. It was in those very bunk beds years later that I would begin to imagine a world beyond the boundaries of Georgetown, a world that came to me by rediffusion radio that my brother Desmond I listened to well after bedtime, huddled close with the volume low so we wouldn't wake the house.

We were very much affected by what you would call modern life but we soon started to make our way and got our confidence when we got the hang of the city. I remember noticing the street lights, donkey carts, buses, and hearing about households that had telephones. We surely but slowly made friends with those people who lived near to us and our confidence grew after a while. I remember especially Mr. Nichols, the vulcaniser down the road who played accordion and had seventeen children, and Mr. Figureoa, the shoemaker with whom I spent a lot of time in his workshop watching him sew with a big cobbler's needle. He was the repairman of the area. Mr. Ferreira just up the street had a donkey cart which he used for his business, carrying loads. His donkey, Bing, was washed and brushed every day and Mr. Ferreira kept flowers in his bridle and fed him molasses and oats. Every night at six o'clock - I could set my clock to it - he would promenade him to the stables down the street.

The Perreiras, unrelated to our family, lived down the street and had a salt goods shop and they sold groceries like pig tails and pickles; I played a lot of cricket in the yard with their son Eugene who was a great player. The Smalls lived across the street from us. Mr. Small ran a dispensary that we called the doctor shop, and he had a daughter who turned out to be a very good basketball player. Further up Russell Street lived Glendon Gibbs, family of Lance Gibbs, who went on to play for then British Guiana and the West Indies and in one test match against Australia. In Broad Street, fairly close by was Rudy Franklin, a very promising off spinner who played one match for British Guiana. In Howes Street lived the Allsop family, a brilliant family who went on to achieve many things. I remember particularly their father who, dressed immaculately in white, rode out on his bicycle every morning. One of the Allsop sons went on to write a dictionary of West Indian English usage. Mr. Green ran a drugstore in a neighbouring area and his son Hamilton who went to St Stanislaus was a good 100 yard runner and later in life became Prime Minister of Guyana and Mayor of Georgetown. Across the road was the Beckles family; Mr. Beckles was a fire officer and his son Lennox became a Guyanese boxing star and a world rated boxer. The Moses family lived next door on Howes Street and the son Ranni Moses became an outstanding footballer and played on the right wing. A corner and a half away on Russell Street lived Olga Lopes-Seale, the brilliant Guyanese broadcaster who ran the Children's Needy Fund programme each Christmas on Radio Demerara and who assisted thousands of families. She later migrated to Barbados and carried out the same programme on Voice of Barbados with equal success and received the title of Dame through the Barbados Government for her contribution to society.

With the help of relatives who had already moved to the city we were eventually placed in our first school, the Brickdam Roman Catholic School which was run by the nuns with Sister Ursula at the helm. I remember particularly Sister Corinne who took an interest in me and picked me for the May procession. But primary school was a challenge to me, particularly as someone who stammered. I had a major problem trying to get through my schooling at a time when the world was not sympathetic to handicaps. Invariably I would be afraid if the teacher were to ask me a question during any given class, but funnily enough, I didn't do too badly in the actual examinations. I was quite bright; I got to fifth standard in primary school, moving up every year by passing my exams and finishing in the top ten. The recurring problem however, was my inability to be able to speak fluently and confidently.

I have very clear memories of spending nights lying in my bunk bed imagining a world in which I spoke without stammering. My mother indulged my fantasies as I pretended to be a sports commentator. She allowed me to lie in bed to do my imaginary commentaries on cricket coming from Australia, and from England at Lords. She would allow me to do imaginary boxing commentaries coming from Madison Square Garden and I would have imaginary fights between Jersey Joe Walcott and Joe Louis, "the Brown Bomber", Sugar Ray Robinson and Floyd Patterson, and all sorts of make-believe international football matches between England and Brazil – calling all the names and doing play by play. She probably understood that fantasy was important and she allowed it. She didn't tell me to shut up, or that I was crazy.

My family was tremendously supportive, but the stammering began to bother me in another arena. As I got older there were parties that were not just family. I'd find myself in a situation where I would want to ask a young lady to dance and the whole process was painful because sometimes by the time I got the words out, 'May I have this dance?' it would take about three minutes, and the Nat King Cole tune that was playing would have ended and I had missed the opportunity.

I left primary school before I finished sixth standard and planned to continue my secondary education. My brother Desmond had gone to St Stanislaus College, one of the leading colleges, and had done very well, but I failed the admission exam so I went to Central High School. I found subjects like geometry and algebra very difficult, very alien. I think my chances of doing well at secondary school were restricted and it was decided that I should go into the working world. By the age of sixteen I was a working man.

I took my first job as a clerical assistant with the British Guiana Credit Corporation. My brother-in-law, Bertie Leung, who was married to my sister Joan, knew the head of the corporation Mr. Yap, and there was an opening for a clerk. This was a lending institution for housing and farming and I would be an all rounder; I would go to the treasury, file documents, go to lawyers offices, pay bills, and handle the overall running of the office making sure we had stamps and that the cheques were written. For all this I was paid the princely sum of fifty dollars a month, which was a huge amount of money for a sixteen year old. The cost of living was nothing compared with today and I didn't have to make any contribution to the home, so the fifty dollars was for buying personal things and my social life.

I think I spent most of that on the little cricket teams I had started to organise. I had a team called Berwick CC that I started with Terry Hudson. We shared a birthday and were partners in crime. We had known each other for most of our lives, we both lived in Charlestown and we created a pitch between the stoop and the gate at his house, bowling from the street. We could not bowl too short because we would hit the wooden posts and inevitably smash a window, as did on occasion happen. We would make ourselves scarce until Terry's mother cooled off and then resume our game. In the case of rain, we had devised a board game using dice and would play an entire test match that way. That is how mad we were about sports.

Later, as Berwick, we functioned as a group that played football and cricket and we organised friendly competitions against other teams. I drew on groups of boys my age, some I knew from school. Organising tournaments meant finding umpires and securing the balls for the matches, organising practices and reserving the playing fields too. In a sense I started to develop some skills that would serve me later in life. But I wasn't thinking of that at the time. I did it because I enjoyed it. In fact my life then seemed pretty ideal. Work was flexible; I didn't keep regular nine to four hours because I was out and about for the corporation.

I rode a bicycle of which I was very proud around Georgetown. I had slowly started to make my way. It was at this time that I got my nickname "Reds". I had flaming red hair. There was a movie that came out called "The Redhead and the Cowboy", and Desmond Martins and his brother Terry started calling me "the redhead" which in the interest of expediency soon became Reds. As I started to get more and more involved in sport, the radio and newspapers dropped Joseph and added "Reds" so that I became known as "Reds" Perreira.

I established something of a name among the business community as a sport enthusiast so that sometimes in addition to making my business rounds I was also providing the scores and summaries of the latest cricket or football games to the various offices. There was in fact a man who was highly placed at the registry who played for the West Indies, Berkley Gaskin who had two test matches in 1948 and who later became a West Indies manager and selector. Every time I came to his office at the Deeds Registry I made sure I knew the score of the latest game because he would always say, 'Young Laddie, what's happening?' and I would be able to tell him, '60 for 2 at lunch', or whatever was happening. It was in fact a very pleasant job; it didn't suffocate my interests, but I never allowed my other activities to interfere with my responsibilities of my job.

In those years, cricket became something of an obsession for me. As early as 1947 I got a glimpse of George Headley the great West Indies batsman at Jamaica versus British Guiana, and I remember being able to get into Bourda to catch some of a Saturday test match in 1948. In 1951, I witnessed the Barbados versus British Guiana inter-colonial match during which Leslie White and Glendon Gibbs made the first class partnership of 390. And in 1953 India came to play. It was my first test match and a significant moment in my life. I was in the presence of the celebrated spinners Vinoo Mankad and Subash Gupte and outstanding batsman Vijay Hazare, the India captain who had that year achieved the distinction of scoring a century in each innings against the mighty Australia.

As a young teenager I spent the majority of my Saturdays and Sundays watching first class cricket at the major grounds in Georgetown and the major trial matches that were played to select the British Guiana team for inter-colonial matches. The selectors were mainly conservative, I felt, and were reluctanct to include new faces, especially in the batting department. The BG team had had a settled an opening pair in Leslie Wight and Glendon Gibbs but with an aging middle order. The fast bowling department was well served by Charlie Stayers and Pat Legall, with the spin department well covered by Norman Wight and Lance Gibbs.

I watched with a sense of sorrow, opening batsmen like Bud Lee and Horton Dolphin, while the middle order talent that could not make the side included the elegant Ossie Gibson, hard hitting Charlie Agard, and the classy Eddie Francisco and Joe Texeira. Guyana was blessed with many wicket keepers and therefore young Joe Hazelwood, despite his neatness with the gloves had no chance. Norman Rampath was a brilliant stroke maker who made runs at the first division level while Julian Archer, Ron Willock and Cecil Pilgrim, three young promising opening bowlers hardly came close to winning a national cap. Sadly Pilgrim was struck with rheumatic fever to end a very promising career. The reserved spin department for Guyana was also in good stock with Eddie French, Leslie Fernandes, Dowlat Ram and the tall off spinner, Sonny Abdool along with the clever left arm spinner Algie Soloman.

To this day, I can still see these men in white playing in the trial matched with good success, but as they played their moment of glory was the trial matches themselves. Some of these unheralded players are still alive and scattered all over the world and whenever possible I enjoy reminiscing about their days in the sun.

By the 1950s West Indies had started to emerge as a force to be reckoned with in cricket. Beating England in 1950 was a major breakthrough for the colonial Caribbean because that was the great success of Weekes, Worrell and Walcott, all of whom were later knighted for their contribution to the sport. This was the time of the early independence movement and the West Indies' success brought great confidence to the region. It made West Indians extremely proud and conscious of cricket because they had beaten the colonial masters at the game they had taught us. But we played in a different style with rhythm and panache and flair. With the introduction of shortwave radio I had started to become interested in commentary. It was not just getting scores. I had started to get attracted to the rhythm and flow of the game.

Guyana was no different from any British colony in the decade of the 50s as political leaders and trade unions fought big business and king sugar for better wages and conditions. As an eleven year old I was conscious through the media of the developing personalities that led the fight in this area. Hubert Critchlow, the father of trade unions was a household name and Cheddi Jagan was campaigning for a seat in the executive council, and I was conscious of the Enmore martyrs, shot down in a confrontation with the police in 1948. The Peoples Progressive Party (PPP) was formed in 1950 and headed by Jagan and Forbes Burnham, but sport was not very far away from my mind as the USA shocked the world in that same year when they beat England in the Football World Cup 1-0 in Brazil. The West Indies were off to Australia in 1951 and inter-colonial cricket held the spotlight at Bourda.

I was in fourth standard at primary school (St. Mary's RC) when it was announced that King George the sixth had died. With adult suffrage instituted the 1953 elections saw the PPP being swept to victory only to be in office for 133 days before the constitution was suspended by the British Government on the basis that they were too left wing. British troops were sent in and arrived with fixed bayonets which surprised the population somewhat as there were no riots or major disturbances to be quelled.

The Australians came in 1955 and they were very strong and really over ran us. I watched the Guyana test match and I saw the great fast bowlers Keith Miller and Ray Lindwall for the first time. Keith Miller was a great all rounder and it was the first time I saw a fast bowler bowl a leg spin. It wasn't typical for a fast bowler and it was my first view of a slow ball. Miller was such a gigantic man of six foot four and he ran up to Bruce Pairadeau and bowled a leg spinner. It may have been my first sighting of a fast bowler delivering a slow ball. The great memory of that game against British Guiana was the budding star Rohan Kanhai scoring a magnificent hundred against the tourists. Keith Miller was a personality that even the Australians could not control but they were in fact a great team. It was a series in which the late Clyde Walcott really distinguished himself with scores of 108, 126, 110, 81, 83, 155 and 110.

In 1956 the West Indies toured New Zealand to be followed by the tour of England in 1957. In 1959 I saw the West Indies Track and Field Championships in British Guiana and through the hardworking efforts of Trinidadian football official Eric James, the West Indies team toured England made up of players from Trinidad and Tobago, British Guiana, Jamaica and Barbados.

My goal keeping days with Juventus Football Team, Guyana, 1961

Chapter 3

A Caribbean Cricket Experience

It was in 1956 that I really caught the bug. With the help of my father, I went to Trinidad for my first real taste of regional cricket. It was the team selection for the 1957 tour of England and players I had only heard about on the British colonial rediffusion radio were to be there. I was now in working life and I had some degree of flexibility to make that decision. I was going to a West Indian event. It was not the done thing; I might have been the only spectator from another country. The others would have been cricket officials who were there with their teams. Such was my interest that I thought to myself: it is not crossing the English channel and I will survive.

I caught an inter-island boat, owned by the British sugar company Bookers that carried rice and timber to Trinidad. It cost fifteen dollars to be on the deck and the journey took 16 to 20 hours. I would not say that I was exactly a great passenger; I was very sea sick and very happy to disembark once we got there. I lived quietly within my budget and I did not do a lot of socialising, returning to the guest house across the road at the end of the day.

The 1956 trials gave me a wider perspective on all the players. For the first time I was seeing Wesley Hall, the young fast bowler, and Roy Gilchrist and Gerry Alexander, who later became the West Indies wicket-keeping captain. I saw Jackie Hendricks who later became a West Indies player, manager and selector; I was again able to see Sonny Ramadhin and Alfred Valentine, along with an emerging Rohan Kanhai, and an inspiring Gary Sobers, Basil Butcher and Lance Gibbs. I was able to watch all the talent of the West Indies including some from the Windward Islands. There was a wicket keeper called Alec Reid who should have gone to England in '57 but wasn't chosen, and Frank Mason of St Vincent, who bowled very quickly but his place went to Wesley Hall. I think they thought he was young enough and would have more opportunities to play.

I saw a young Trinidadian batsman called Hammond Furlong cry his eyes out when the names were announced on the final afternoon and he wasn't selected, though he would later have an opportunity. They had instead chosen Andy Ganteaume. I felt that a bad deal was done against him because in 1948, in his only test match, he made a hundred against England but was never picked again; you felt that the selectors made a make-up selection but at that time Ganteaume was forty and might have been considered past his best. It was a very moving thing to see a man so disappointed and so passionate when he was not on the side.

I stayed opposite The Oval in a little guest house on Tragarete Road and I think I paid the princely sum of about twenty dollars for staying there. I was able to just walk across the road to watch the trials. Mr. Sonny Murray, related to Lance and Deryck Murray, (I didn't know then) gave me a pass so I could come into the old colonial oval. I sat in the pavilion and watched each day of play for three weeks. I could not have passed my time any more ideally. The Joseph Charles Solo soft drink factory was nearby and I was able to meet the family, as the two sons were cricket enthusiasts. I remember being very impressed by a tour of the place, seeing the soft drink production line as bottles came out on conveyer belts out of the washer and then were filled and corked. The Steel Band yard where I spent most of my evenings was nearby, and if I was not there, I was at the Rocky Cinema catching the latest film or roaming the stands around the Oval enticed by the aromas of delicious cheap eats like roti and arepas. I did go down into Port of Spain on the off days and saw the huge Salvatori Building just off Marine Square later to be called Independence Square and then the Brian Lara Promenade.

When the trials were done I made my way by boat back to Georgetown, really enlightened and enthused that I had seen the people who were knocking at the door for a trip to England in 1957. I returned to Guyana with a new fervour and interest in all things sport. It did not matter the discipline, or the arena, I followed it. That is how I came to follow hockey. In 1958 the Trinidadian and Jamaican women's hockey teams came to Guyana to play the West Indies Women's Hockey Championship. It was a significant regional event because Jamaica so infrequently came to the Eastern Caribbean. I knew all the Guyanese players, so naturally I attended. Little did I know how that choice would once again initiate a series of decisions that would set me on a trajectory I never could have anticipated.

A group of us all went to watch the matches. We knew the Guyanese women on the team and appreciated the skill of what Jamaica and Trinidad had to offer. I met a Jamaican hockey player called Winsome Marrett and we got to know each other quite well. She was intrigued by my passion for sport and impressed, I suppose, that I had some sense of the history of Jamaica and its sporting achievements. She invited me to visit her in Jamaica for Christmas that year. That was not something that was common then, a young Jamaican lady inviting somebody from the other end of the Caribbean to come and spend Christmas with her family at the end of 1958. I was delighted for the opportunity.

I applied for my vacation and received a verbal consent, so I arranged for free passage on a rice boat with a company called John Fernandes, the agents for the boat. Just before the trip I was told that my leave was not granted, but by then all the arrangements were in place and I had told this young lady that I was coming. I had a choice to make. I remember sitting down at my desk contemplating this dilemma. But the decision was clear. I resigned from my job and went to Jamaica.

I spent five days as the only passenger on the boat. It was me and the wide expanse of the Caribbean Sea. I saw snatches of life, of other vessels passing and I was fortunate that I didn't handle the sea travel too badly. The crew was extremely pleasant and the captain was from the Cayman Islands, Captain Scott. I remember he had a toothache for the five days I was onboard, but he would not go to a dentist even when we went to Trinidad to pick up bitumen, asphalt and oil. He just drank to numb the pain. The chef on board had a very effeminate manner and would introduce his coffee cakes and ackee with flourish. It was my first experience of meeting a person who was homosexual. I was totally unaware that there were gay people in the world; it was a foreign concept to me.

We arrived in Jamaica after five days at sea and the boat stopped at St Ann's Bay at the eastern tip of Jamaica. There were to be many stops before we would arrive at Kingston and it would have meant another two days on the boat. I realised that if I got off at St Ann's Bay I could probably make it to Kingston by land in less time. The boat could not come alongside the wharf so two men rowed me ashore. When they spoke I could not understand a word, it was my first introduction to Jamaican patois. Now, of course, I can understand it but then I felt they could have been speaking French. When we made it ashore I handed my passport to customs and I was waved in without hassle. The security man asked if I was from BG and I said yes. He said, 'Well look it, there's a young man', he spoke to me in broad patois, 'There's a young man who just came to look for you and him soon come back.' I was perplexed, nobody knew I was coming and I insisted it could not have been me. He said, 'Well look; aren't you from BG? Look man, a young man came to look for you, him soon come back, him have a sports car.' Lo and behold ten minutes later a young man appeared in a sports car. He introduced himself a friend of Winsome Marrett and explained that she'd asked him to meet me.

She must have had a crystal ball to just guess that I would come off at St Ann's. Her friend took me to a great house on an estate, arranged lunch and I fell asleep in this huge four poster bed that they gave me. Winsome drove over in her Mini Minor and from St Ann's Bay I went to Kingston. There I was in Halfway Tree at 12 Hill View Avenue and I met the Marrett family. Her mother was very serious, like most mothers; the father was very nice, he worked at Bata and was keen on football and the sister Joy was friendly.

I spent Christmas with a lot of personalities, and met many of the sporting fraternity including the respected Foggy Burrowes who published a magazine called Sport Life. At the end of Christmas it was time to come home on another boat that was going back to Guyana. We went back via Nicaragua which was then under the dictatorial rule of Somoza. We went through Curacao and then came to Port of Spain and then back to British Guiana and that was the end of my sojourn to Jamaica. It was in fact almost the start of a love affair with the place and many more trips to Jamaica.

The following year, my brother gave me $200 and I went on a charter flight to the next regional hockey tournament. I was still in contact with Winsome and had the pleasure of meeting the well known Jamaican Prime Minister from the colonial days, Sir Alexander Bustamante. He came to Sabina Park and I was introduced to this towering character. He had fought in the Spanish American War and he was in fact the leader of his party and then Prime Minister. He was one of many Prime Ministers that I was going to meet later in life.

When I came back to B.G it was with a renewed energy and to a new job which continued to allow me the flexibility I needed to be able to pursue my sporting interests. Mr. Burrowes, a contact whom I had met in Jamaica published Sports Life Magazine and I sold it in British Guiana working on a commission basis. Even then I recognised that the magazine's focus was not broad enough to appeal to a wider Caribbean audience. Though the content was heavily Jamaican I was able to go to the major Guyanese sports clubs and institutions to sell subscriptions to the publication. That was my job until I went to Suriname.

I had convinced my father to allow me to go to neighbouring Suriname where football and basketball were very well organised. I spent a year there living with a Guyanese family and being attached to football coach Andre Kampervene, who was later executed during a coup, and Ludwig de Saunders who was the head basketball coach and had trained in Europe. I had early on recognised that I would myself never be a great footballer. I was five foot eight and a half and no great athlete, but that time I spent in Suriname improved my knowledge of both football and basketball in that short period. During that time I was able to see Holland play Suriname in Paramaribo plus the national basketball team entertaining overseas countries. Where I did not speak the language of Suriname, I spoke the language of sport and this was a great learning time for me. The language barrier was not insurmountable. Suriname was a very musical country and I was a good dancer; I danced a good merengue. Suriname was my first experience of a culture so entirely different from my own. The food was different and I certainly enjoyed all of the Indonesian food and Suriname creole food. I was trying to make my way, attend the sessions I had to attend and take full advantage of every moment of being there. I returned to B.G prepared to take up the mantle of a well-paying job at Coca Cola, at that time engaged in a mighty struggle against Pepsi.

As a guest player with the Bookers Cricket Team in England, 1963

Chapter 4
The Atlantic Crossing

In late March in 1962 I came home from a day's work for the Coca-Cola Company; my father informed me that he was sending my siblings Monica, Yvonne and Brian to school in England, and that I was to accompany them. It was an opportunity I seized and one which was to have a profound impact on my life. On April seventh, we boarded a charter and landed at Gatwick which was not more than an air strip then. My uncle, who had gone on to England several years before, met us there and within a matter of weeks of my father's decision, I found myself immersed in a new life and a totally different culture.

In those early days I saw to my brothers and sisters and that they were settled in school. Once I was satisfied that they were okay, I gravitated towards some friends who lived in the Bayswater area: Vic Gonsalves, Lloyd and Cutie Ferreira, Ivor De Freitas and Johnny Lee who were residing at 34 Leicester Square. In the basement there was a Grenadian girl called Margaret Evans and a Trinidadian called Carol Dupres, whilst in the choice flat which had a balcony overlooking the road there was a trio of crazy Australians, Kevin Mac Intyre, Bob Campbell and Eric Angus, who got up to all sorts of pranks but they were, as they say, fair dinkum Aussies.

Kevin, the shortest of the trio was the most outrageous, as he would meet me coming out of the busy Queen's Way tube station. As persons made their way home in the evening he would shout out, looking directly at me, asking whether I had gotten off the assault charge or how the divorce went. The entire station would stop for a moment and stare. The Aussies would have raving parties and the next morning they would be so broke they would have to collect bottles to get a refund at the Prince Alfred Pub. They ran a travel agency from their bedsitter flat called Viking Travel and since they worked with Air Italia and British European Airways, they were able to divert bookings through their travel agency and earn substantial commissions. Those of us who lived in the building were well briefed to answer the phone as, 'Bayswater 2158 this is Viking Travel can I help you?' And invariably they'd ask for Kevin or Bob. It all came to an end one day when some clients decided to visit Viking Travel to find it was a bedsitter. Their friends in the building had to act very quickly, saying Kevin was sick and they entertained them in our own flat until they decided to leave. The incident was just too close for comfort, coupled with the fact that the airlines they were working with would have soon started to query the existence of Viking Travel.

It was a period of adventures and misadventures. We had fun, even if money was always in short supply, we knew how to make it stretch. We used to manipulate the heater to get away without paying by picking the lock of the gas metre, passing the shilling through two or three times then allowing it to drop, gaining a lot of gas credit. When the landlord came to clear the metres he would find some money, though he might have been surprised to find we were not using as much gas as he would have expected. Some Trinidadian friends did this but they never allowed the shilling to fall and the landlord on a surprise visit caught them and they had to write an I.O.U note for three pounds. In spite of our tricks to keep warm, being cold was just a way of life.

I remember once almost freezing to death. It was during my time at Selfridges, when I was working pre-season with Chelsea. I had gone to a Chelsea versus Manchester United football match at Stanford Bridge and the expected crowd was 56,000. Eager to get there before the crowds, I made my way there too quickly and found myself in the grounds at one p.m. for a three o'clock kick off. A tea bar not too far away saved my life – I was virtually frozen. At the end of the game at five o'clock on a Saturday afternoon, I could hardly walk down from the terraces and had to use the metal bars that stopped the crowds from crushing each other to support myself.

There was a strong Caribbean community in London at the time and everyone knew of some relative or friend who had gone on before. I was lucky to be able to initially share a flat with this group of friends, a situation which was good for me because I was able to learn the ropes. England was a strange new world; these friends taught me how to get about London, using the buses and underground, knowing the connections. Luckily in those days, not like today, there were fewer underground lines. It was not that it was hard but it was new and it helped having friends who could show you how things worked. It was in fact a very exciting time to be in London. There was the unique sensation of going to places for the first time and meeting old friends. In spite of the cold and some of the challenges, I was enjoying being in England and had quite the vibrant social life. I remember going to Barclays Bank on Moscow Road every two weeks and finding my account shrinking and shrinking. My friend Johnny Lee and I had found there was no lime anymore, that everyone had gone to work, that we were the only two enjoying the good life and it was time to get our acts together and find a job.

Johnny Lee joined me in the job search and we both got employed in a factory in Harsden, which produced metres that recorded how much power you burnt in a factory or home.

My job was to do daily checks on the outbound metres and track their shipment. I had once again become a working person. Now I was up early to catch the seven ten Central line. If you didn't catch it, it was trouble because you could not possibly make it to work on time otherwise. The discipline I had set aside for those first few months had to come back into focus. Of course I managed to get myself involved in sports. I ran the factory football team which played other factories in the area. It was good for the morale of the group.

Johnny Lee and I were working for fourteen pounds per week. It was good to have money coming in again. Our first commitment was paying the rent. That was a cardinal rule: pay the rent and own the key. Rent was about three pounds. Then you put aside something for transportation. Every pay day we bought the basics: coffee, tea, bread, cheese, milk, the basic breakfast type stuff. Some evenings I might bring in a pork chop or a steak, but I never had the luxury of having an apartment with a freezer or fridge. I ate very few vegetables, except for special treat of the three and six Chinese meal of roast pork and vegetables that we had at a restaurant on Westbourne Grove. It was a low budget establishment that had no frills in its service. You learned to order by number from the menu which we knew by heart and when the waiter brought your meal, he would virtually slide it on to the table and force you to grab it – you had to serve yourself water and cutlery, and no tip was expected. But the food was excellent, healthy and balanced. Eating out in London was fairly expensive and one had to choose such events sparingly. By Thursday of each week, when supplies were getting low and we were flat broke, we would head over to the apartment of a New Zealand girl named Jan Sterling. Jan was always able to produce toast and baked beans with a little bit of cheese and some coffee. Jan was the great saviour and pleasant company and my one regret was that I never got her home address in New Zealand, a country which I had the pleasure of visiting three times later in life.

We found little shortcuts to make our money stretch. For example, you quickly learned how to outsmart the London underground. My system was to buy a threepence ticket in the morning though I was at Queensway station, and that I would use in the afternoon for my return trip to the adjoining Notting Hill station. I would simply say, with two hundred people behind me pushing through the barriers, 'nine pence' at my North Acton station. There was no way that that ticket collector was going to stop to query my station of origin.

I did have the embarrassment, when I first came up, of being caught out. The Dixieland Steel Band was playing down in Porchester Hall and some friends and I decided that we would go and hear them. I was a rookie in England so I had been led. We had no ticket and when we got to Lancaster Gate, there was a Barbadian underground collector. 'Four three please' we asked, meaning four tickets at thruppence and gave him the equivalent. The Barbadian asked us how we had come down to the platform to test whether in fact we had paid the correct fare. Stumped by the question we said by escalator. In very dry Barbadian humour the ticket collector said, 'Well they must have built that last night'. The embarrassment came over me in particular because I was new, and he did not allow us to go. People kept passing us and we were held up at this ticket office. When he had held us good and proper

– after fifteen minutes – he decided to let us go saying, 'Go ahead, have this ride on London Transport'. I pledged to myself from then that that would not happen to me again. If I called a station I had to know whether you came to the platform by stairs, lift or escalator.

On longer trips out of London you would not take the chance. Though very often you would go unmolested, there were checks along the route. But if for instance you had paid a pound and then arrived at your destination to find the collector away from his post and a sign saying 'gone to tea', with a heavy heart and hand you put your ticket down because there was no point keeping it now.

At Bayswater Station there was a female Jamaican collector I used to chat with who had migrated in the early fifties. I had often talked with her about Jamaica and she got to know me by face. I would greet her and she me, and if I had come from Paris and said thruppence, she would believe me, wish me a happy day, and so it worked out in my favour.

When I first came to England I looked forward to seeing the famous English landmarks like their test grounds, Westminster Abbey, Buckingham Palace, but never did I expect to see up close and personal, The Old Bailey.

On a cold Friday afternoon in the middle of February 1963 my friend Curtis Pierre, leader of the Dixieland steel band from Trinidad, a well respected orchestra that had played for the Queen and had represented the Trinidad Tourist Board in Europe, was arrested 20 yards from his front door at Inverness Terrace. Curtis, who was by far the neatest dresser you can imagine, was stopped by two British police men and arrested and taken down to the Paddington Station where he was charged for loitering, peering into cars with intention to steal, possession of a firearm and using the said firearm to resist arrest . The magistrate felt that this was a serious charge and ruled that the case must be tried by the central criminal court at the Old Bailey.

Curtis was refused bail and spent the night in a cell at Paddington, next to an Irish prostitute who spent the night cursing the police, the Queen, the Pope, white people, niggers and everything that moved. His one permitted telephone call brought a swarm of friends: Vernon Delima, Desmond Allum, Tony Jacelon, Rolland Delima and members of the Dixieland steel band. He also got a visit from Pat Castagne, famous for writing the Trinidad & Tobago National Anthem and with an association with the Trinidad embassy, who informed him that the Trinidad & Tobago Government would post his bail. On Curtis' release he wrote to the Trinidad Prime Minister Dr Eric Williams whose government offered to pay for his defence team. It was made up of Queens' Counsel Dingle Foot, a former UK Attorney General, and a Trinidad born lawyer Jeff Barth.

On a visit to Dusseldorf in Germany, Curtis had bought what he thought was a starting pistol to scare off the German teddy boys. He was in fact walking to my home to give me the pistol since I was involved in the world of sport, as he felt he had no use for it, when he was arrested.

In order to prepare for the trial night we gathered in the Bayswater to do a night court rehearsal with Vernon Delima and Curtis acting as judge. When the trial started Curtis was fortunate on two counts: the Trinidad Government had flown his wife to London and the former West Indies cricketer Learie Constantine, then High Commissioner to Britain attended the trial.

The evidence given by the British police portrayed Curtis as a poor steel band leader with no one to take him in. In fact, the defence was able to produce a bank statement from Barclays which showed him to be very solvent. They also claimed that they saw him 26 yards away trying to get into cars while visibility that afternoon was recorded at 15 yards. The advice given to Curtis by Learie Constantine was not to laugh or smile during the proceedings because it would be perceived as arrogance. I was his key witness and after giving evidence for the defence the jury retired.

When they came back to announce the verdict, Curtis was found not guilty of being in possession of a firearm, but on the second count of resisting arrest with a firearm he was found guilty. The judge intervened to tell the jury that he was surprised that after being found not guilty on the first count, that Curtis could be found guilty on count two when he was not in possession of a firearm.

The judge's ruling was that Curtis Pierre should pay 20 pounds or spend 40 days in jail which his defence team was extremely happy with. Curtis however, appealed in order to clear his name totally, but lost the case. The whole experience was a bad nightmare for this talented musician and shortly after he packed up and headed back to Port of Spain; I lost my job for taking too many days off to give evidence at the trial but was happy that Curtis did not face a ten or fifteen year sentence.

I worked at Harsden for about a year. I did not make a lot of money but I made sure that I managed my budget and I worked overtime just to ensure that I could enjoy some of the benefits of living in London. I would get reasonably priced tickets to go and see Ella Fitzgerald, Johnny Mathis and Oscar Peterson, the famous black Canadian pianist. I was able to take in concerts of Sammy Davis and Sarah Vaughn. Fridays were great, you half hoped you would not be called in for overtime but there was the conflict of wanting the time off but needing the money.

On Saturday afternoons Grandstand Sports was on TV if you were not attending them live. I found a jazz pub in Earl's Court called the Colhern and whether it was winter, spring, summer or fall, every Sunday morning I would get up and go down because they would have live jazz and calypso. There was the added incentive of buying a cheap roti and that would be your lunch. At two o'clock when that was over there was always somebody who would have a lime, an after lunch party somewhere, so your social plan would sometimes develop as you went along. Sundays were hard, the cycle was starting again. On Sunday nights we watched the BBC or ITV news. The reality of the week, the hard grind ahead was especially difficult in the winter months. The shared experience with a group of West Indians made it bearable.

My West Indian connection really was through the West Indies Student Centre where I later became sports coordinator. My initial attraction was that I could meet Caribbean people, some of whom I had known from before. I could read the Caribbean papers, and eat Caribbean food. There was a Barbadian cook, Ms. Prescott, who provided dinner at the Student Centre. For 'three and six' there was a three course meal starting with a soup (split peas or black eye), a main dish and a sweet (more often bread custard). They also had the luxury of a warm shower which was a welcome reprieve from the horrors of the tub. The Student Centre, run by Barbadian warden Pony Hyman who lived on the premises, was an interesting institution, and an important germination ground for Caribbean leadership. There were a lot of students who later emerged to play significant roles in Caribbean life. Tom Adams, who frequented the Centre, later became Prime Minister of Barbados, and Antigua's Lester Bird who was also reading law later became his country's PM. David Simmons, now the Chief Justice in Barbados was at the Student Centre and he was in fact the captain of the cricket team and a great trumpet player. Dennis Patterson who was from Guyana went back and became the Chief Evaluation Officer and an outstanding Secretary to the West Indies Table Tennis Association. David Klautky studied engineering and went back to Guyana to establish a very successful engineering company. He incidentally also played football for a team I ran in Guyana. Richard and Hugh Small, Jamaican brothers, did law and returned to Jamaica. To this day they still have a respected legal practice. The later Attorney General in Antigua, Gerry Watt was also at the Student Centre. He had been our fast bowler.

The Student Centre was an important institution, a way to stay in touch while you went about the English way of life. We played cricket together and kept up with what was going on in Caribbean life. As Sports Coordinator it was challenging to motivate everyone under the constraints of English weather. On those cold days it was a struggle to get eleven people to line up to make up a side. We had a table tennis team and I ran tournaments in the basement of the Student Centre as much as possible.

My love for sport was not shared to the same degree by the rest of my friends. If I wanted to see England versus Brazil at Wembley Stadium, maybe Johnny Lee might come with me; on occasion he might come with me to watch Arsenal play at home at Highbury. If I wanted to go to cricket I would probably end up going alone. I did not want to drag my friends to things that they did not naturally gravitate towards. It was easier to go see a Johnny Mathis or an Ella Fitzgerald or a Sammy Davis; that was not a hard sell. You had to be very much in love with sport because there was a physical effort to get to where you were going, as well as the challenge of budgeting for the ticket.

I also ran a basketball team called the Guyana Celtics with the help of an English man who lived in Bromley Kent, John Blundell, whom I met by accident at a basketball tournament. He helped to get us into the South of England League. I was able to pull together guys from Guyana mainly but we had guys from Trinidad playing. It demanded a lot of sacrifice. Getting to games was difficult.

The summer of my first working year I went hitchhiking in Europe. A lot of my friends were going on tours to Europe on organised pre-paid plans but that did not interest me. I did not like the idea of spending a hundred pounds for a week on the continent. I set off alone across to Holland from Dover and over into Belgium. Hitchhiking was a challenge. Nobody was obligated to pick you up; you had to present yourself well if you wanted to get a ride.

I learned that you do not hitchhike with too many people because that was a handicap. I stayed in youth hostels and met lots of people. It was much more rewarding as a personal challenge and I certainly saw more natural life in Europe by going that way instead of on a planned tour. I remember on my first hitchhiking trip a Belgian business man stopped and gave me a ride. We got on so well he took me all over Brussels, bought me a meal and then dropped me off at the youth hostel. I suppose he took his time because he had never met anyone from the Caribbean before.

That adventure reinvigorated me and I was happy to return to the real demands of my London life. I took on a variety of jobs over time including a stint at the Heinz 57 factory and at the famous Selfridges Department Store on Oxford Street. That job enabled me to enjoy enormous flexibility and the opportunity to indulge my sports fascination. My boss, Mr. Burst at Selfridges, allowed me time off. When there was a game, I was given the opportunity to have an observer attachment with the Chelsea and Arsenal teams. For two months during the pre-season, three times a week I would clock in at nine o'clock and then head off to the training grounds, at Stanford Bridge for Chelsea and the Highbury grounds for Arsenal. I'd be back by three o'clock to work the rest of the afternoon.

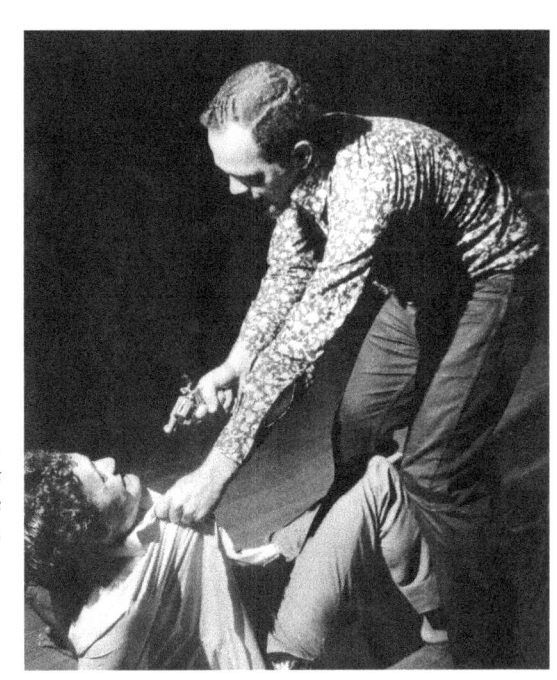

My solitary acting role in the play, "Hello Out There", about to shoot Ken Corsbie, at the Theatre Guild, Guyana

Fundraising project for the University of Guyana, 1970

Chapter 5
Returning to Guyana

I decided to return to Guyana in 1965, earlier than I had planned but keen to impart the knowledge I had gained at the pre-season opportunities at Chelsea and Arsenal, along with the general experience in organising for the Student Centre. I was ready to put down roots in the place for which I had such nostalgia. I had never intended to stay in England. I threw myself into activity, becoming involved with the second division football team Santos, a YMCA operated team with a reputation for losing their tempers, a team that fell short of its potential because of a host of distractions.

The team was in Albouystown, an economically depressed area of Georgetown; the expectations for their success were low. I was ready for the challenge and became involved in re-organising the club structure, ensuring that the administration was separate from the playing arm. We eventually made it to the first division but were suspended, unfairly I thought, because our secretary had failed to attend three executive meetings. I decided to launch a one-man demonstration, reluctant to implicate the players and jeopardise their ability to play any further. I took my advocacy quite seriously; I felt that the team's performance was handicapped by factors that had little to do with ability, and set about to start addressing those issues. Through a social development drive I assisted the players in securing employment, and invited speakers to come and share their wisdom with the team. I spent my evenings and weekends visiting with the players and their families, enlisting their relatives to support their endeavour, making sure they attended practices, kept decent hours and had clean uniforms. It was thrilling to watch the community mobilised.

All the work bore fruit. Santos enjoyed great success and won the League Cup tournament in the first division. The attention such an accomplishment garnered propelled me into the limelight and I was invited to coach the Under 23 National Team. I immediately began to implement some of the modern coaching techniques that I had picked up in England with Arsenal and Chelsea. We played a short passing game high in technique. The team toured Guyana playing exhibition matches and culminating in a victory against the hitherto unstoppable British Army team whose players had UK club experience from the various third and second divisions. This success brought me to the attention of the powers that be and I was appointed national coach to the National Football Team. Sadly though, my powers were limited; in fact on reflection I found I was severely compromised and this eventually led to my being banned from the sport for life, a predicament which left me embarrassed and temporarily defeated.

When the selections were being made for a side to represent Guyana in Barbados in a three way tournament involving Barbados, Guyana and Trinidad I was not included in the selection committee. This did not sit well with me and my instinct was to withdraw, but B.L Crombie, then the premier sports commentator in British Guiana and someone I respected, urged me to be patient, to accept the responsibility and bide my time. I decided to take his advice and accept the post of coach, but later found out that the football association had ruled that I was not to have a say in the starting eleven.

Looking back on it I realise now I was in a very weak position and that undermined me as coach. I tried hard under the circumstances in the practices and blackboard sessions but the fact was that we performed poorly. We missed many goal scoring opportunities and could not muster a strong defence, simply because I would have gone for a younger, more mobile defence had I had a say in the initial selection. Kensington was a bigger ground as opposed to the Georgetown Football Club grounds, the main playing venue in British Guiana. Morale was low as we were not winning so I made a decision to cancel our final practice session. My reasoning was that the players were not in a good mental state and that a rest would be more beneficial than a practice at that juncture, and I was hoping for an improved performance in our last game against Trinidad. We should have been leading at least two-nil at half time, having missed many opportunities in the six yard box, but we did not perform in the same way in the second half and lost in the end to Trinidad by four goals to nil.

On return to Guyana the manager made his report to the association and based on his report I, and the team's captain Monty Hope (a Caribbean representative to England in 1959) were suspended for life from participation in any form of football. I was ignorant of the decision until it was public. I had been at a volleyball party at Lennie Shuffler's house when a friend brought in a copy of the Daily Chronicle. The front page bore the headline: *Reds Perreira Banned for Life*. The FA felt that I had no reason for cancelling the last practice session and held me accountable for the overall poor performance of the team which they had selected. Monty Hope's suspension was based on a report by the manager that he had refused to leave a reception put on for all the teams. In fact Hope was in conversation with the Barbados star Reggie Haynes at the time the manager announced we were leaving the reception, and might have spent another few minutes ending his conversation with his former Caribbean colleague before heading for the team bus, causing no major delay and in no way refusing to leave the venue. Monty Hope and I had no opportunity to appear before the FA to answer the allegations and I felt disillusioned and dejected by what had transpired.

At this point I decided to return to England. It was with a heavy heart that I drove to the airport in September of 1966. My brother Desmond drove me out and B.L Crombie felt so moved that he drove the twenty-three miles to Atkinson Airport to say goodbye and express his regrets.

Though I was to look back on that year with an overwhelming sense of disappointment, on reflection it was not a complete loss. I learned something about myself and resilience. I had also been home to witness Guyana's independence on May 26th 1966. I had gone to the flag raising ceremony and watched a friend, Desmond Roberts, then a Lieutenant in the army, raise the Golden Arrowhead over a new independent nation. The occasion was at the national park; it was a windy evening and that helped the new flag to billow over the landscape. Though there was the disappointment towards the end of my time in Guyana, I had in fact witnessed the dawn of a new Guyana.

A younger self at Kaiteur Falls, 1973

My one man protest against the Guyana F.A.

Chapter 6
A Sad Return to England

I returned to England as autumn set in, utterly despondent. I was not entirely sure what I wanted and the miserable weather did not help. I had to find a job and a place to live and this was not the best time as job and flat hunting were better in the earlier part of the year. I resumed my contact with the West Indies Student Centre and the friends who were still in London, while spending most of October, November and December watching the English first division and the international matches at Wembley.

I felt that I wanted to experience life in another European country and headed for Holland to visit an ex-girlfriend, Yolande Nijste. We had met in Lyon, France in 1964 where I had been some years before on a cultural festival when I was part of a West Indies Student Centre delegation. Though her family was welcoming and her home very comfortable, I was no happier there. She had taken the trouble to get me a job in an Amsterdam hotel; I felt it was too close to England. I had it fixed in my mind that I would set out again and that it should be to Denmark. On my last night in Amsterdam we went to see "Dr. Zhivago". The weather seemed mild as we got to the cinema but when the enjoyable movie was over we came out to find two feet of snow; the weather had changed for the worse in Holland. The next day, on February 8th, Yolande fixed me some salami sandwiches and off I set on an intrepid, albeit cold, adventure.

When you hitchhike, you learn to develop a personality that enables you to interact easily with people. In some cases, the people who picked you up did not speak English. I got a lift from the Dutch-German border with a truck that carried frozen goods. The man looked out to me from his window at the checkpoint and I yelled out, 'Copenhagen'. 'Yah, yah', he said and signalled to me, and I got in and he drove off onto the big autobahn. For the first fifteen or twenty minutes I talked, commenting on the journey and my adventures, but I realised after a while that he had said nothing. It suddenly occurred to me he did not speak English; he had given me the ride for companionship and to make sure that he did not fall asleep at the wheel. I did not want him to fall asleep either, so if I could not talk to him, I would sing. I sang every Sparrow song I knew, Harry Belafonte, Nat King Cole and Frank Sinatra. I made sure I made enough noise that he could drive through the night, alert.

At one point late in our journey, he gestured to a restaurant. We ordered a meal without conversation, finished eating and then went back to the cab. He indicated that we should nap for a while before continuing. When we woke up we drove on across the width of Germany to Pud Garten where we crossed by ferry into Denmark. On the ferry he was kind enough offer me a token which would get me a warm shower. It had been a long haul and that refreshed me. When we got into Denmark, we cleared customs and immigration and headed for the capital. About 23 km from Copenhagen, the driver pulled off the road and pointed to a cottage. It was February, 11th, very cold I remember; we had arrived at his home. His wife met us at the door invited me in. They had a nice wood fire and she offered me Danish pastries and tea. I had a book with a world map and I was able to show them which part of the world I was from. They looked as if they had invited a Martian to tea.

I took my leave after sharing their warm hospitality and walked onto the main highway. A Fiat with a young couple passed and they turned and passed again, and on this occasion stopped and inquired where I was going. When I said Copenhagen they offered to drive me the twenty or so kilometres into the city. At the central station a sign advertised one pound per night lodgings and I registered at the Norland Hotel. I looked forward to a hot shower, clean sheets and a soft bed. It had been a long journey. The next day I found a youth hostel and the company of a few other travellers. Some of them were from South Africa and I had held a strong position against South Africa because of apartheid, but I soon realised that they had not done anything to me personally, and in fact did not necessarily support apartheid. It was off season and the manager of the hostel made a deal with us that we could stay for free until the season opened, in exchange for keeping the place in good order over the winter. I eventually got a job at a restaurant as a busboy, clearing and wiping tables.

I was earning and twice as much as I would have done in England and the arrangement with the hostel continued until April when the tourist season started up again. During that time, I was waking up in the mornings a Norwegian guy who was working on a construction site. He could not get up on his own so I had to shake him awake. I used to call to him, 'Norsk', which was short for Norwegian. When our hostel arrangement came to an end he told me about a camp site that charged one English pound a week to stay and he gave me his tent; he was off to Spain to see his girlfriend. I lived on a camping site virtually until the end of summer until winter came again; I didn't have any overheads and I was making thirty pounds a week. I had a problem with what to do with the money because the krone was under threat because the Japanese had started to build ships and Denmark had had a great tradition of ship building. The competition meant the krone was unstable, so I decided to keep my money in sterling. Living on a campsite meant absolutely no security. I carried it all on me along with my 12 LPs.

During my residence at the campsite, I met two Americans at a jazz club who were dodging the military draft. They had burned their cards and they were spending a lot of money on rent. I had a big tent, and happy for the company, I invited them to bring their sleeping bags and to come stay. They stayed about four weeks. Because I worked in the restaurant I was able to bring home food and I fed them every night. The camp site had a cooking facility and hot showers; they stayed with minimal expense. One day I came back and they were gone. They left a note saying they had decided to face the music and they had gone to Holland where there was a major American embassy. At around the same time, Abdullah, the dishwasher from Egypt had hurt himself earning extra money grinding coffee and I found myself promoted from busboy to doing his job.

It was during my sojourn in Denmark that I started to overcome my stammering. By then I had worked out that my trouble was with the letter "r" in Richard or Rodriguez, and that I was having problems with the "s", as in Sri Lanka. I had to learn a technique, breathing hard to overcome the start of the word. As I got better at that, the confidence came and the stammering abated; I was over the first hurdle. I had not been able to say Rodriguez to save my life then all of a sudden it was like being able to breathe.

The Danish would come in to the restaurant in the morning and have a Carlsberg beer and a Danish pastry, I was amazed by this. I would have my tea or coffee. When I finished my washing I would run across to the central station and buy my copy of the Guardian and The Telegraph and I would be stay in touch with what was happening in the sporting world. I travelled all over Denmark hitchhiking. I went to Norway and Sweden and up as far as Gothenburg and Stockholm. At the end of the summer I hitchhiked back to London and met my sister Joan and her husband Bertie. In the following months I simply enjoyed what England had to offer and felt I had made the right decision in choosing Denmark as I found the people open-minded. Although I had a brown complexion and brown eyes, they were generally interested in my culture and the part of the world that I had come from. I returned to Guyana on a chartered flight on December 12, 1967.

My early days as a sportscaster, GBS, 1968

Chapter 7

Becoming a Real Broadcaster

When I came back to Guyana in 1967 it was not with the same enthusiasm as the time before. I was, however, happy to be back, a lot wiser since I had returned to a false start in 1965. I was looking forward to Christmas and to a fresh start in 1968. Christmas was enjoyable away from the cold, among old friends. I tried to get a job as a sport administrator and went from personality to personality, but I did not seem to be getting anywhere. A small window of opportunity presented itself when the Government Information Service offered me a spot in their programming to do a feature on sport. I think it paid the sum of fifty-six dollars a month. I had obtained a bicycle and that was how I got around to do research for the feature. The programme was well listened to and I was pleased that finally I had the opportunity to do something relevant to the world of sport. I reconnected with the world of cricket and football, basketball and sport in general. For a long time it seemed I had not achieved a great deal but I had to be patient.

I was lucky then to be able to have a very close relationship with my brother Desmond who was an engineer at a sugar estate on the east coast of the Demerara called Enmore. It was an outlet for me to be able to go up there on a weekend, spend time by the pool, play table tennis and enjoy nice, juicy hamburgers. I would go up with a Canadian volunteer teacher from Winnipeg, Sharon Edey whom I was then seeing. She had ample opportunity to go out with a number of affluent gentlemen with motorcars, who earned a lot more money, but for some reason she liked me and the fact that I was involved in sport for the betterment of youth. She worked with the department of the ministry that dealt with delinquent youth and was heavily involved. Though she could have afforded a motorcycle, she chose to ride a push bike as it would allow her to peer down the alleyways and ghettos of Georgetown as she passed by in order to identify those who might have been in her programme. Sometimes she would ask me to come along and speak to the kids and to their parents. These were kids who might have dropped out or who were having problems with school and showed signs of going down the wrong route. For a long time in 1968, that was the pace of my life.

When I returned to Guyana, the question of the ban instituted by the Guyana Football Association was still hanging over me. I wanted to clear my name and get some justice. Two lawyers, David Decaries and Miles Fitzpatrick, were involved in an organisation called The New World, a left of centre group that produced a quarterly, and they took up my cause. They were interested in the type of work I was doing with players in terms of self development, employment, and lectures in the evenings with different personalities like writers and trade unionists. I suppose they saw that I was on the right track, trying to uplift and give the players a feeling of importance and self-esteem. They saw me as someone who was progressive and they gave me their support. We were able to get the matter heard in front of a judge named Sir Kenneth Stoby and when the evidence was provided, the matter was thrown out for lack of any substance. The ban was overturned. This was the platform for a new beginning.

When I look back, I have to acknowledge that 1968 provided a major breakthrough. In September of that year, I went to a party one night and coming back I ran into Hugh Cholmondeley. He informed me that a new radio station was starting called the Guyana Broadcasting Service and that he wanted me to come and be part of the sports department. On October 1st 1968, some thirty odd people gathered in a very small studio in 68 Hadfield Street and the concept of the station was outlined and the members of the staff, handpicked, were introduced: the news department, sports, commercial world, cultural world, operations, the chief technicians. This was the first dream team that included now Sir Ron Saunders, Cecil Griffith, Matthew Allen, Beverly Rodrigues, Christopher Dean, Clairmont Taitt, Ken Corsbie, Wordsworth McAndrew, Ron Savory, Cecil Thomas, Terry Holder, Sheila Marshall, Joan Green, Carl Ng Yen, Keith Barnwell and Pansy King among others.

It was the making of a very strong creative team and eventually the station opened. I was part of the sports department which was headed by a former Guyana footballer and cricketer, Cecil Thomas; I was to be his young back up. Very soon we did a nightly programme called "Action Line" and I handled Monday night where I answered queries from the public regarding the world of sport. I addressed questions about various sports disciplines in Guyana, as well as what was happening in international sport. It proved to be very testing because you had to be very much on top of things. I had to follow local and international events, and to anticipate the types of questions I might be asked. There was a commitment by the producer that all questions were to be addressed so if there was a query I could not answer, I would be prepared to answer it the next Monday. The policy of the station was to be fair and balanced to administrators, competitors, referees, judges, and etcetera. In order to ensure that nothing defamatory went out, the technicians had instituted a ten second delay that gave an opportunity to stop any slander.

I also helped to produce the morning, midday and evening sportscasts and sometimes a special feature in the afternoon's information hour which covered every aspect of Guyana life. There was also a mid-week evening programme which came my way, called "Night Ride". It started at nine and went into the night. This was not a sports programme but a general culture and lifestyle show. For instance, I would bring a steel band into the studio and feature them, or a guitarist or other interesting personalities, especially in the culture and music fields. Ken Corsbie fronted the programme, but it was shared by a number of us. The opportunity brought out a new dimension in me. I was able to explore my interests outside of the sporting arena.

GBS was ahead of its time. It was in fact a very progressive station, and I do not think we realised at the time how far ahead we were compared with the rest of the Caribbean. GBS was already doing talk shows when most programming at the time was centred on news and music. The wonderful telephone permitted a lot more involvement from people and the programme extended into the world of sport, agriculture, culture. News gathering in 1968 and into the early '70s was not a simple exercise. For example, with the West Indies touring Australia in 1968, the test matches were carried on radio, but for the matches against the Australian state sides, I had to be up by four in the morning to record Radio Australia on the shortwave band which provided a summary of the day's play. This was done in my front gallery thanks to my father's faithful GEC radio, and I always kept my fingers crossed that the nearby donkey "Bing" owned by Mr. Ferreira, would not start his early morning braying, or a group of dogs would not have a major barking dispute. If a vehicle did pass, I would hope that at that hour of the morning there would be no horn blowing. What would the listeners have thought? That material then had to be brought down to the station which would provide listeners with the up to date information.

Another source of information was a Chinese cricket fan named Vivian who ran a parlour on King's Street in Georgetown. He mounted a large blackboard on which he chalked in the latest scores from all the first class venues in the world. It was an astonishing feat and a labour of love because this was not the time of the internet or the mobile phone. In those days there was no television in Guyana. Hundreds of people would be inside and outside of his shop stretching onto the road in an orderly manner following the events of the day especially if the West Indies were playing in Australia, India or New Zealand. I am not sure the shop itself did much business but it certainly was popular.

Things were looking up for me. I upgraded from my sister Pat's bicycle to a small 125cc Honda motorcycle that I bought second hand for three hundred dollars. I remember riding around with my heavy German recorder; I would strap it on my back and find interviews. It was a thrill and a challenge to try to be as creative as possible in terms of programming and I attended all the events myself. I think it was important as a young journalist to do so. One gained a certain amount of respect and credibility with the listeners to be able to go on the air and say, 'At football this afternoon, x beat y; at boxing last night, so and so knocked out so and so.' But I still needed to do a fair bit of networking with trusted friends to get the final scores on all the events of that day. GBS covered a great deal of sport including live cricket, football, boxing, basketball, table tennis, hockey, motor racing, horse racing and rugby.

When I had come back from England in 1967 I found that the BGCC no longer existed as a football team. The people who had taken over had not maintained the level of interest and that along with migration and players moving to other teams meant that things had virtually died, and all the work of Basil Arno, Robin Davis and Charlie Stayers who assisted me was lost. There were other challenges for me as in 1969 I became president of the Guyana Basketball Association. It was a busy time for me for at the same time I had agreed to coach the Santos Football Club. I enlisted my mother who would launder the team jerseys in preparation for a match. There was a famous clothesline in Russell Street which featured the team colours and no one dared touch them for fear of the wrath of team supporters.

At the time of becoming president of the Guyana Basketball Association, this popular game was at a very low level but thanks to vice presidents Joe Singh, who was later made head of the Guyana Defence Force, and Harry Dyett, who served in the Ministry of Foreign Affairs, Faye Gaskin, treasurer and secretary Francis Knight, we were able to turn teams into clubs. We requested that for the new season all club executives be non-players. All of a sudden we found insurance salesmen, teachers, and private sector executives being at the head of these clubs which became stronger and in turn made a stronger association. The results were amazing; by the 1970 season we had a core of high-functioning clubs.

We were able to build a strong Basketball Association which saw us going to Venezuela in 1971 to play in the Caribbean and Central America championships. It was quite an exciting time. We played Trinidad in Caracas, and our ambassador Ann Jardine was delighted to witness our triumph. We were not totally overwhelmed by Venezuela and were 48-48 at half time but lost eventually by not having depth on the bench. The experience of playing against Cuba, Puerto Rico and Panama was a dream come true for the players and officials, as these were excellent and strong countries. It was in fact a very important beginning.

We had to work very closely with the private sector; we played on a public court. One of the commitments I got from the team in Venezuela was that each national player would be associated with a secondary school on our return to Guyana and commit to working with them. We were soon able to have a secondary school competition with some thirteen secondary schools, two of which came from outside of Georgetown. The initiative brought out a great deal of talent which eventually flowed into the national junior and senior teams. At this period Guyana would have been ahead of Trinidad, Barbados and Suriname and this was further emphasised in 1973 when Guyana was the only English-speaking Caribbean country to attend the Caribbean and Central American Games in Puerto Rico, and similarly in 1975 when the championships were held in Santo Domingo.

Chapter 8
A Fresh Start

I decided to leave my job at GBS in 1972 after four enjoyable and exciting years during which time I had learned a great deal. I felt a job evaluation exercise that had been done that year had not provided a fair assessment of my work and the increment offered was much less than I had expected. There was also the matter of Hugh Cholmondeley moving on to an appointment with UNESCO in Jamaica and with one or two others heading in different directions for different reasons. The dream team was no longer the same. I did not have another immediate job prospect, but Christmas was approaching and I decided to enjoy the season and wait until the new year to begin my job search in earnest. In early 1973 an opportunity arose for me to go to Jamaica to cover the Sunshine Showdown, a heavyweight fight between George Foreman and Joe Frazier. I made my way to Jamaica independently to witness a world heavyweight fight in the Caribbean and I got myself an attachment to the JBC, the Jamaica Broadcasting Corporation, through Lindy Delapena, a Jamaican who had played professional football in England for Charlton and Middlesborough.

I had met Lindy at the Commonwealth Games in Edinburgh in 1970 when carrying out an assignment for BBC Caribbean Service, and he for JBC. Our team was made up of the later well known television presenter Trinidadian Trevor MacDonald, and the former Olympic bronze medallist Emanuel MacDonald Bailey who also hailed from the land of calypso and steel band. Covering the games was most enjoyable as I was able to meet so many personalities. The Scottish weather, however, was cruel to all who were involved in the event, as a gale force wind blew through the two weeks of August. The one lasting memory of that event was the performance of then unknown athlete Hasley Crawford. He had come to represent Trinidad and Tobago in the sprints and only had the experience of running on grass before attending the games. The tall, unassuming Crawford produced a great performance by picking up the bronze medal in the 100 metres. It was an early signal that there was better to come from this "Trini" boy as he showed in 1976 in the same event in Montreal when he took gold.

I was associated with JBC for the Sunshine Showdown which was held at the National Stadium in Kingston. Pearl Bailey sang the national anthem and if my memory serves me right, US President Lyndon Johnson died the same night.

As a young broadcaster, I was faced with a dilemma, as George Foreman surprised everyone, stopping Frazier in two rounds to become the new champion of the world. I could have simply joined the crowd and headed out of the Jamaica Stadium, but instead I decided to seek permission from Lindy to go into the V.I.P area where a number of outstanding boxing personalities were still chatting about the surprise outcome. I took advantage of the situation to do a number of interviews, first with Angelo Dundee who was associated with Muhammad Ali, Bob Foster, the light heavyweight champion of the world, heavyweight contenders

Ernie Terrell, Thad Spencer and Jimmy Ellis, plus a voice from across the Atlantic, British boxing commentator Harry Carpenter who was also at ringside.

The JBC management team were very impressed with the fact that I took the initiative to run around to interview all these personalities. The interviews were aired that night at eleven thirty. Lindy Delapena, who was also aware of my cricket interest offered me another attachment to come back to cover the West Indies President's Eleven against Australia at Montego Bay. The panel included Hugh Crosskill, who was an excellent young talent at the time, and later distinguished himself with cricket commentary and current affairs radio both in Jamaica and in Barbados for the CBU and later in England at the BBC. It was quite an experience to see Montego Bay, a world renowned tourist destination; the drive to Mo' Bay was in itself an education as it was the length of the country.

We stayed at a nice hotel called the Upper Deck which had a great view. JBC then further offered me an opportunity to cover the test match at Sabina Park the following weekend. I was on a roll. They provided the accommodation, everything; I also did Jamaica versus Australia and then West Indies versus Australia. Because of my exposure in Jamaica, I got a call from Jerry Richards, Head of Sport at the Caribbean Broadcasting Service in Barbados to be part of his station's team to cover the Australian match against Barbados and the West Indies. I was pleased to be invited to work with Jerry as I greatly respected him and felt that he was an underrated commentator with a strong voice and distinctive style. The CBC team also included Tony Cozier, the much respected Australian Alan McGilvery, and Algie Simmons.

When I returned to Guyana, I was minding my own business alone at Russell Street one day when the horn blew from out on the street. I came out to find a vehicle idling and its driver addressed me saying, 'The Minister of Sports, Shirley Fields-Ridley, would like to meet you. Can you contact her secretary Pat Thomas?' I was perplexed and intrigued. I called the next day and was invited to meet with the minister. That was Wednesday; our appointment was for Thursday. At our meeting she said that she had been following my progress and knew my background. I had gone to primary school with her brother Rudy, and she knew of my work with Santos and the Alboystown YMCA. She knew that I was on top of what was happening and why I had left GBS. She had just been appointed Minister of Sport in the Guyana government and she wanted someone who could at any given time provide advice and an opinion on the state of any discipline or association, and general advice on what would be advantageous or detrimental in decisions about the world of sports. She offered me the post of sports advisor.

I could not have imagined such an opportunity. I would still have the flexibility to do my broadcasts because it was important that I stayed in touch. The Minister did not want me to remove myself from these areas of life because she felt it made me current and relevant, the type of person she needed as an advisor. I simply had to inform her of my movements. Well, I would move from earning $300 per month to $1000 per month, and I would be eligible for a duty free car. It would be a step in the right direction. But I also knew in taking that job as sports advisor I would probably have a thousand enemies. When you have the ear of the Minister, you become the focus for many people who have personal agendas. I would be called on sometimes to offer opinions that I knew would not be popular. I decided to accept the challenge.

It was a time where if you really were serious, you could provide the information that would elevate sports in Guyana. I was not a party person. She respected the fact that I did not have affiliation with any particular political party. She was interested in independent information. I really enjoyed working with the Minister. We engaged the national associations to make sure they were having their AGMs, their national trials, that they were functioning in a democratic manner, and that there was some effort being made to spread the disciplines country wide. We focussed on the club structure. It was that kind of uplifting of standards.

During that time we engaged an Italian architect to design a velodrome, to be named for former cyclist Barry Massey, and badly wanted by the cycling fraternity who were still riding on grass while the world was moving on. The architect came through the Olympic Solidarity Committee, but we did not get the cooperation of the then cycling fraternity. I think there was a mistrust that we were trying to take over. Then there was the world oil crisis, and third world OPEC countries had to cut their budgets and the velodrome was never built. But we made great progress in table tennis with the help of the Embassy of China. We got the Chinese to provide us with a table tennis coach from Bejing, and the standard was lifted. The Ministry employed a lot of coaches to carry out the coaching programmes, national associations developed outside of Georgetown, and we were able to provide teams with badly needed equipment.

One of the major projects that we were successful in carrying out was the building of the National Indoor Auditorium which seated 4,000 spectators and provided the sports of boxing, basketball, volleyball, table tennis, hockey, football, karate and judo a venue for national and international competition. This was later renamed after outstanding former boxer Cliff Anderson who fought unsuccessfully for the British Empire Bantamweight Title and lost under controversial circumstances.

The Minister was able to demand more from the associations. Her policies strengthened their organisation and structure, demanded more accountability and challenged them to take on more responsibility for fundraising. She established a wider national sports base, extending the reach of sports development outside of Georgetown and building courts and playing fields. She appointed me a member of the National Sports Council (NSC) under the chairmanship of Basil Arno, and of which I later became chairman. I later renamed it the NSDC adding a D to stand for Development.

A cherished photo as Lance Gibbs (second from right) walks off the MCG in Australia after breaking Freddie Trueman's World record, 1975-76

Chapter 9
The Broadcast Circuit

I continued my work as commentator and my involvement in community level sports during this time. England came at the end of 1974 and played a test in Guyana. I was one of many commentators along with Tony Cozier who by this time had established himself in the world of cricket journalism and commentating. The major event looming in the distance and one for which we would once again be paired, was the first ever World Cup. The tournament started out with 60 overs, which in subsequent years changed to 50, and it was sponsored by the Prudential Insurance Company. The teams played for the Prudential Cup, and all the major cricketing nations of the world, to include Canada and East Africa, were to meet in England.

The Caribbean Broadcasting Union had been formed earlier to look at broadcasting standards and programming changes generally; this event motivated an examination of the broadcasting of West Indies cricket, especially coming from abroad. Where stations put together their own teams, the CBU then coordinated the coverage with the help of the BBC. Tony Cozier, Jeff Charles from Dominica, and I were chosen to be the Caribbean Broadcasting Union team. Jeff Charles was on an attachment to BBC and had done a lot of broadcasting. We met with Alva Clarke, a St Lucia-born who was at the head of Commonwealth Broadcasting, and following a detailed meeting our accreditations were provided along with the English commentators who would be part of our broadcast. They were John Arlott, Brian Johnson, Christopher Martin-Jenkins and Henry Blowfelt. The former English players Freddie Trueman and Trevor Bailey rounded out the team.

During the 1975 World Cup the West Indies manager Clyde Walcott saw Tony Cozier and I as people whom he and the team could embrace and trust, and on many occasions we were invited to travel on the West Indies bus, which was really quite an honour. That does not happen anymore because I think the relationship between commentators and players, and the commentators and the Cricket Board, is somewhat different. Right now the West Indies coach is really off limits to everyone except those who are directly involved and in a sense I can understand that.

It was during that World Cup tournament that I experienced my most testing, demanding stint as commentator. The West Indies had beaten Sri Lanka in their opening game at Old Trafford by nine wickets, to meet Pakistan in the next round at Edgbaston. It was a game that promised excitement and good cricket and it certainly delivered. Pakistan won the toss and batted and made 266, which was not out of reach for the strong West Indies side of Roy Fredericks, Gordon Greenidge, Alvin Kallicharran, Rohan Kanhai, Clive Lloyd, Viv Richards, Bernard Julien, Deryck Murray and Keith Boyce. But we found ourselves, maybe because of lack of concentration, or perhaps from complacency that there was enough talent to get the runs, at 203 for 9 with Roberts walking out to join Murray.

The reality of a loss was heavy in the atmosphere, and with it the end to all chances at the World Cup. It was extremely tense; Roberts, who was more known for his aggressive, skilful fast bowling was in partnership with Murray who was a more accomplished player and had a lot of first class and test runs under his belt. They got together and slowly but surely the scores mounted. The West Indies were 40 runs away, then 30, 20 but even then it only would have taken one ball to end it all.

When the target was being approached by the West Indies, everyone in the ground was standing. The place was charged; eventually Murray and Roberts were able somehow to reach the target and the West Indies won. Later, then manager, the late Clyde Walcott said that at one point they had more or less given up, but that when it started to look like the West Indies might just pull it off, players did not want to move from their original seats because they felt to move would bring bad luck. Even if they wanted to go to the bathroom they did not leave. At the end of it there were tears in the West Indies dressing room.

From a commentary point of view I can tell you it was drama on the field. I remember when my stint in the commentating box was finished, what had prevailed in the West Indies dressing room was mirrored in the box. I cannot remember who was to take over next but we decided not to change and I went on for about forty minutes until the final run was made. There were tears of joy in my eyes. It was a very emotional, dramatic play and it was tense. It was a great escape from obscurity in that tournament and we left a very happy team.

Clive Lloyd and his side then won an important game against Australia at the Oval in London in a Group B match, dismissing the Ian Chappell led side for 192 and acquiring the runs for the loss of three wickets before meeting New Zealand at the same venue in the semi-final. The Kiwis were bowled out for a 158 and the West Indies got the required runs with the loss of five wickets. Australia qualified for the final in a dramatic low scoring match at

Headingley as England sent in to bat were all out for 93 runs with Gary Gilmour taking 6 for 14, while Australia lost six wickets in acquiring the winning total of 94.

The first ever World Cup Final was played on June 21st, the longest day of the year. It was a great day for cricket with excellent weather; the match finished just after eight o'clock. The West Indies were initially in trouble: they had lost Fredericks who stepped on his wicket after hooking Lillee for six to be followed by the early loss of Kallicharran and Greenidge. The West Indies were 50 for 3 on the board when the greying former West Indies captain Kanhai came in to join Lloyd. He was not originally chosen in the final eleven but was brought in to the team to replace Garfield Sobers who had had an injury. Kanhai played a beautiful secondary role to Lloyd. He did not try to compete; he just skilfully turned the strike around. Lloyd was at an outstanding best. He made one of the best hundreds in World Cup cricket, a real captain's knock, and that partnership turned the West Indies batting disaster into a very healthy competitive score.

Australia got within range but of course one of the outstanding performances was by Viv Richards who was more known as a batsman, but had been brilliant in the field that day and ran out five Australians. When Lloyd departed for 102, the West Indies were 206 for 5 and eventually scored 291 as the lower order added some important runs. The task of scoring 292 was not beyond Australia. They did extremely well to reach 274 after being 195 for 6 with Dennis Lillee and Jeff Thomson providing resistance at the end in a tense evening at Lords.

The image of the Duke of Edinburgh, Prince Philip, handing the West Indies captain Clive Lloyd the World Cup trophy will be imprinted in my mind forever. I remember his putting the trophy on the head of Kallicharran with all the players around him. Tony Cozier and I found ourselves in the Australian dressing room drinking Foster's lager and then in the West Indies dressing room drinking something a little stronger. I also remember somebody presenting Vanburn Holder with a huge cake. It made a brief appearance in the West Indies dressing room where it was devoured; there were a lot of hungry bellies filled with a lot of drink and no food.

That was indubitably one of the more memorable days in my life, and a magnificent day for West Indies cricket. I am sure Tony Cozier would attest to that. We were part of broadcasting a world event and a victory that meant so much to Caribbean people all over the world. I cannot remember how I got back to my B&B on Gloucester Road. I woke up the next morning at about nine and it was a beautiful way to wake up. I opened my eyes realising the enormity of the victory: the West Indies had won, and I was part of it. Everything seemed to be so right on the Sunday morning. It was perfect. I rushed out and bought all the major English papers.

The West Indies team were brought back to the Caribbean, and to Guyana. The then Prime Minister Forbes Burnham made sure the team was honoured and presented with gifts. The World Cup itself was flown by helicopter all over Guyana to pay tribute to the achievement of the West Indies team and to involve the rural cricket supporters.

It was a much simpler World Cup than the tournament we know today. The early competitions were 60 overs and fewer rules and regulations prevailed. The World Cup then was played in England, in '75, '79, and '83. It was not until '87 that it left England to be jointly hosted by India and Pakistan before returning in 2000, with Ireland and Holland co-hosting. By then the World Cup enjoyed more financial inducement for the players and the boards who were taking part through sponsorship and television rights.

What the West Indies got for winning the 1975 World Cup was a small token in comparison. There was glory there that money could not buy. If they had been the losing finalists and each gotten 10,000 pounds, I do not think they would have traded it for being the winning team. These were a bunch of guys who were extremely proud of wearing the maroon cap and committed to being the best. They played as a collective unit; there was no one playing for himself.

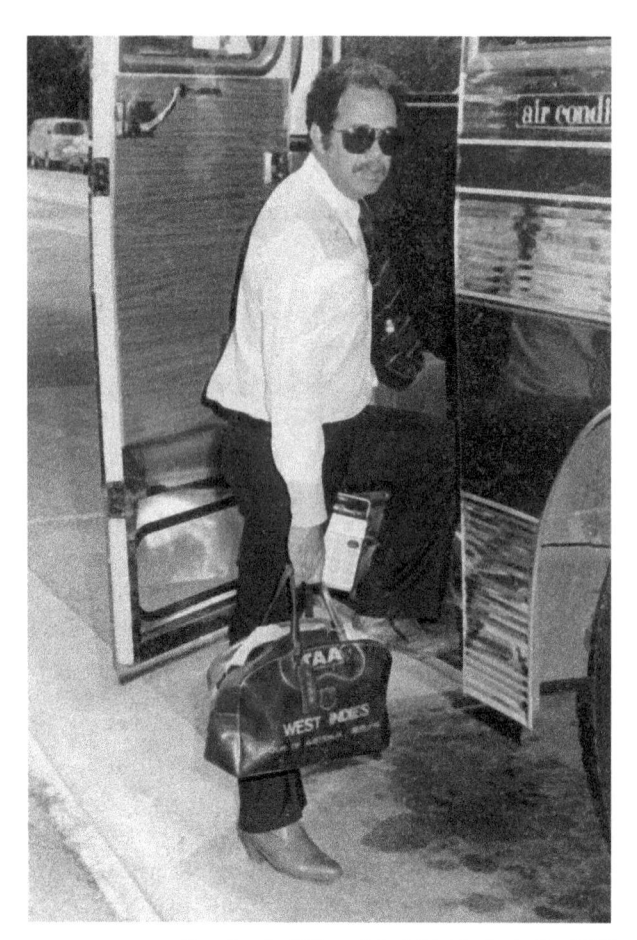

Boarding the W.I coach in Adelaide, Australia, 1975

Chapter 10
Down Under

In 1975 I accompanied the West Indies team for the first time on their tour of Australia. The value of the exposure was immeasurable. There was no CBU team selected to go to Australia for the 75-76 tour, it was on my own initiative. A friend of mine named now Sir Ron Saunders helped me to raise the required financing by working with the private sector in Guyana. All the same, I was on a tight budget. I called the Australia Broadcasting Corporation and spoke to Bernie Kerr who was the head of cricket broadcasting for ABC radio. Having heard me during the 1975 World Cup he initially agreed that both Tony and I would be part of the ABC panel. However, when I arrived, it was clear we could not both be retained and the natural choice was Tony Cozier who had been there in 1968 and was more experienced. I did all the first class matches for the ABC which was very enjoyable because it was broadcasting from some of the major grounds in Australia. It was also an opportunity to go up country. In those days there were many more first class matches in between the tests.

Interest was high because of the West Indies versus Australia final earlier that year. The West Indies team was a drawing card. They had always been because they had always played aggressively but sportingly. It was attractive cricket, never dull and they were good sportsmen. I think the early West Indies team set a very high standard, especially the Frank Worrell led side in 1960-61.

The tour was challenging to me in terms of being able to maintain a reasonable standard of living. My budget was tight and I could not afford the luxurious hotels and travel lodges that the teams were staying at. I used little pubs with a few rooms above for rent. It reminded me of the old Jesse James movies with the swinging doors and the parlours; but they were clean and decent. I had a bed and breakfast arrangement and then I would head to the West Indies hotel and was welcome on the bus to go to and from the various test grounds. I knew my place and did not get involved in team matters, but I had gotten to know all the players personally. At the test grounds the players would keep lunch for me. If there was a social invitation, it would be extended to Tony Cozier and I; on rest day if there was a barbecue or a visit to an interesting site, the invitation would be extended to us. It was on the rest day of the Adelaide test that there was the great tradition of the players, officials and press visiting a South Australian vineyard. It was quite a well-planned event which included a large barbecue lunch, tennis, music and wine to last a lifetime.

The West Indies team had lost their opening test in Brisbane due mainly to a first innings collapse on the opening day; they were all out for 214 after a mad opening session which saw them 120 for 6 at lunch. There were just too many attacking shots in that period instead of digging in in that first session and scoring at a slower rate. Australia went on to win by eight wickets but there was a positive when the West Indies batted a second time, as the two young batsmen, Lawrence Rowe and Alvin Kallicharran scored 107 and 101 respectively in this losing cause.

The second test in Perth was scheduled to be played on the fastest pitch in all of Australia if not the world. It was always a good batting surface and Australia winning the toss, managed 329 thanks mainly to a superb 156 by Ian Chappell against some excellent bowling of Andy Roberts, Keith Boyce, Bernard Julien, Michael Holding and Lance Gibbs. The West Indies replied aggressively shaking off the psychological damage that might have been done in Brisbane, and amassed 585. The W.I. selectors had dropped Gordon Greenidge after failing badly in the opening test, but that left Clive Lloyd with a dilemma of who should be Roy Fredericks' opening partner since there was no other recognised opening batsman in the final eleven. After a prolonged debate, Bernard Julien the all rounder, volunteered to go in with Fredericks. Julien's bravery allowed the West Indies to put together an opening partnership of 91 though his innings of 25 ended with a broken thumb after being hit by Jeff Thomson.

The West Indies victory in this important second test match was mainly due to a brilliant 169 by the left-handed Fredericks. He virtually took on Lillee, Thomson, Gary Gilmour and Max Walker. On this flier of a pitch with a brilliant display of cutting and hooking, this knock by the West Indian opener is still rated as one of the top four innings ever played in Australia. Fredericks' brilliance was further supported by a stroke playing display by Captain Lloyd of 149 to put West Indies in a match winning position. The pressure was just too much for the Australians who collapsed for a paltry 169 with Andy Roberts taking 7 for 54 from 14 overs.

It was one-all and we were heading out to Melbourne. It was in fact a good visit for me also to Western Australia because other than seeing world class cricket and witnessing the West Indies win, I was extremely fortunate with my accommodation. I had chosen a pub close to the WACA ground which was owned by a Dutch immigrant. The rates for bed and breakfast were within my budget and the atmosphere in the saloon was lively and friendly. The clientele was mainly of a European background, the pub obviously attracted people from that part of the world and football was the main talking point, not cricket. Since I had followed English and European football I might have surprised my Dutch landlord with my knowledge of the Dutch and German clubs, and on the morning of my departure he was kind enough to waive all charges.

During the test match at Perth I was able to do commentary on an FM station which had surprisingly received permission to carry the match. This further improved my capacity to earn and this was important as it was a long tour with six test matches and lots of travel ahead. Melbourne might be recorded as the turning point of this tour. It was crunch time for both teams. Australia was thinking of dropping Thomson who was their outstanding fast bowler and the partner of Lillee who was destroyed by Fredericks and Lloyd in Perth. They thought long and hard about that and decided they would keep Thomson in Melbourne. The West Indies eventually lost the match; Thomson and Lillee bowled a much fuller length and did not bowl so short to Fredericks and company who were accustomed to a short game. It was frustrating because I felt there were some decisions that went against us. Had the rulings been favourable, the result might have been different.

For example, Gary Cosier, a young batsman brought in by the Australians, who eventually scored a hundred and gave Australia a fairly strong position in that game, seemed to be plum leg before to Bernard Julien. He was later fortunate also to survive a caught behind appeal; the ball had swung in and trapped him on the back foot when he was seven. Ian Redpath was thought to be also fortunate with a similar decision. There were other instances of leg before appeals by Lance Gibbs as the Australian top order tried unsuccessfully to sweep the West Indies off spinner. The West Indies left the state of Victoria still hopeful that they could do better in New South Wales.

Despite the loss of the test, the visit to the MCG proved to be a high point for my own professional career. The crowds were huge; in some cases almost 90,000 people, which was really significant. I had never seen anything like that before. You hear of the Maracana Stadium in Brazil which then had a capacity of 130,000 persons for football, but you never really perceived cricket grounds as being that big. Later when I went to India, West Indies played at Eden Gardens in Calcutta which holds 100,000, and it was as big as that, and that was really a major spectacle. The crowds in Australia were immense but I was taken aback by the level of beer consumption during the day's play. The cricket-mad Australians who were very macho overall, entered the turnstiles with coolers full of beer. What was even worse was the sight of them staggering away at close of play with sun-burnt bodies in search of the tram or the train which was quite a walk from the grounds.

The day before the test match, by sheer accident, I had the opportunity to meet probably the greatest batsman that ever lived, Sir Donald Bradman who had a test average of 99. That day the mayor of Melbourne had had a reception for both teams at the City Hall. After the official function I was trying to leave very quickly because I had a television interview with Channel 10. Lo and behold, ducking out at that time because he had another appointment across the road at the Windsor Hotel was Sir Donald Bradman. We had a brief chat and I simply asked him whether he had seen most of the tour, but I did not want to burden him with a barrage of questions. He was dapperly dressed in grey. He looked remarkably fit for his age after retiring in 1948. We came down the steps together, waited for the traffic and crossed the road; he went into the Windsor Hotel and I headed to Channel 10. It was a great moment.

It was during my stay in Melbourne that I was able to make contact with ex-girlfriend Mary Francis, whom I had dated in 1963 in England, and my next door neighbour Kevin McIntyre in Bayswater. I had remembered that Mary was working in London for the shipping line that brought out the English immigrants to Australia. I visited the corresponding office in Melbourne and looked for the most senior person there and inquired whether he knew a Mary Francis who had worked with the company in England. He did not hesitate to say yes, and told me that she was working at a travel agency called Crossroads in the city.

Before heading over, I called and was told that she had gone to South African Airways in Collins Street to deliver some tickets. I decided when getting there to surprise her on her arrival, only to be surprised myself. When the office door of the South African Airways manager opened and Kevin Mc Intyre from the old flat in Bayswater stepped out, I might have been very surprised, but Kevin was dumbstruck. It was as if he had seen a ghost, and I remember his false teeth dropped from his upper gums. It was sheer luck that in one hour I had reunited with people I had not seen in thirteen years, having had no contact information for them when arriving in Australia.

The other significant thing about that test match was that by the third day of the tour the Australian Board could have handed the West Indies Board their guaranteed fee. It became apparent that the cricket boards all over the world were making money and I think the issue started to germinate in the minds of the players. 'Hey,' they argued, 'We are the main actors and we're not the ones being paid'. I remember Ian Chappell telling me in 1973 that he got two thousand Australian dollars for leading Australia in the W.I. The West Indies players in 1963 were then the unofficial champions of the world, and their per diem allowance in England was one pound a day, except for the professionals Gary Sobers, Rohan Kanhai and Wesley Hall who got six hundred pounds as reported in the press. This was the number one team in the world with huge crowds in England and the question of compensation was later to become a major issue.

Melbourne was then followed by Sydney, where we were once more competitive. Sydney was a beautiful city, the beaches, the restaurants along the coast; Harbour Bridge and the Sydney Opera House were also stunning landmarks. Remarkably the migration of West Indians to the place earlier had created a few roti shops. It was a fun city. Melbourne was the cultural hub of Australia but Sydney was the tourist city: warm temperatures, fantastic beaches and a great deal to watch in terms of sporting events. I was not surprised in my later life to see them stage the Olympic Games.

We lost that test match when we batted a second time, being bowled out for a paltry 128 after Australia only led us by 50 in the first innings. This was mainly because we were trying to hook the Australian fast bowlers. You can play hook shots on small Caribbean grounds and easily hit the ball for six, but on the big Sydney cricket ground, which was probably my of all the test grounds I have worked at in Australia, we invariably got caught down at the boundary. One newspaper even called us the 'Happy Hookers'.

We were now 3-1 down, when we headed from Sydney to Adelaide. The change of location brought the luxury and comfort of a motor car, a Holden on loan from Jeff Glover, the West Indies Board liaison officer. In fact, our first stop on that tour had been in Adelaide and since he and his brother had moved away from their parents' home, he suggested that as avid cricket fans and former school teachers that they would love to have me as a guest. The hospitality of the Glovers proved beyond my dreams. As an early riser I was served tea at six, had dinner with them most evenings and they would drive me to the Adelaide Oval. As far as the test match was concerned we were again doing well; we had Australia on the run. At 272 for 6 we had a good chance of bowling them out under 325 on a pitch that always favoured the batsmen, but Gary Gilmour came in and played a whirlwind knock and just took the game away from the West Indies. There was just nothing we could do to get him out and Australia got a huge first innings total. I think by that time we started to lose a bit of spirit. It was, however, a good test match for Keith Boyce, the West Indian all rounder who took 3 for 75 and 2 for 74, scoring 95 and 69 respectively. The Adelaide test was also a landmark for the great West Indies off spinner Lance Gibbs as he equalled the record of Freddie Trueman of 307 test victims, Gibbs in 78 test matches while Trueman had taken 67. The truth be told, the off spinner achieved his success mainly on pitches good for batting while Trueman had benefited from the green pitches in England in the early part of his career, when there was little covering of the square.

For some reason the boards had agreed to a six test match tour. If the series was close this would have been a great grand final; that was not the case, we had a number of players carrying injury even before we got back to Melbourne for the final game and I think that if they had taken any kind of a poll most people would have voted for ending the tour then. We had to play the sixth test match and by that time I think all hopes of beating Australia again were shot. People just looked forward to returning to the West Indies. I would say we were overall outplayed and that Australia was the more experienced side, but if one or two decisions had gone our way it could have been a closer series. It was at least for Lance Gibbs a defining moment as his 2 wickets for 68 (Gilmour and Redpath) took him past Trueman to a world record to join Gary Sobers, who in 1957-58 against Pakistan at Sabina Park became the first West Indian world record holder when he surpassed Len Hutton's score of 364. Gibbs' achievement did have a bit of an unfortunate end however.

An overzealous West Indies fan jumped the fence, bottle of champagne in hand and sought permission from Clive Lloyd to offer his fellow Guyanese a toast. Lloyd nodded in agreement and what seemed to be a spontaneous but harmless action caused a major fracas. Neither Lloyd nor Gibbs had remembered that this contravened the policy of this ground. The champagne-bearing intruder somehow managed to outrun the pursuing security guard and got back over the fence and into the stand. The police however, had their orders to arrest him. The crowds in solidarity formed a barricade of bodies to protect him, but after a period of almost an hour he was eventually arrested and charged.

It is after all a small world and much later in my career at the Pietermaritzburg Ground in South Africa, during the West Indies tour of 1998 I met a young Guyanese with his English girlfriend who in course of conversation told the story of his father's arrest at the MCG in Melbourne. When I informed him that I had seen the whole episode unfold he could hardly believe that I was telling the truth.

An historical moment W.I. team first series' win in Australia at Adelaide, 1979 (Tony Cozier far right)

Chapter 11
Establishing Myself

The West Indies returned from the Australia tour disappointed, after their great showing at the 1975 World Cup. There had been great optimism that they could have beaten Australia on their home ground for the first time. Arguably the relative inexperience of the team manager might have contributed. A manager who had been to Australia before, or had played a fair amount of test cricket and had had great success, like Clyde Walcott or Gerry Alexander, might have been able to assist the players, not only technically but also psychologically. The manager was the former West Indies fast bowler Esmond Kentish, a good board man, but he had not played a great deal of test cricket, nor had he been to Australia before and so he did not have knowledge of local conditions. That, coupled with the fact that the West Indies team was a comparatively young side under Lloyd who had taken over in 1974, and was meeting a competitive Australian side led by Greg Chappell on Australian soil, proved an insurmountable challenge. When we returned everyone wanted to talk about the tour and I did a lot of press interviews, but I had to resume my job at the Ministry of Sport and I looked forward to getting back into the rhythm of my work after so long away.

India were touring the West Indies that year but my job had to take precedence then. I was invited to join the Minister of Education Ceciline Hercules Beard along with Eustace McBean, the Chief Physical Education Officer of that Ministry, to attend the first ever UNESCO conference of physical education in Paris, an event which clashed with the test match in Guyana. I was away for three weeks and I enjoyed the opportunity, but the conference really only paid lip service to the Third World. It was the Third World that needed the upgrading of physical education in schools, the infrastructure development and equipment, but the European agenda dominated the conference. Though the Third World did make interjections, I do not believe the final document that was produced reflected the imbalance, the training needs, and financial needs of the Caribbean, Africa, Asia, India, Pakistan. There were not a lot of opportunities to see much of Paris, the days were long. I often had to keep the company of the Minister of Education, so where I might have gone out on my own I had to consider the protocol with the Minister. Mr. McBean, an avid photographer quickly disappeared with camera in hand to shoot the sites of Paris.

As far as the India tour was concerned the West Indies had beaten India quite thoroughly in the series as Sunil Gavaskar simply did not have the same success against our bowlers as he had enjoyed in 1971.

It was in 1976 that Guyana took the decision to withdraw its Olympic team, already assembled in the Olympic village in Montreal, because of the controversy about the games between New Zealand with South Africa. Guyana had a strong anti-apartheid position and had given a substantial amount of aid to the South African liberation forces. When the meeting was being held at the office of the Prime Minister that evening, my advice to my own minister was that before deciding to withdraw we should check to see what Cuba, Trinidad and Jamaica were doing. At that time Guyana was closely aligned with the three island nations who shared a position on the apartheid policy of South Africa. I advised that we should first coordinate our stance, but the next morning the decision was announced that Guyana would withdraw. It was a very difficult decision to have taken with regard to the athletes. The team included a Guyanese athlete by the name of James Wren Gilkes who had won the gold medal in 1975 in Mexico in the Pan-American games, and Kenny Bristol was a boxer who had won a gold medal in the middle-weight division. They both were very competitive and had a very good chance of winning medals in Montreal.

When the decision came down, the athletes had already received their accreditation; they had been through the draw, they knew which heat they were in and were immersed in the life of the Olympic village, but they had to return to Guyana. Gilkes tried to appeal to the I.O.C to allow him to run as an independent neutral athlete. They considered it for a while but then it was denied as the I.O.C decided that the Olympics was about competition between nations and not individuals. My job was to go to the airport to meet those athletes and it was not an easy task. All I could say with any conviction was that the sacrifice they had made then would help the many millions of black South Africans to one day see freedom. I really could not say anymore. I thought if Jamaica, Cuba and Trinidad had gone we could have maintained our position on apartheid but not cut our noses to spoil our faces. To this day Guyana's only Olympic medal is a bronze for boxing in Moscow in 1980.

As manager with winning National Rugby Team, Jamaica, 1969 (centre)

Chapter 12
A Cricket Revolution

The question of players being paid what they were worth had been germinating from the early seventies. The Australian players had already met with Bob Hawke, the head of that country's trade union movement in Melbourne in 1976, and after hearing their grievances agreed that they were being underpaid. The issue brewed for several months. In 1977 the Australian media tycoon Kerry Packer entered a bid to the Australian Cricket Board for broadcasting rights. Though his bid was significantly higher than that of the ABC to cover test cricket, the contract was awarded them instead. Packer, head of the famous Channel 9, was furious and did not feel a private channel should be denied the opportunity. Packer's Channel 9 had successfully got the rights for tennis and golf in Australia; he enjoyed success both with acquiring the rights and in attracting viewership for the events, and obviously felt that the same could be done with other sporting disciplines. In early 1977 players were being contacted in Australia by Packer associates about possibly joining World Series Cricket and unknown to the West Indies Board, Packer men that included Austin Robinson, John Cornell and Tony Greig were in the forefront of selling World Series Cricket to some of the best players in the world. Grieg himself lost the England captaincy as a result, although he continued to play for his county Sussex and England, but he was not a popular person in England, especially with the English test administrators.

On May 8th 1977 Kerry Packer officially announced the launch of the first World Series Cricket, and proceeded with his efforts to sign some of the best players in the world. I was doing commentary in Guyana, Trinidad and Barbados at the time. It was an exciting, competitive series between West Indies and Pakistan. It was during this tour that Irving Shillingford from Dominica made our test team. He had debuted in Port of Spain in the second test scoring 39 and 2 but produced an attractive 120 in good batting conditions at Bourda in a drawn game. Surprisingly by the fifth test in Jamaica he was dropped. Had he come from one of the larger Caribbean territories he probably would have been kept in the side. The larger countries enjoyed a lot more clout and influence than the smaller islands that were producing some very promising players. Nevertheless it was a great series, decided in a final test match in Jamaica. It attracted large crowds and quality cricket, very competitive and brought the best out of the West Indies.

News of Packer's recruitment during the series soon became public and the reactions were varied. Australia and Pakistan took hard lines, dropping most of their leading players from their sides. The first season of World Series Cricket was the promotion of the personalities pitting the great batting stars against the outstanding fast bowlers. It got branded as a circus for one reason or another and just did not attract large crowds although the cricket was fierce and competitive with no quarter given. Players were playing for more than money, as personal pride was involved. There was no love lost among these men of different nationalities. The initial 1977 series was made up of a World eleven, a West Indies team and two Australian sides, but despite the heavy promotion and the problem of not getting the official test grounds, the first WSC series was a financial disaster for Packer. The one encouraging feature was the improved crowds at the day-night matches and this was no doubt remembered when his planners came to putting together the second season of World Series Cricket.

In contrast the Australian Cricket Board revived the career of former batting star Bobby Simpson to lead a new look Australian side against India in a home series and led them to a 3-2 victory with the series decider taking place at the Adelaide Oval in the final test. It was just what the Australian Board needed at the time, and Simpson was later appointed to lead Australia in the West Indies.

The West Indies Board had taken a softer line on the players who had initially signed with Kerry Packer, and included them in the first two test matches of 1978 against Australia, easily won by the West Indies. However, by the third test in Guyana the West Indies Board announced they would leave out Desmond Haynes and Colin Croft and Deryck Murray. It had become known that Haynes and Croft were the new signings to the Packer group, and Murray who was the Secretary of the West Indies Players Association, was seen by the board as an agitator who might have helped recruit these two bright stars. When West Indies Captain Clive Lloyd met with the selectors, chaired by Joey Carew with co-selectors Clyde Walcott and J.K Holt, he objected strongly to the omission of these players and withdrew as captain of the West Indies team in protest. The other senior players joined Lloyd in solidarity and the board then had to ask the selectors to name a new West Indies side under Alvin Kallicharran.

The new look side included Alvin Greenidge, Basil Williams, Larry Gomes, Irving Shillingford, David Murray, Sew Shivnarine, Norbert Phillip, Vanburn Holder, Sylvester Clarke and Derek Parry who was the only survivor of the previous test. With the absence of the stars the series appeared to be much more even with Australia winning the third test at Bourda, thanks to some super batting by Graeme Wood with 126 and Craig Serjeant who got 124. The West Indies made it two all at Port of Spain by winning the fourth and retaining the Frank Worrell Trophy. The fifth ended in a draw and on a sour note when spectators invaded the ground following the dismissal of Vanburn Holder just before close of play on the last day.

A lot of young Australians and young West Indies players had opportunities to showcase during the tour, but the world was more focussed on how the Kerry Packer series was going to unfold. The Packer organisers tried to attract spectators by bringing in tremendous innovations: first of all they played with a white ball and a black sight screen and they played under lights for the first time. The series was not able to get the official test grounds and had to be played at country grounds and football stadiums. Packer financed it and though it lost a lot of money, he was confident that the tournament would only grow in popularity.

The following year Packer did not only get a few West Indian players, he got an entire team. There was an entire Australian team, and an international team led by Tony Greig. The result was a super series. The innovations were instituted: a new set of fielding restrictions created opportunities for fast scoring, and pioneering batting and the introduction of coloured uniforms. It was a totally new presentation of the game and the players were being paid and paid well. Not only were the players benefiting, the umpires earnings moved from a hundred pounds a game to seven hundred pounds.

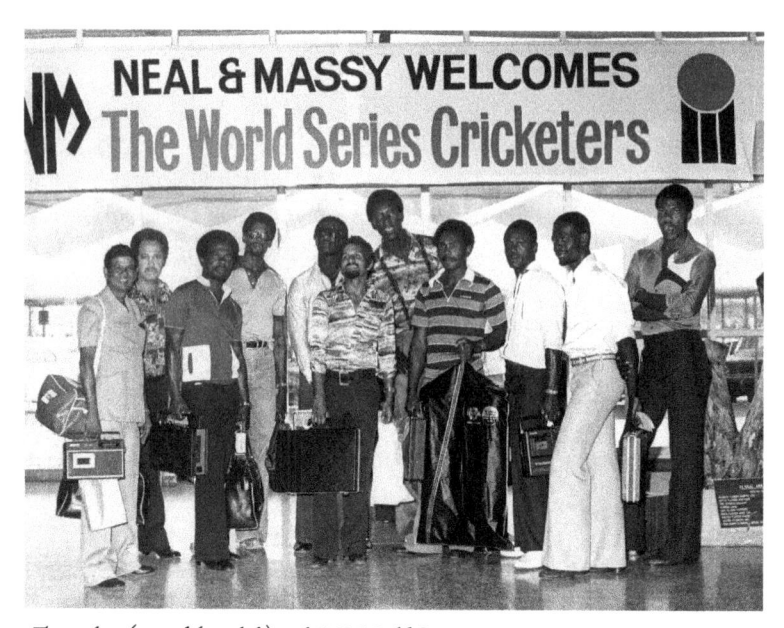

The author (second from left) with W.I. World Series team, Jamaica Airport, 1979

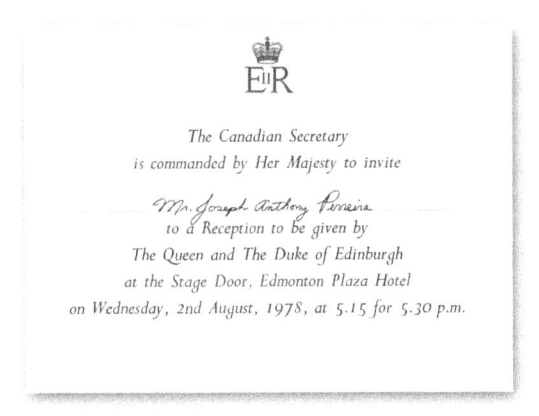

A surprise invitation from England's H.R.H Queen Elizabeth II during the Commonwealth Games in Edmonton, Canada, 1978

Chapter 13
Meeting the Legends

In the middle of 1978 I was given an opportunity to cover the Commonwealth Games in Canada. My relative Dave Martin arranged for me to stay with a Trinidadian couple during my stint in Alberta. My hosts met me at the airport when I arrived out of Toronto in early afternoon and took me to their home where we had a typical "Trini" dinner of chicken pelau. They then explained to me that they were both working nights and so I would probably be on my own for most of my one week stay. I could hear them coming home at about five a.m. on some occasions; at that hour they certainly did not want to chat, but to head straight to bed. Because of this timing we hardly saw each other, but I was able to acknowledge their hospitality by leaving tickets for track and field, cycling and swimming as there were West Indians in those events.

It was on this visit to Canada that I met Wilt Chamberlain the Philidelphia 76'ers centre, but interestingly enough his presence there was wholly unconnected to basketball. He was there to promote the game of volleyball during the games and take advantage of the presence of a huge press corps. It was a great opportunity to interview him and he agreed. The scene of the interview was almost laughable. I was glad that no one was there to take a picture as I had to get this seven footer to sit down whilst I conducted the interview standing up with my hand held recorder.

To my surprise I received an invitation from the Queen of England who was attending the games as the head of the Commonwealth and was putting on what would have been a traditional reception on the rest day of the event. Although it was quite an honour to meet the Queen and Prince Philip and her children, the major highlight of the event was meeting Dr Roger Bannister, the English runner who first broke the four minute mile barrier. He was tall as I remember him, and walked gracefully. What surprised me was his ability to talk with passion about those very cold days in England when he had to prepare for his attempt on the mile barrier. While he trained for this event set for May 6th 1954, he was also enrolled in a medical degree programme and had to carefully divide his time at Oxford between studies and track activities.

Flying to Alberta gave me an idea how vast Canada was as it took more than three hours after taking off from Pearson International Airport in Toronto before we landed in Edmonton. The city was not as built up as Toronto as it was still very much on a development trend and seemed to have lots of space. I spent a lot of time at the luxurious MacDonald Hotel as the headquarters for the Commonwealth Broadcasting office was located there, headed by Alva Clarke. The other journalists from the Caribbean who attended the games included Hugh Crosskill, the brilliant Jamaican broadcaster. In later years I had the pleasure of broadcasting cricket with him. Alvin Corneal, well-known regionally for his football career with Trinidad and Tobago, and also bearing the distinction of representing Trinidad and Tobago at cricket for a number of years in a strong batting line-up, was also covering the games for radio for the twin island republic.

On my return to Guyana, I was approached by Tony Cozier who by then had written a book on fifty years of West Indies test cricket from 1928-1978. Tony had received sponsorship from a Trinidad company, and support for a proposed radio programme that was to follow the outline of his book. He wanted me to share the task of conducting interviews with the players who were still alive. This meant a substantial amount of travel in the region and spending close to a month in England in an attempt to interview players who had played for and against the West Indies in the thirties and the series that followed. The visit to England also provided the programme with material from Pakistan and India players who were either working or residing in England after their playing days. For me it was quite an experience as it was almost like turning back the clock. I was able to meet players who up until that time had been just names in cricket annals. At times it was difficult because I was asking players to remember performances, scores and incidents that took place almost forty years before. In fact it was a credit to some of these former test players to be able to recall and provide the relevant information.

The project also took me to Port of Spain and among the interviews I conducted there was Clifford Roach, the outstanding West Indies batsman who recorded our first test hundred against England in Barbados 1929-30. Roach told me a marvellous story about the same tour. Following his century at Kensington he then recorded scores of 0 and 0 in the following test at Port of Spain. These two low scores prompted the selectors to think of omitting the West Indian opener for the third test in Guyana, but the appointed captain for that test match, Maurice Fernandes pleaded on his behalf to the selectors. Clifford Roach then took the opportunity, by scoring 209, to support Fernandes' faith in him, and had in that game a major partnership with George Headley who contributed 114.

There was also a funny story told by the Barbados and West Indies leg spinner Bertie Clarke about his captain Rolph Grant when he invited him to bowl during the second test in 1939 at Old Trafford, Manchester. The captain said, 'Now young Clarke, I'm not setting a field for leg breaks and googlies, you have to decide what you are going to bowl, you can't bowl both.' The Trinidad and Tobago Grant was a well-respected captain and expected his leg spinner to stick to the game plan. Clarke said that he started with the intention of obeying his captain's instructions and bowled only leg breaks, but George Headley, fielding at short mid-on by the third over was advising him under his breath to bowl the googlie. Clarke ignored the senior West Indies batsman for a while until he had built up the courage to go against his captain. The first googlie had the outstanding England batsman Walter Hammond caught by wicket keeper Derrick Sealy off an inside edge, and as celebrations took place on the field Rolph Grant came directly to Clarke, oblivious of Hammond's departure through his change of delivery, reprimanded him, and reiterated his instructions that he could not bowl both leg break and googlie.

The other moving experience from this broadcast venture was meeting with the former West Indies fast bowler Hophnie Hobah Hines Johnson, who stretched well past six feet two and still carried strong shoulders. When playing at his home ground in Jamaica, he had taken 5 for 41 and 5 for 55 in the 1948 test match against England at Sabina Park to help the West Indies win by ten wickets. Surprisingly he was not included in the West Indies '49 tour to India as Prior Jones was preferred. He had only played three tests for the West Indies but turned up for the interview with four solid scrapbooks on his career and extremely proud of his cricket achievements although he might have been treated badly by the selectors. One of his victims in that '48 test match was the England opener Len Hutton whom he bowled for 56.

Regrettably our tight budget did not allow us to offer recompense to the interview subjects and as a result we missed the opportunity of interviewing George Headley and Sonny Ramadhin. Tony had had an agreement to interview the great Jamaica and West Indies batsman Headley, but overnight someone must have indicated that we were in no position to compensate. The other occasion was when the former West Indies wicket-keeper/ batsman Clairmont Depeiza had arranged for Sonny Ramadhin whom he knew very well, to agree for me to come up from my London base to the north of England to carry out the interview. I was almost about to leave my brother Victor's Finsbury Park flat to commence my journey when the phone rang with Depeiza on line to say that unless we could offer three hundred pounds, the mystery spinner would not carry out the interview. The sponsorship just did not allow for payments of these amounts, yet we understood the player's positions.

When the interviews were finally done and carefully edited, the programme was recorded at the Caribbean Broadcasting Corporation in Barbados. The finished product was later presented to the sponsors at a special ceremony in Port of Spain for distribution to regional stations.

Chapter 14
A Near Miss at Jonestown

For many, November 18th 1978 will always be remembered for the loss of 909 American lives at Jonestown, a community in the north western part of Guyana run by the Reverend Jim Jones of the People's Temple. The majority of the people who died there were made to participate in a mass suicide when they were forced to drink a cyanide concoction prepared by the medical officials who were part of the community. It was significant because it represented the largest loss of civilian life in any one day in American history, and thrust the little known Guyana into the spotlight, but it was more significant for me because it represented a narrow miss.

One week prior to the tragedy, I had been to the People's Temple Community to offer recommendations for their basketball programme and had subsequently accepted an invitation for the following week to be there along with a karate black belt instructor who had been asked to provide an assessment on their karate programme.

The initial invitation had been made by two members of the commune, Debbie Adams and Karen Clayton, both of whom I knew from their visits to the Ministry of Sport where I was working. I actually knew Karen socially as she was very keen on attending sporting events and was quite a good dancer.

In 1977 the People's Temple had organized an excellent concert at the National Cultural Centre in Georgetown which attracted almost a full house of 2000 persons. They had put on show all the talented musicians and singers and for those attending it was almost as though we were in Los Angeles or New York as the standards were so high. It was good PR for the group as they had faced an embarrassment at the Sacred Heart Catholic Church in Main Street when the Reverend Jones staged curing a woman of cancer only for the press to find out that he had used chicken breasts when he allegedly extracted the cancer from the woman's chest. The Catholic Community were not happy that this highly regarded Cathedral which ran a school in the same compound had been secured by the People's Temple for such a purpose, and the concert helped redeem the organisation's image with the public.

Instead of repeating the concert in 1978, the group decided to sponsor a basketball tournament at the National Indoor Centre in Georgetown that would include the leading clubs in Guyana. They were however, somewhat concerned about the standard of their team's performance and invited me to fly up to the compound as a Ministry of Sport official. I reported to the Ogle Airport on the east coast of the Demerara and on arrival discovered that Jim Jones' wife's mother and father were also making the trip. We began the journey to Port Kaituma by plane and then travelled a further six miles to the commune on a fairly dusty and uneven surface. The pilot, who flew by visual, kindly pointed out the outstanding landmarks and communities as we crossed over many rivers and vast areas of this somewhat underdeveloped area.

At the Port Kaituma airstrip I was met by Debbie and Karen and we travelled in the back of an open small truck that was pulled by a tractor. It was just about midday when we arrived at the People's Temple community and I was struck by the cleanliness and what appeared to be a happy and industrious group of Americans far away from their original hometowns. Lunch was served and I was impressed to learn that they were in fact preparing over 3000 meals each day, and using the heat of their wooden stoves to assist in the drying of their laundry. In the middle of the commune there was a substantial pile of lumber which was earmarked for the building of more small apartments to further improve their living conditions and provide greater comfort for the members. It was indeed a pleasant Saturday afternoon and I noticed that many African American members in the latter years of their lives were enjoying sitting in the sun possibly forgetting arthritis and other issues that they may have faced in the USA.

Jones had come to Guyana with good recommendations for the work he had done in improving housing for the black American community and poor Americans in general. The group had the support of the Burnham Government and moved quite easily around Georgetown with their headquarters in a large house in Campbellville where new members would spend some time before being taken to the commune itself.

After lunch I was taken to watch the People's Temple basket-ballers play in a match on a wooden court that they had skilfully built. After viewing the game for about twenty minutes, I had no doubts of their readiness. I informed the planning committee that they had nothing to worry about as the standard displayed by the former junior college students, who had been taken to Guyana by their parents, was of a high standard. They acted very quickly on my recommendation and they seemed to be ready to move ahead with the plans for the tournament in conjunction with the Guyana Basketball Association. The following morning, a group of players, including Jones' biological son left for Georgetown on their boat, the "Albatross".

That evening there was entertainment for those of us who were visiting and the community in general and their talented musicians and singers performed for about an hour while dinner was had. The seating arrangements were such that I was seated next to Jim Jones. He spoke slowly but coherently and wore black pants and a flaming red shirt and a neat hairstyle. The one feature I could not observe was his eyes as even at that hour of the night he wore dark glasses. When dinner was finished I could have had no inkling that this American commune was on the verge of collective suicide.

However, when I turned in to my one bedroom apartment I was surprised to hear an information hour. The official on the PA system kept reminding the entire community that the CIA would always be a threat and that the Guyana Army may come at any time to disrupt the work of the People's Temple. I was certainly taken aback by this and when Karen came to see if I was okay and happy with my accommodation, I questioned her about what I considered indoctrination. The conversation led to a major row between us as she attempted to justify the programme. I felt deep down that Karen was not entirely convinced or necessarily in support of this aspect of the organization, but went along with what was taking place because of fear. Still I had no problem sleeping that evening mainly due to the length and activity of my day. While at breakfast the following morning I was asked to return the following week with a qualified karate instructor as they wanted verification on style they were actually practicing.

On my return to Georgetown I contacted Sensei Dacosta who was a teaching black belt at a dojo opposite the Bourda test ground and he readily agreed to come to Jonestown and carry out this exercise. However, by Thursday of that week I received a call from Karen indicating that Congressman Leo Ryan was to visit the commune with his own entourage and a strong US press corp to verify allegations that members were being held at Jonestown against their will. I did not feel it was a good time for me and Sensei Dacosta to visit as they had to prepare a programme for the visiting congressman.

Later that evening I was at the Pegasus Hotel in Georgetown when Congressman Leo Ryan arrived with his group and the foyer was filled with the television equipment of all the major American networks. Since I was not going to return that weekend I was co-opted to broadcast a football game at Linden, the bauxite town some 60 miles up the Demerara River. The tournament was between a visiting Chinese team from Peking and a national selection, and when the players walked off at half time a Guyana Defense Force lieutenant who was stationed in the area came up to me and quietly informed me that there was some trouble in Jonestown. He told me that at least 300 people were killed and the rest had run into the nearby surrounding areas. By the time I got to Georgetown some two hours later, the rumours were rife. Someone who had flown out from the airstrip as the attack on the congressman and his party was taking place was able to confirm that shooting was ongoing as he became airborne. The rest of this story is well documented but I was able to confirm through an army source that Karen did not drink the cyanide but was shot through the back of the head for refusing.

The following weekend I left for Australia and as I flew out from the Guyana international airport I shivered thinking of what might have happened to me and how it might have ended tragically if Sensei Dacosta and I had got caught up in those hours of madness at Port Kaituma or at the commune itself. It was ironic that sitting next to me at the back of the BWIA jet was one of Jim Jones' lawyers, Charles Garry. He had escaped with his life after he convinced a guard to let him go free so he could tell the world about this great deed by the community. He had walked all six miles through the bush to get out on that bleak afternoon and showed the scars of being cut by razor bush and branches. He seemed tired, drawn and almost overwhelmed by the experience of what had taken place which no doubt was traumatic, but he was happy to be flying out with his life, out of Guyana. He did tell me that he had advised Jones to allow the small group of persons who wanted to leave with the congressman to go unobstructed as this itself was a vote of confidence against all the allegations that hundreds of people were being kept in this People's Temple Community against their will. It was when I got to Australia that I really was struck when I saw coverage on their television of the stacks of dead members and the large number of former members departing in body bags.

Chapter 15
My Involvement with Kerry Packer

I was at home one night in my Charlotte Street cottage in Georgetown a month before the second Packer Cricket World Series was about to begin, when the telephone rang. It was a voice identified from Australia asking me whether I would like to come and do radio commentary for the Packer Series. For the first few seconds I thought it was a prank, but I then realised it was a genuine official who introduced himself as Lynton Taylor from PBL Marketing in Syndey. I jumped at the chance as I was still freelancing. He gave me instructions about where to collect my ticket in Georgetown. I was to fly into London and go to the Quantas desk to collect my ticket to Perth.

Out of the storybook of life, I was about to be part of a major event in the world of cricket. I got to Perth where we were playing this first game at the show ground, and should have headed to the Sheraton Hotel where I was being put up. A driver would be sent to meet me. When I checked in at London I had to show my yellow fever vaccination and all my inoculations but when I got to the airport at Perth and the health department asked me for the vaccinations, they could not be found. I was frustrated and told them I had been there in 1975 and indicated that my ten year shot would have covered the time period. The authorities accepted that to a point but they simply demurred politely, saying: "Mr. Perreira, with all due respect we need to follow procedure and unfortunately we're going to have to put you in quarantine for three days".

There was a newly upgraded quarantine bungalow and I was to be the first guest. With the series started, I had to stay isolated for this period with two full time nurses, to be visited by a doctor every morning and every evening to check my temperature, look at my eyes and to make sure I wasn't turning out in any funny way until the period of quarantine was over. I was alone with the nurses who were on shift; one was younger than the other and the more pleasant. She brought her long playing records and entertained herself, and I suppose entertained me too. The officer from the Ministry of Health said: "Mr. Perreira, order what you want: caviar, champagne; Quantas is going to pay this bill because they have lost your vaccination". I did not get into caviar, I just wanted to get out. The door was not locked but I was obligated to stay. When my three day quarantine expired, I departed to the Sheraton Hotel only to have to fly off to central Australia that afternoon.

Lance Gibbs was there and saw the funny side of it. He told everyone to be careful of this young man who had just come out of quarantine in Perth. It was quite a reception; everywhere was this huge laughter. There I was waltzing in on the last day of the test which coincided with my last day of quarantine to get all kinds of teasing at the Sheraton.

We played in Australian rules football grounds. The Packer organisation turned these grounds into cricket grounds and actually used a helicopter to drop a pitch into the middle of the square, which was developed elsewhere. It was a matter of having financial backing because the turnout was not great. For example in Melbourne we played at the Waverly Stadium seventeen miles out from the centre of the city, and Lawrence Rowe made a magnificent 175 against Lillee and Thomson. It was watched by only 2000 people though this was class batting. The same pattern continued: we enjoyed very competitive cricket, the best of England, Australia, the West Indies and the Rest of the World and the best of umpires. But the Packer controversy was to plague the tournament.

England were then touring Australia and it was cheese to chalk when you looked at the spectators for the England team playing the Australians. The best cricket was on the World Series but the crowds were simply not coming. This was partly because the conditions were not the traditional cricket grounds. Kerry Packer managed to get the Sydney Cricket Grounds, the only test grounds used during the series. We never got the Adelaide Oval, the Gabba in Brisbane or the Melbourne Cricket Ground, but World Series was able to acquire the Sydney Cricket Ground as this was not controlled by the Australia Cricket Board. It was there at the one day international between the West Indies and Australia, black sight screen, white ball, coloured clothing, that a revolution started in this day and night contest.

The revolution was talking place in the commentary booth as well. Commercial radio was different from the radio commentary I had done before. Where you would broadcast six balls in an over in a normal cricket game, you had to get your commercials in and sometimes you would miss three balls in an over. Apart from this Kerry Packer never interfered. He said: "Listen, you've got a job to do, make it sound attractive and enterprising, sell the product but do not tell the public any false stories".

The match started at two in the afternoon at the Sydney Cricket Ground and by about four o' clock the crowds began to emerge. The picture is this: it is now eight o' clock and well over 45,000 people have gathered. Lillee is bowling to Fredericks and Greenidge with the moon above. The lights of the Sydney Cricket Ground are on all around and the blood curls in your veins, the hair stands on your arms. You cannot believe what you are seeing. It was almost witnessing something of an impossible dream. The mix finally came together, the innovations, helmets, all kinds of razzmatazz to attract the crowds. There was a team song specially done: "Come on Aussie, come on, come on…", and other inducements for people to come and enjoy, to have fun. The atmosphere was perfect, the cricket was fierce and competitive with the West Indies winning the contest. Packer himself was delighted with the final breakthrough to success and ordered champagne for all and sundry. He later organised a Christmas party at his home in Sydney, a well-arranged affair with entertainers from as far afield as Los Angeles. It turned out to be quite a night.

Chapter 16
Barbados

In the early part of 1980, though cricket was very much part of my attention, I decided to make a move to leave Guyana for Barbados. I felt that as a freelancer I needed to experience life in the Caribbean, improve my knowledge of the region and place myself geographically in the centre. The decision became even more necessary when the then Guyana government added a fifty percent tax on airline tickets which meant that if anyone wanted my services and was willing to pay for me to travel, there would be a huge additional cost; as a freelancer I would not have been competitive. I had resigned from the Ministry of Sport as sports advisor at the end of 1978, but kept the role of Chairman of the National Sports Council. Most people believed I was still employed by the Ministry – because it was still a high profile role with a fair amount of responsibility. My coaching and administrative staff was almost forty, and NSC Secretary Derrick Whitehead had to be actively involved to keep up the momentum of the council. When I decided to make the move I went to the Permanent Secretary and informed him that I was going to leave. It was the right time for me to step down and do something different.

I tied in my departure with coverage of a world boxing fight between World Champion, Mexican-American Salvador Sanchez, and a very talented, promising Guyanese by the name of Patrick Ford who got a world title shot in a Mexican American town in San Antonio, Texas. It was in fact a very great opportunity to be ringside to do television coverage for Trinidad and Guyana. Patrick Ford was managed by a Trinidadian Richard Fara and was very popular in the twin island state, and of course he was a national hero in Guyana. The fight itself was close to the very end. Patrick Ford did an excellent job against the very experienced Mexican-American fighter. Sanchez was at the very top among champions in that division, and Ford boxed beautifully, jabbing continuously and occasionally surprising his opponent with right crosses and shots to the body. I think he surprised not only the opponent but certainly everyone around the ringside and silenced the Mexican-American crowd until the tide turned against him.

Maybe a little bit of inexperience in his preparations contributed. Instead of resting, he had gone out with his fiancée to shop on the afternoon of the fight – or perhaps he started a little too quickly and should have kept back a little bit of energy for finishing, but Sanchez started to take charge of the fight. It was in fact a great performance and a great opportunity to be there. I also had the pleasure of meeting the outstanding and outspoken American boxing commentator Howard Cosell, who had had his clashes with Muhammad Ali but lost most of them, and had a reputation of being opinionated and cocky. But speaking to him at length before the programme got underway I must admit he did not come across that way to me. He had a calm personality. He obviously knew his boxing very well and was keen in a genuine way to learn more about the somewhat unknown Patrick Ford.

After the fight I travelled to Barbados which would be my new home and stayed the first two weeks with Guyanese dramatist Ken Corsbie in Belleville before moving to my small flat in Rockley. In my first weeks, I made contact with a friend with whom I had played cricket in England and became very close to David Simmons. He was a law student in the sixties and we had met at the West Indies Student Centre in London – he later became Attorney General and Chief Justice of Barbados. He helped me apply for a work permit through the regular channels and it was approved. Cricket is almost a lodge in the Caribbean and I think through cricket my application might have been expedited. Later I applied for immigrant status as I felt that it was more secure. It also afforded me the flexibility to change employers if I wanted.

I was invited by the CBC to join them, mainly in radio with an occasional spot on television. I worked with Sam Wilkinson, a vibrant sports-loving Barbadian journalist who had also played cricket at the second division level in Barbados, and was extremely keen on table tennis. We formed a dynamic team at "The Pine" and we really transformed radio in Barbados. I applied some of the techniques I had learned in the 1960s at GBS and we introduced the telephone a great deal as a means of reaching officials, sponsors and competitors and the sporting community in general. All of a sudden CBC was able to bring the voices of sporting personalities to the listening public.

We had flexibility with the programme department and with the news persons, like Jean Lewis, the programme director from Jamaica who liked what Sam and I were doing. They saw that we were willing to go the extra mile and to work without regard for the clock. At lunch time we were given as much as twenty-five minutes against the previous time of ten and sometimes in the evening we would have close to thirty minutes, which gave us the time to really get to the issues and highlight quality performance. We had less flexibility in the morning because of the structure of the programming as we had to be out in time to join the BBC for the World News and of course, the famous pips. People appreciated the new approach and responded favourably, making themselves available for interviews and providing contact numbers where necessary.

Sam eventually left the CBC - he had been disappointed at the lack of support on an initiative that he had put forward to cover the Caribbean Table Tennis Championships - and decided to work with a car dealership. His popularity served him well in that world. I was then faced with programming for six days a week and it seemed there was no movement to bring on a replacement. The work took its toll and eventually I suffered from a bad septic throat which I discovered on a visit to Doctor Ahmed Patel. He immediately said I was liable to get sick with high fever if I did not take a break from being on the air. I informed the radio station, called from the doctor's office and he certified my leave. The next morning I drove up to "The Pine" at CBC though I had a bit of a fever, to ensure there was enough news for the morning announcer Wynn Callender. To my surprise I found the sports department of one had expanded to three in a matter of hours. It underlined an inconsistency in their treatment of me. Had they brought on someone to replace Sam I would not have fallen sick.

My brother Desmond had called to check up on me and suggested I visit Toronto, and watch the 1982 World Cup Football with him on television, which was eventually won by Italy. I didn't think I was breaking any rules when I decided to go. I relaxed at my brother's home, took my medication and followed the tournament, and I remember sending a postcard to CBC, something to the effect of: feeling better, see you on the appointed date. I returned to Barbados as scheduled and called the CBC to let them know that I would be resuming work the following morning. At about 4 o'clock a CBC driver arrived at my home in Ventnor Gardens and delivered a letter which ended the contract with me and paid me to date. I could not understand why. I had done nothing wrong and I decided to take the matter further.

I spoke with my friend David Simmons who felt we had a very good case. I had my doctor's letter, and had secured the postcards I had sent to CBC when I went to clear my desk. But a legal hearing takes a long time to get settled and by the time that the case was ready to be called, no one who had been part of the decision to terminate my contract was still on the CBC board. I felt that it did not make sense to take the board to court. I decided to withdraw the case.

A few days after the letter came ending my contract with the CBC however, Harold Hoyte from the Nation Group, which owned the Voice of Barbados, offered me an appointment, so I was not without work very long. One of the first things I did with VOB was to cover the CAC Youth Athletic Championships. I remember getting Alison Leacock, a former athlete herself and a popular VOB announcer, and former national athlete Orlando Green to be part of the broadcast, as well as a Barbadian track and field athlete who spoke Spanish, and we were able to interact with the Spanish speaking sports community to provide very extensive coverage.

I had developed a strong relationship with VOB and did a morning show from my flat at Ventnor Gardens in the morning with Julian Rogers, the early morning man to whom I delivered my broadcast by telephone. My move to VOB was further enhanced when the Nation Group were able to attract Tony Cozier away from the CBC and we were able to work together again, along with Erskine King, the former Barbados player who had joined VOB as sports editor. We began to attract a growing listenership which helped the sales department and it turned out to be a golden period. One year we even had what we dubbed a "dream team" which included Sir Garfield Sobers. In a way the jolt of the letter from CBC did not turn out to be such a disaster.

In 1982 VOB covered Jamaica versus Barbados at Kensington, and the Windwards opposing strong Barbados at the same venue. Barbados easily beat Jamaica by an innings and 95 runs after scoring 465 mainly through an outstanding 172 by Alvin Greenidge. Jamaica in reply could only muster 242 and 128. Joel Garner was the main destroyer when Jamaica batted the first time taking 6 for 73. The Windwards produced an outstanding performance to beat Barbados by 4 wickets in a tense and dramatic four days that surprised the Caribbean cricketing world. The Bajans had in fact taken first innings lead as the Windwards, replying to the 269 scored by the home team, fell short and were only able to put together 213. Thanks to some hostile and sustained fast bowling by Norbert Phillip who ended with 4 for 21, and clever off spin bowling by Stanley Hinds (3 for 62) and Thomas Kentish (2 for 44), it was a "game on" situation when Barbados was bowled out for 184, leaving the Windwards to get 241 for victory on the last day.

The players from the banana producing islands had got off to a bad start, losing Lance John for 2 and Lennox Lewis for 1 before Lockhart Sebastian first got support from Shane Julien (20) and Will Slack, the Middlesex Vincentian-born player who was not out 60 at the end, as Norbert Phillip again came back to play a vital role in the Windwards victory by scoring 62. In all my days of covering cricket I have never seen a manager so overjoyed as was Dominican Tom Lafond. He was happy but crying in the Kensington dressing room and it was no doubt tears of joy as he tried to take in the tremendous feat of his team, as it was not often that visiting contingents beat Barbados at Kensington easily.

The other game I covered that year was Barbados against Leewards at Warner Park. The scores in that game were Leewards 194 and 284 while Barbados recorded 308 and 173 for 6. There were some excellent bowling performances on what is normally a very good batting track at Warner Park, with Garner taking 5 for 56 and Andy Roberts 4 for 53. Richie Richardson who had failed to score in the first innings produced an innings of class when scoring 76 against a quality Bajan attack of Garner, Ezra Mosley, Franklyn Stephenson, Albert Padmore. However, what will always linger in my mind from that game was a truly magnificent display of batting by Stephenson who was eventually run out for 165. The most talented all rounder never to play for the West Indies displayed some shots off the back foot that took me back to watching the great Clyde Walcott.

One of the projects I was happy to be part of during my time in Barbados was getting BWIA to sponsor the combined secondary school basketball team in the BBA first division competition. I would often attend matches at the YMCA and felt the unsponsored secondary school talent had tremendous potential but needed to be backed by a private sector grouping if they were going to improve. I had gotten to know basketball coach George Shepard and discussed the possibility of approaching BWIA for possible sponsorship. We met with Cleveland Mayers, a keen sports enthusiast who was in senior management of the company, and after two weeks of intense discussions the sponsorship was approved and the players provided new playing outfits carrying the logo, and basketballs and equipment that would assist in their team practices and warm up drills.

Chapter 17
My Reputation on the Line

Wednesday, January 11th, 1983 began as a typical beautiful Caribbean day. I had been in the habit of listening to the morning news from Barbados and around the region on various radio stations because I was producing the sports news cast for VOB and voicing it by telephone each morning. Later that morning I left my apartment in Ventnor Gardens, Rockley and headed for Kensington where the Barbados team was practicing for their upcoming match against the Leewards. I had just gone past the Immigration headquarters in Bridgetown when the traffic slowed for pedestrian crossing and a deep throated gentleman whose information I trusted came to my vehicle and informed me that a rebel West Indies cricket team was leaving Barbados for South Africa the next day. As he walked away he said, "Do your homework."

If this were true it would have a significant impact on West Indian cricket and society. Those who believed in bridge-building had always tried to attract the top West Indian players to South Africa, but the issue had always been pride and not money with the players because of the South African system of Apartheid. My thoughts as the Barbadian team practiced just below the Kensington stand were not on the activity in front of me but on the sensational news I had received earlier in the day.

As a cricket journalist I felt I could not wait until this development became known after the players had departed Barbados, or from international wires. But I needed more substantial proof before I could break the story. It was about noon when I called a friend at BWIA who had looked after my travel arrangements over the years and enquired about the passengers booked for Miami out of Barbados on the following day. I was requested to provide some names and in a matter of minutes a list of well known cricketers appeared on the screen of the BWIA reservation staff. I felt I had enough to work with to break the story on VOB and consulted Julian Rogers who was the "on air" announcer at the time.

It was 1:05 p.m. on that day that Julian and I decided to go with the story; the telephone lines were tied up for about two hours. A number of callers challenged that if my story were false my career as a journalist and broadcaster would be irretrievably damaged. What I did refrain from revealing while on the air, were the actual names of players who were scheduled to leave on the following day. I felt it would not have been right and proper to put names out into the public domain at that time because it was a very sensitive issue. The news that a West Indies rebel team may have been heading for Apartheid South Africa was a major discussion point for the rest of the day and the evening. The Barbadian press no doubt worked overtime to confirm the story, while the phone at my residence rang off the hook.

The following morning just after 8:00 a.m., I headed for the Grantley Adams Airport to see what would unfold and whether the information I received was in fact accurate. Every sport-related and current affairs journalist was already there when I arrived and we all waited for the BWIA plane from Trinidad to come in which was the scheduled flight for the players to take on their way to Miami. The Sun Jet Aircraft arrived on schedule, passengers came off who were either heading into Barbados or simply in transit, and after a while there was the first boarding announcement, but there were no players in sight. The Miami-bound aircraft took off on time and with no players on board, the pressure began to build as my career hung in the balance. A small number of the press did depart the airport but the majority stayed as other airlines had flights to the American city. I walked around the airport constantly looking for some lead when I was told by an airport worker that he had seen the family of Alvin Greenidge, the Barbadian opener who had played for the West Indies against Australia in 1978 and toured India under Alvin Kallicharran in the same year, check in a suitcase at the American Airline counter much earlier in the morning. This was an encouraging bit of information and straight away I headed to the American Airlines counter. The manager on duty confirmed to me in confidence that the players were in fact on his flight and I promised not to reveal the information. I quickly realised that the BWIA booking was a clever decoy.

The drama heightened as the American jet arrived, but there was still no team at the airport; and again there was the same pattern of persons deplaning either as in transit passengers or visitors to Barbados, followed by the announcement for passengers to assemble in the departure area. A few minutes later a small van came to a stop with screeching tyres in front of the departure area and much to my relief I saw Sylvester Clarke leading the charge to the immigration door. It became obvious that the players were all pre-booked well prior to getting to the airport.

The drama that filled the atmosphere at the airport experienced another twist as after the players were safely on board and the cabin door closed, we heard another sound of screeching tyres. It was the former West Indies off-spinner Albert Padmoore who emerged from a taxi to join the same flight. I did try to get him to give me a short statement about the decision to go to South Africa, but all the way to the immigration door he simply keep saying in a polite way and with a slight smile "no comment, no comment." He made his way out unto the tarmac, the airline door opened once more, the steps were wheeled back into place and "Paddy" as he is known had boarded. In fact Harold Hoyte, editor of the progressive Nation Newspaper at that time was able to get his passport sent from his home and bought a return ticket to Miami in order to secure a major story for his paper. It was later learnt that Lawrence Rowe and Colin Croft had departed Jamaica and the players would all join up in Miami.

I breathed a sigh of relief as I headed back to my Rockley home, and silently thanked 'Deep Throat' for sharing the information which brought the best out of me as a journalist.

Chapter 18
Last Years in Barbados

1983 was possibly the most busy, challenging year for me in my career as a broadcaster. The year started with first class matches at Kensington Oval in Barbados, and later the visit of the Indian cricket team, followed by the World Cup in England, the Pan-American Games in Caracas, and ending with a three month stint in mythical India. It was a rewarding year for a freelance journalist and I was able to participate in some quality events.

The first class season for 1983 got going in the third week in January and the Leewards came to play Barbados. While the game itself was important, of greater interest to fans and the board alike was the question of who would go to India as the reserve opening batsman. There were two candidates in people's minds, young players Richie Richardson from Antigua, and Andrew Light from Guyana. The Leewards game was played out amid much anticipation. Against what was a fairly good Barbados attack that included Malcolm Marshall and Wayne Daniel, Richardson marked his name very well, because out of 253 he scored 102 and in doing so had impressed the selectors.

Barbados did in fact win that game by 56 runs because the Leewards collapsed rather badly in the second innings at 189 with Wayne Daniel, who had 7 for 55 in the first innings, finishing with 5 for 33 in the second. I think in every respect Richardson virtually won a place to India later on in the year with that performance. Andrew Light also presented himself as a candidate for India when Guyana played Barbados at Kensington in early February. Opening the innings against an attack that included Marshall, Neil Phillips, Roddy Estwick and George Linton, he recorded a 112 and batting a second time for good measure, got 53.

But when it came down to the final selection Richardson got in, a selection which led him to many runs for the West Indies all over the world and eventually led him to the West Indies captaincy. Light unfortunately never won a West Indies senior cap and though he continued to play for Guyana, he was surely disappointed that he did not get an opportunity to play at the highest level. The selectors obviously had their reasons in terms of who was mentally stronger, and consideration of all round ability probably came into focus. Light passed away some years ago but his legacy is being carried on by his young son who is seen as a promising prospect in Guyanese cricket.

As the first class season continued, people were turning their attention to the arrival of the Indian cricket team in the Caribbean. That test series started in Jamaica, and Sabina Park with its fast conditions favoured the fast bowlers. India were bowled out on the first day for a fairly average 251. West Indies did not reply with anything much better than 254 and when the fourth day's play was completely washed out, Sabina Park was in fact a lake. Everyone thought this would be a very boring draw. The commentators and press turned up to find the ground staff working very hard to get the grounds into condition, and the fifth day was playable from the start, but the spectators expected did not show. Marshall and Roberts really bent their backs and their great effort saw India being bowled out for 174 with the Antiguan taking 5 for 39 while Marshall finished with 3 for 56.

It was a good but somewhat slow start by Gordon Greenidge and Desmond Haynes. Clive Lloyd was not happy with the pace of scoring the runs and sent out a message with the water cart to Greenidge. He asked him to pick up the run chase so that the West Indies could have a chance of attacking the total. Lloyd wanted him to try to win the game even if it meant getting out in the process. So he did, Greenidge going for 42, Haynes departing shortly after that for 34. Then Viv Richards came in and smashed 61 in about half of the deliveries he faced and then it was match on, the West Indies were virtually underway to winning the match.

In the meantime people who had been listening on the radio started to dash down to Sabina to get there as quickly as possible. Gus Logie came in and hit the first ball for 4 and he went for 10: Jeffery Dujon hit a six over mid-wicket. He was not out on 17 and at the end Marshall was there with him and the West Indies had won by 4 wickets. It was in fact a marvellous fairy tale end which only about 2000 people witnessed at Sabina. The authorities had thought it might be a boring draw on the last day and had only opened one gate, so when the pile up came to get into Sabina, gate collectors had to be mobilised to try and cater for the crowd. What looked to be a dull draw with a fourth day totally washed out, turned into some of the most exciting cricket ever seen at Sabina and to this day about 10,000 people will tell you that they were there to witness it.

The West Indies arrived in Port of Spain for the second test, a game that ended in a draw but one that had a little bit of a twist very much in India's favour. They had batted first and scored only a 175 with Gavaskar who was key to their batting, falling to Holding for 1. When the West Indies batted, they got off to the most disastrous start ever seen at this great ground. Greenidge was bowled by Sandhu without scoring, Haynes fell for the same score caught Kirmani, and when Richards fell to Kapil Dev for 1 the Oval scoreboard showed the West Indies 3 wickets down for 1 run. But in a typical fairytale recovery, two left-handers, Larry Gomes (123), and Clive Lloyds (143), in a partnership of 237, got West Indies to a respectable score of 394. India replied strongly with 409 for 7 in the second inning thanks to Mohinder Amarnath and Captain Kapil Dev who scored some easy runs to reach 100 when the game looked like it would end on a no decision. West Indies were really on the edge with 3 wickets down and one run on the board, and had Gomes and Lloyd not got together, India could well have squared the series, but the match ended on a draw.

The day will also be remembered for an earthquake which hit Port of Spain during the actual day's play. It seemed to have gone on for about 30 seconds but it might have been closer to 15. At first it was thought that the shaking of the commentary box was due to heavy machinery being moved along the roadway just behind the media centre, but we quickly realised from the buzz and movement of the crowd from their seats, especially in the double decker stands, that we were experiencing a mild tremor.

The third test was held in Georgetown, a high scoring game hit by rain with the West Indies getting 470. Richards had a bit of revenge on the Indian attack getting a 109 and in reply India got 254 for 1 when the rains came. At Kensington it was a West Indies victory by 10 wickets. By that time West Indies had really seized control of the series. Gavaskar again failed to make the anticipated runs and India were all out for 209. Thanks to Gus Logie West Indies scored 130. Greenidge got 57, Haynes 92, Richards 80 and the West Indies racked up 486. In the second innings India scored a paltry 277 with Roberts getting 4 wickets, Holding 2, Marshall 2, and the West Indies fast bowler attack was just too much. The West Indies needed one for victory and this was achieved via a no-ball which was almost an anti-climatic ending.

The Antigua test as we expected turned out to be a very high scoring draw. India scored 457, Ravi Shastri leading the way with 102. Kapil Dev hit the ball all over the ARG, scoring 98. The West Indies replied fairly strongly with 550. The interest point there was a partnership of 296 between Greenidge and Haynes which was only broken because Gordon Greenidge's son back in Barbados had fallen ill. He had to retire because of the situation, not out at 154 and it was 296 when he left the ground and flew back to Barbados. Although India did score 247 for 5 in their second innings, that game was destined for a draw. The West Indies won the series, and with a possible meeting at the World Cup in the coming year it was a good psychological win, inspiring Caribbean hopes a lot further.

We had all arrived in England by the end of May, early June and the West Indies were in Group B. In their opening game of the 1983 World Cup, after dominating the men from the sub-continent in the West Indies, they were beaten by India at Old Trafford. It might have been an indication of things to come, but the West Indies did bounce back at Leeds, beating Australia by 100 runs. One must note the performance of Winston Davis, the Windward Islands fast bowler, who had a record performance taking 7 for 51. The West Indies then had a fairly easy victory against Zimbabwe at Worcester winning by 8 wickets. We then moved south and opposed India in Zone B at the Oval, a venue which will always be a happy hunting ground for the men from the Caribbean. This was a crucial game for the defending champions and one they had to win. An outstanding innings of 119 by the West Indies vice-captain Viv Richards from 146 balls after Greenidge and Haynes had gone for 9 and 38 respectively, pushed the West Indies to a competitive 282 from their 60 overs. Captain Lloyd at the end contributed 41 from 42 balls to further support the early work of Richards, while Larry Gomes had a bit of a cameo hitting 27 from 22 balls. India's reply got off to a bad start with Srikanth and Shastri falling to Roberts for 2 and 6 respectively. Armanath did hold the Indian innings together for a while with a polished display of 80, but India fell short of their 283 target and were bowled out for 216 with Roberts and Holding sharing most of the wickets.

The West Indies beat Australia in their return Group B game at Lords. Batting first, Australia felt they had a chance of upsetting the West Indies when they scored 273 thanks to Kim Hughes' 69, David Hookes' 56 and Graham Yallop's 52, and towards the end Rodney Marsh smashed 37 from 26 balls to give Australia some further hope. However, Greenidge and Haynes gave the West Indies a solid start with an opening partnership of 79 before Haynes fell for 33. Then a partnership of 124 between Greenidge and Richards got the West Indies in sight of victory before Greenidge departed on 90. The Antigua 'master blaster' was left not out 95 as first Gomes and then Lloyd assisted in securing the victory off 57.5 overs.

When they played Zimbabwe, West Indies won very easily by 10 wickets: Zimbabwe scoring 171, and West Indies 172 without loss, with Haynes getting 88 and Faoud Bacchus 80. The semi-final line up was India against England, and West Indies against Pakistan. India versus England was played at Old Trafford in Lancashire and West Indies versus Pakistan at the Oval in London, which suited them well because the majority of West Indians lived around the Oval ground in London. India beat England quite easily in the first semi-final in Manchester. England sent in to bat, scored a below par 213 of which many of the top order got starts, but no one went on. India got the required score for the loss of 6 wickets and must have felt quite confident of doing well in their first ever final. At the Oval, Pakistan like England, failed to record a sizeable total after they were also sent in scoring 184, Marshall blowing away the middle order with 3 for 28 off 12 after Roberts collected two Pakistan scalps for 25 off the same number of overs. The West Indies got the required 188 runs for the loss of only 2 wickets, Greenidge (17) and Haynes (29), with Richards undefeated on 80 from 96 balls; while in contrast the dependable Gomes was quite prepared to turn the strike over and was undefeated when victory came with 50 from a 100 balls.

At the final there was every feeling within the West Indies camp that a third World Cup victory was well within their reach. They managed to have recovered from the psychological difficulty in the opening game against India; they had beaten them in the return Zone B game, and they had had some very impressive wins along the line. But one had to acknowledge that having beaten the West Indies in the early part of the tournament, India had also played well with victories over Australia and England in the competition.

The atmosphere at Lords for the final on June 25th was electric, noisy and colourful, mainly due to the supporters of both teams. The West Indies began well with Clive Lloyd winning the toss in his third final and deciding to insert India. This decision looked to be the correct one for after Roberts removed Gavaskar for 2, the rest of the Indian batting order struggled against the attack of Roberts, Marshall, Holding and Gomes with India all out for a paltry 183 that did not look at the time like enough runs to lift the World Cup. It was a good, economical all-round bowling performance by the West Indies, with Roberts taking 3 for 32 from 10, Garner 1 for 24 from 12, Marshall had 11 overs, 2 for 24 and Holding from his 9.4 overs at 2 for 26. Gomes also chipped in by grabbing 2 important wickets in the middle order for 49 runs from 11 overs. As the West Indies walked off to their dressing room to prepare for their reply, most Indian spectators and supporters all over the world had virtually written off Indian chances.

The West Indies were in early trouble losing Greenidge for 1 and Haynes for 13, but maybe the turning point in the game was when Richards, who threatened to counter attack, was brilliantly caught by Kapil Dev running back from short mid-wicket out towards the boundary taking a marvellous athletic catch after he had scored 33 from 28 balls with 7 fours. I think maybe the West Indies lost the plot at that time. Marshall and Dujon did try to produce a rear guard action but the West Indies were all out for 140. Armanath turned out to be the Indian bowling hero, taking 3 for 12 off 7 overs and his solid 26 from 80 balls gave him the "man of the match" award. India to their delight, had won their first ever World Cup and the West Indies spectators were in a deep gloom.

That gloom was to follow all the journalists because we were all invited to attend a West Indies reception on the road across from Lords. Obviously the West Indies board had anticipated a win and had planned ahead. The Indian team was celebrating as we got in to the foyer of the hotel with their tassa drums, whistles and horns and anything that could make noise, while the West Indies, on the floor below milled around in dejection. It was such an anti-climax in atmosphere, the contrast between the total gaiety and celebration of the Indian team and fans, and our silent morgue. There was hardly any conversation, there was little to say really. I spent maybe about twenty minutes commiserating with the team, but I believed our loss was due in fact to complacency.

If India had made a hundred more runs the whole approach of the West Indies batting might have been totally different. What if Kapil Dev had not taken that great running catch? Richards might have just turned loose on the Indian attack and that target of 183 might have been swallowed up in an hour and a half. A friend of mine who had flown all the way from Toronto to watch the World Cup joined in my disappointment. I suggested that we go down to Edgeware Road to cheer ourselves up with a curry and we called a taxi to take us there. I remember distinctly when the taxi driver stopped and we got in the car that he was a black Englishman, obviously of West Indian parentage though he spoke with a strong British accent. As we moved off, he looked at us and exclaimed, 'You lot didn't play too well today, did you?' He had simply distanced himself from his West Indian roots and we thought it was very funny. We buried our sorrows in a curry in Edgeware Road.

There was great debate on our return to the Caribbean: did the West Indies pick the right team? Was it complacency? Did we underrate India etc.? But we had won twice; we had to accept these defeats. The win for India was good for world cricket. What it started to indicate was that England could not be the automatic venue for future World Cup tournaments. When India got to the finals, the Indian Board had requested more tickets for their supporters and the request was refused and I think the Indians decided then that the next time the discussions on the World Cup came around that they would challenge England hosting again. They were part of a host bid for the 1987 World Cup so ideas were starting to germinate about it becoming more of a world event and not a world event played in England.

The Pan-American games in Caracas in the month of August, was a contrast to cricket. It was my second visit to Caracas having taken the Guyana basketball team there in 1971. Although there was infrastructure development overall, one still was conscious of the shanty towns and red brick buildings with their aerials that shot up above them. Although Venezuela was an oil rich country, the Venezuelan Bolivar had lost a lot of its value. In '71 it was 8 Bolivars to the dollar and in 1983 it was something in the vicinity of 200 to the dollar. But despite that the games were well run.

One of the early shocks we had was that the West Germans had given the Venezuelans some modern scientific equipment to do drug testing, and so a number of athletes were disqualified, having failed the urinalysis, from the US, Canada, Cuba, Colombia, Argentina, Puerto Rico, Nicaragua, Chile, Venezuela, including US Olympic weightlifting hopeful, Jeff Michels. Before the track and field competition commenced, several athletes withdrew from the games and returned home without explanation. No information was given, the athletes did not take part and maybe actions speak louder than words. It was felt by the press corps that it might have been the result of the new drug testing process and an attempt to avoid being detected.

The games were themselves multi-sport. There was track and field as well as boxing, cycling, football and hockey, with a lot of Caribbean countries participating and it was in fact totally enjoyable again to be part of a Spanish speaking world. It was a challenge though as one had to learn some basic Spanish to get around to venues and to understand what was going on. There was a small Caribbean media contingent made up of myself, Alvin Corneal and Selwyn Melville of Trinidad, with Selwyn's basic knowledge of Spanish being extremely helpful. Caracas was in fact a major step forward for the small countries of the Pan-American world.

Despite the withdrawal of many of the US competitors, they were able still to secure a tally of 38 medals made up of 14 gold, 11 silver and 13 bronze. Cuba carried the Caribbean banner with four medals less made up of 12 gold, 12 silver and 10 bronze, while Trinidad and Tobago picked up 1 silver for the 4 by 100 metre race and a bronze for the shotput event. Bahamas rounded up the Caribbean medal tally with a bronze medal in the men's discus.

Chapter 19
An Indian Odyssey

After World Cup it was time to return to freelance work in Barbados. My mind turned to the West Indies tour of India and I was contacted by the Caribbean Broadcasting Union who had decided to relay commentary for the six test tour. They contracted Tony Cozier and I and we did not cover the first session of play but started just after lunch. Along with respected Indian voice Dickie Rutnigar, we would carry the broadcast, which was in the wee hours of the morning in the Caribbean until the close of play. It was in fact quite a technical exercise because it meant booking lines from India that had to pass through Montreal and be beamed down to a central spot in the Caribbean, like the CBC in Barbados, and then they would split the services to the very many stations in the region.

India had always been very mythical for me. I had seen the first India team visit the West Indies in 1953 and though I had seen other Indian teams in the intervening years, there was always that wonder about what the actual country was like. I had heard mainly negative things about India, particularly about the poverty and people getting ill because of bad water and food but still I was not sure exactly what to expect. Coming from Guyana where the majority of the population had come as indentured workers from India I had some idea about their attitudes to life and the importance of the Hindu religion. I had been exposed of course to the Friday call to prayer for Muslims so in that respect it was not a culture shock. We knew the work of Mahatma Ghandi in the Indian independence movement, his non-violence philosophy and his work in South Africa, especially in areas like Durban. Curry and saris were very much part of most West Indians' lives, especially in places like Guyana and Trinidad, and Indian wedding celebrations with their sumptuous colours and food was part of my experience. I knew that India was a vast country with a huge population but arriving via London that night, I still was not prepared for what I could expect.

It had been a long journey and it was the middle of the night when we arrived. I was really taken aback by the vast number of people at the airport at four o'clock in the morning. It was almost as if it were four in the afternoon, and families had gathered to see relatives off. The West Indies team were well received by the Indian delegates who displayed a tremendous hospitality that extended to me and Tony Cozier. We were garlanded with flowers and began the long journey by a comfortable, modern coach from the airport. It was a forty-five minute drive and though it was dark there was much to see along the way. There were large groups of people standing along the road perhaps waiting for transportation or waiting for an opportunity to get a job somewhere or simply having nowhere to go. When we arrived in Bombay we were extremely comfortable, the myth of the disaster of Indian hotels was washed away because we stayed at the very modern five-star Taj Hotel.

Wesley Hall was manager and Clive Lloyd was captain, and the feeling of being close to the West Indies team was very special. We felt it was an honour to be in the same hotel with the team. We were warmly received by the players if we went to a room to chat with someone. If there was a team affair Tony and I were invited. Cricket at that point had not been spoilt by the issues that later crept into the game.

As Tony Cozier was also there in the capacity as print journalist and had to write his copy for various newspapers, I felt I should be the one to do some of the ground setting legwork. I contacted All India Radio, who had been advised of course by the CBU that we were coming, to double check arrangements and broadcast positions and to ensure that the technical lines were booked and tested. I also had to see the programme director. It was not just a matter of turning up at the ground and walking in. The CBU had sent us and they expected that the broadcast would come down the line at the appropriate time and without disruption.

I also had to monitor from a technical point of view the quality of the broadcast sound. With the vast crowds, commentary could sometimes be drowned out. This was nothing we had ever experienced elsewhere. The crowds in the Caribbean were never that large, Trinidad Tobago might have 20,000 people but most grounds in the Caribbean held less than 12,000. What we soon discovered was that the Indian operator, thinking he was doing a great job by riding the volume control up on the crowd when a wicket fell or a six was hit, overpowered the broadcast, and it was only by listening and keeping an eye on the operator that we realised what was happening. It literally took black tape to keep the levels down to ensure they could not be changed. We of course catered for low levels for smaller crowds at the start of a test match or the start of a one day international. It was not as easy an exercise as covering cricket out of Australia or New Zealand, or England or South Africa.

The first test was out in a small area of India called Kanpur, a long journey by coach out of Bombay. What we noticed first was the step down in quality of accommodation. We had to be able to adapt to conditions because it was not going to help you if you kicked up a fuss. I kept my eating habits fairly simple; the further away from the city the more one had to watch food preparation. I made sure to peel my own fruit and stick to coffee and tea. We lunched with the West Indies team whose food was carefully prepared and we learned to stay away from oily things and lots of gravy and ended up eating a lot of biriyani meals.

While in Kanpur, we received news of political stirrings back home in the island of Grenada that ran shockwaves through us all. The news about the death of Grenada's Prime Minister Maurice Bishop reached the West Indies team on the eve of the opening test at Green Park Kanpur. Before I left the region I was aware that there was great tension in "the Spice Isle" and that Bishop was under house arrest, as the Bernard Coard faction attempted to take control of the government and country. I knew Maurice Bishop well before the New Jewel Movement and later when his Peoples Revolutionary Government (PRG) was formed. We met in London in the early 60's at the West Indian Student Centre at Collingham Gardens set between Earls Court and Gloucester Road. In those days he was studying law and after we both returned to the region I often met him at Bourda during regional and test matches. As a Caribbean man he obviously saw the importance of cricket and liked the game but once confessed that he was a better card player than anything else in terms of his sporting talent.

The news of his death sent me reeling and I recalled my associations with the once peaceful Grenada. On the day the West Indies played their World Series game against Australia as part of the Kerry Packer programme, there was a crowd riot at Kensington, and we heard that the Eric Gairy government had been overthrown by the PRG in a bloodless coup. After the new government was formed under Prime Minister Bishop, Jackie Creft was named Minister of Sport. She contacted me in the early 80s about her wish to establish a progressive national sporting structure for Grenada that would ensure country-wide programmes and activities. During this period I was in communication with the new minister from my home in Rockley, Barbados and visited Grenada on quite a number of occasions, staying privately with my long standing friends Sandy and Alma Taylor.

About two weeks prior to my departure to India I had visited Grenada for the purpose of a meeting with Minister Creft as she had reached a conclusion regarding a national sporting structure. It would have involved her ministry, a national sports council, national associations and a parish structure to ensure balanced development. When I arrived at Pearls Airport there was a car from the Ministry to meet me as arranged prior to my departure, but on arriving at the Ministry of Sport Minister Creft was not in office. This surprised me as she was not one to miss her appointments. After waiting for about thirty minutes I called her home and found that she was not there either so I returned to the home of Sandy and Alma Taylor and waited for her to contact me. I was unaware that that day the central committee of the PRG was meeting to decide leadership and possible sharing of power between Bishop and Coard. I later understood that this had been a proposal from the Coard faction for a substantial amount of time since Bishop may have been thinking of changing his foreign policy.

On the third and final day of my visit I received a call from Minister Creft apologizing for her absence and asking me to meet Blondel Church, an officer of the Ministry of Sport. He was a young, friendly Grenadian obviously interested in sport and outlined basically what his minister had decided on. After the meeting was concluded I headed to the airport for my trip back to Barbados only to realize two days later that the PRG was falling apart as a group. I got a call from a friend who told me to listen to Radio Grenada immediately. Normal programming was suspended; unbroken music was being heard interrupted only by recorded statements from the head of the Grenadian Army Hudson Austin. The news later got out that Bishop was under house arrest and the situation in Grenada had turned tense.

A day later I departed via London for India and headed for Kanpur to prepare for the broadcasting of the first test. With a mosque which was situated near by our hotel calling on the community via a loud P.A system to attend morning prayers, I found sleeping beyond 4 a.m. difficult. I decided to have an early morning coffee and turn to my short wave radio which I always carried on tour, and waited for the BBC World News at 5 a.m. Indian time. It was second story of the news when I heard that the Prime Minister of Grenada Maurice Bishop and other Ministers of his government had been executed by a firing squad.

I was obviously shocked by the information I just heard as the English speaking Caribbean did not have a history of such drastic action to change leadership. I felt an urge to share this unbelievable occurrence with somebody and left my room and went down the corridor to knock on the door of Viv Richards and Winston Davis. I felt as persons from the Leeward and Windward Islands they were likely to appreciate, even at the early hour, the news of Maurice Bishop's death; they were both visibly moved. Later that morning at breakfast I informed manager Wes Hall and the rest of the West Indies team.

The West Indies had in fact played India in the early part of 1983 at the old large Queens Park Ground in an ODI which Bishop had attended and had presented trophies and the "man of the match" award. I was asked to be master of ceremonies and got Maurice to say a few words, attended by both sides, after he had presented Winston Davis with the "man of the match" award. His security men in the main pavilion were not happy with my impromptu invitation to the Grenadian leader but he did not seem to mind. That was the last time that the West Indies players and I would have seen Bishop alive.

Kanpur was not a great game for India; it was one the West Indies won very easily. The late Malcolm Marshall missed his only possible test hundred when he was bowled and caught by Kapil Dev for 92. The West Indies selectors on tour took a decision to drop Andy Roberts which was a bit of a surprise. It was not very often that he was left out unless he was injured, but it seemed they felt that Marshall, Holding and Winston Davis along with Eldine Baptiste should be the quartet. They say that fast bowlers hunt in pairs: Hall and Griffith, Statham and Trueman, Lillee and Thomson. Andy Roberts and Michael Holding had a special relationship, not just as fast bowlers but as friends and one could see that Holding was sad and upset that his colleague was left out.

We had moved to Dehli which was cooler and played the second Test at the very small Dehli Ground which was by no means as big as Kanpur but situated in the much more modern Indian capital. We enjoyed being in the seat of the Indian government after Kanpur. There were massive modern buildings and roadways and of course lots of traffic. India is a place where two o'clock in the morning is just as busy as two o'clock in the afternoon, and the holy cow really does rule the roadways. Whatever you do, you do not hit down a cow or else you would be in very real trouble.

From general talk it was felt that Roberts was not in the best form and that they would have gotten more out of Baptiste who was a genuine all rounder, with good experience with Leewards and Kent. For the second test Wayne Daniel came in in Baptiste's place to join Marshall, Holding and Davis, keeping Roberts out which was very surprising to us and to the Indian crowds. I am not sure the Indian batsmen were unhappy about this because Roberts was highly respected great thinking Antiguan bowler.

India is big but the world can be small. All the major embassies of the world are represented in Dehli and the Guyana High Commission was based there. A friend of mine who had played basketball with me back in the early days in Guyana, Errol Lee, was in fact a career diplomat and he invited me to come and spend the week with his family in their home in Dehli. It was a pleasure to get out of the hotel and live in a home environment. They had brought a Guyanese house keeper who cooked West Indian food and Errol turned out to be a very positive contact not just for me but for the West Indies team, because he entertained us with a party with all the calypsos and the Caribbean rhythms, a welcome taste of home for us all.

The visit to Dehli was of some historical importance for cricket. The game itself ended in a draw before the West Indies moved on to Gurjarat state. This was a state which had not had major test cricket before, and they in fact had built a brand new ground. The pitch was not all that well prepared and it turned out to be a winner for the West Indies who won very easily, with India failing to meet the W.I fast attack. The W.I had put together a fairly ordinary score of 281 but India fell short when they replied with 241. India gave themselves an outside chance when they dismissed the W.I for 201, as Kapil Dev took 9 for 83 off 30 overs. Their hopes were short-lived when they were bundled out for a paltry 103. It was a test match that Jeffrey Dujon will always remember as he was 98 and flicked Kapil Dev to fine leg for 4 for what he thought was his test hundred, only to find the umpire signalling leg byes. He was out in the next over he faced, caught Kapil Dev, bowled Shastri at the same score.

One of the things that we were able to observe was the importance of the Ganges River which ran behind our hotel. It was used for baths, washing of clothes, and most famously for spiritual purposes. People believed that this river cleansed them and improved their lives. The river was very much part of their lives.

It was there that I found out that India had dry states. Where Mahatma Ghandi had done a lot of work there was no alcohol and for the team to have a casual beer you had to sign a document. If Tony Cozier and I or anyone else from the touring party wanted to have a beer or any alcoholic drink we had to sign a form so that if the police came to check there would be a record that we had requested permission.

We returned to Bombay for a test and there I was extended an invitation by the manager of the Indian team. Hanumant Singh, of India's once royalty, had played for India and had scored a debut of 100; I had met him in the West Indies and got to know him well. He invited me when I got to Bombay to come and spend a week with his family. It was not very far from the Taj Hotel. By six o'clock in the morning a houseboy would bring tea, and my laundry would disappear as soon as I put it down. I was not entirely comfortable with the all the attention though I appreciated the hospitality.

Bombay is a fascinating, complicated pace. The traffic alone is overwhelming. I had thought the traffic was bad in Paris when I visited in 1964 but India made it look like child's play. It was as they say in wrestling, catch as catch can. Traffic police efforts were futile because hardly anyone bothered to wait for too much instruction. There is organised begging in Bombay. Beggars are coordinated and have to give their proceeds to the bosses who give them a portion. You never wanted to look lost because as soon as your face revealed you were unsure, people would swarm you and hands would be all over you. You needed to look busy like you knew where you were going even when you did not.

Bombay had very famous clubs that we were permitted access to as adjuncts to the West Indies team called the CCI. They served great Chinese food and it was a welcome reprieve from the heavy Indian diet. The CCI had lots of facilities and they served great teas in the afternoon. I remember when the W.I team travelled upcountry I did not accompany them because that game was not being covered by radio. During that time I would to go to the CCI and enjoy afternoon tea.

The manager of West Indies team Wesley Hall, had a lively personality and was a man of all parts: fast bowler, minister of government, member of the opposition, then a preacher. He was a character; he had played in the famous tied test in 1960-61 in Australia and he could tell many stories about it. He also had a strong interest in horse racing and his son Sean, a jockey, had come out to India while the tour was going on. Hall was able to get Sean some mounts but it meant also that he had to go down to the tracks in various parts of India at five in the morning, and as an early riser I would volunteer to come along. I was surprised by the number of Australians in the racing industry whom I found at Indian tracks as jockeys and trainers and grooms and owners.

Calcutta was a profound experience. I was very moved by the poverty and suffering I witnessed. One of the mistakes I made arriving in Calcutta was succumbing to my curiosity. Seated at the back of the coach I looked hungrily out of the window taking in this fascinating world but as we approached the city the sights became more and more dismal. I saw scenes at the side of the road which are hard to forget and they made me despair because they were so pitiful. There were hundreds of people with nowhere to go, nothing to do and nothing to eat, waiting as if they were expecting to die. It did have a very sobering effect on the mind.

When I got into Calcutta to the contrasting Oberoi Grand, I decided never to let it happen to me again, never try to see everything in the coach. In India you have such extremes of wealth and poverty, you could be staying at the grandest hotel and just a few yards away are people living under tents with open fires boiling water for tea and life goes on. I was also very conscious of the caste system – I knew of it a little bit from my Guyana and Trinidad experience but to see it in India was something very different. The liaison officer, who was in fact a Christian and worked with the travel group that arranged our travel, took me one day to see the Mother Teresa operation. She was a very busy woman and I said no more than "hello" but just to see her in person was a very moving experience. It was a great demonstration of caring. She had a lot of people around her and she was giving orders left, right and centre. I did not overstay my welcome. We stayed about five minutes in the large area that she occupied and realised it was not necessary to stay. It was busy, there was so much to do, telephones were ringing.

W.I picked up a much easier victory at Eden Gardens as India batted poorly against our fast attack which saw Roberts included for the first time. We scored 377 with Lloyd leading the way with a superb captain's knock of 161 in reply to India's 241. When batting a second time India were all out for an embarrassing 90. Marshall was almost unplayable taking 6 for 37 from 15 overs.

The tour was fairly long and we ended up playing six test matches. Three months was a long stint away from home and you needed to have a strong mind as well as a strong stomach. It was the time of the monsoon and we had to watch the rains a lot, and play would often be washed out. That meant more time to kill. There is only so much television you can watch, and the nights and evenings could be very long. Invariably I would rise early and go for a coffee and look forward to the hours of light so that I could keep busy. We spent Christmas in Madras which could have been very difficult in a non-Christian country but the hotel manager made every effort to reflect the Christmas season and facilitated our celebrations even erecting a Christmas tree in the lobby. The player's wives flew in for Christmas and they cooked lunch and we were made to feel as much of the Christmas spirit as was possible in a very Indian world.

The large crowds were very intimidating and the sidewalks were packed. I remember one day going shopping with Clive Lloyd's wife Waveny and it was not a pleasant experience because it was not easy. The players were very careful about going out. In any major hotel city whatever hour of the night, there would be two to three hundred people just sitting outside of the hotel waiting to see the players come or go. The West Indies won the series. The sixth test in Madras was December 24, 26, 27, 28, 29.

The test itself was badly hit by the weather and the relations between the teams deteriorated. It all came about when India were 54 for 3 on the opening day and Gavaskar fended a rising Marshall delivery off the glove and was taken by Dujon, only for umpire Swaroopkishen to turn the appeal down. The outstanding Indian batsman went on to make 236 undefeated as India scored 451 for 8 declared in reply to W.I's 313. West Indies was 64 for 1 when the match ended in a tame draw. The incident on the opening day involving Gavaskar did for the first time in this series bring about a bit of bad blood and the West Indies fast bowlers produced a fair amount of short pitch deliveries on this docile track.

Chapter 20
Moving to St. Lucia

In mid-1984 I made the major decision to leave the freelancing arena and after twenty years of being first and foremost a cricket commentator, to accept a job as Sports Coordinator at the OECS in St Lucia starting September the 1st.

The year had begun with the visit of the Australian side to the West Indies, an event that produced some marvellous performances. The first two test matches in Guyana and Trinidad and Tobago ended in draws. In Guyana I thought the West Indies might have just pushed on through to win. Gordon Greenidge and Desmond Haynes had got into the eighties and nineties when the run chase was on which tends to slow batsmen down. It is quite natural for a batsman to become very selective with those types of scores on the board and with the added pressure of the crowd and responsibility to the team. Eventually Greenidge was at a 120, Haynes got the 100 just before the end; they were both undefeated. The West Indies were 250 without loss but I just felt that if they could have gone through the 80s and 90s more quickly we would have been able to attack the target they had given us and would have headed to Port of Spain one up.

Port of Spain in my mind will always be about the brilliant 130 by Jeffery Dujon. It was a Rolls Royce innings, and exciting to watch. Gus Logie got 97 but it was not a fluent run chase; he was fighting in the typical busy Logie style, always seeming to be working extra hard when Dujon at the end was so much in contrast. His elegant 130 for those people who saw it at the Oval that day will long be remembered. Also noteworthy was the batting of Alan Border who was not out 90, and got an undefeated 100 in the second innings. This gutsy lefthander virtually stood between West Indies winning and the game drawing. Border refused to be dismissed and got good support from the lower order Lawson and Hogan.

The series then changed quickly because at Kensington Oval the West Indies won by 10 wickets which suggested that it was not much of a contest. Australia did score fairly heavily. I recall in the first innings they made 429 with young Wayne Phillips the South Australian making a stylish hundred, but the West Indies replied very strongly and very quickly with 500 for 9 with a good start by Greenidge and Haynes of 132; Haynes with Richardson pushed the West Indies on to 509 with 154 and 178 respectively. Batting a second time the Australians collapsed to 97 and the West Indies had to get just over 20 to win, but the main feature of the West Indies bowling in the second innings was 5 for 42 by Marshall; Holding chipped in with 4 for 24 and the West Indies had taken a sizeable lead in the series.

The Antigua Recreation Ground which has been known over the years as a batting paradise was not quite so for the Australians. The West Indies won at the ARG by an innings and 36 runs, a comprehensive defeat. At that time one was very conscious of the dominance of West Indies cricket. This was truly a great side, well led by Lloyd and completely overwhelming Australia. The team from Down Under scored 262 in the first innings and the

West Indies replied with 498; Australia batting a second time cold only muster 200 and that gave W.I a victory by an innings and 36 runs thanks to Garner's 5 for 63 off 20.5 overs.

If they thought that Antigua was a bad performance the next match was not much better because at Sabina Park the West Indies won by 10 wickets, again Australia failing in the first innings with 199. West Indies got a small score of 305 and Australia only made 160 in the second innings. Again, we had a situation where Marshall was the tormentor, 5 for 51 from 23 overs with good support from Garner and Holding who got 2 each. The West Indies were 55 without loss and won by 10 wickets. The series from a West Indies point of view was very successful. Australia's performance was somewhat disappointing after promising a lot more. Certainly on paper their side looked a lot more competitive, but their batting on that tour let them down and the West Indies had very good starts from Greenidge and Haynes in the top order.

Success followed success because a few weeks after completing that series against Australia at home in early May, the West Indies were again in test competition in England. I did not cover this series as a journalist, but went up to take in a couple of test matches. The West Indies saw another high quality performance by Clive Lloyd and his team and they actually won that series 5-nil. There was another victory at Lords by some 9 wickets, an 8 wicket victory at Headingly and as the third test finished the West Indies won by an innings and 64 runs. In the fourth test W.I won by an innings and 64 runs, and when the fifth test came the West Indies won by 172 runs at the Oval in London. It was a clear cut 5-nil "blackwash" as they say.

The Olympic games were coming up in L.A. that summer. I had missed an opportunity to go to 1976 games in Montreal because of all the controversy with Guyana eventually withdrawing. I am glad that I did not in fact get accredited to go because I was working with the Minister of Sport when Guyana decided to withdraw and I would have been in an awkward position. In 1980 there had been a lot of controversy with the West boycotting Moscow. There was a lot of negativity and information was hard to come by in terms of travel and accommodation.

I decided that I would not let the opportunity to go to L.A. pass by, that I would go and cover stories for the Caribbean radio stations and got my accreditation. There had been a lot of talk about room shortages and overcharging so I arranged to get into L.A. a few days before the games so that I could do the legwork myself. From the press centre it was close to the hotel community. I simply left my suitcase in secure storage and walked around, and I found a Chinese-owned bed and breakfast with my own direct line. It was nice, tidy and clean with good rates and allowed me to function easily with the filing of my stories. It was only 10 minutes away from the press centre. I think I had made the right decision.

The expected smog and bad air did not materialise. There had been a lot of speculation prior to the games about health standards, and concern that the athletes might struggle with the industrial pollution and smog but that did not happen. The expected traffic jams also never materialised. The bus that took the press from the stadium back to the media centre

Chatting with West Indies Opening Batsman Desmond Haynes during World Series in Australia, 1978

Broadcasting with Jack Cameron scorer (left) and Bobby Simpson (centre), Melbourne, 1979

Left to right: Colin Croft, the author, Andy Roberts, Michael Holding and Umpire Stanton Paris, at Governor General's reception in Jamaica

Left to right: Colin Croft, Andy Roberts, Lawrence Rowe, the author and Deryck Murray and family during World Series, Australia, 1978

Accompanying Sir Garfield Sobers at Queen's College, Guyana

JOSEPH 'REDS' PERREIRA 83

Ladder access only; the ABC booth in Tasmania

As President of the Guyana Basketball Association with the National Squad

Attending the 1976 UNESCO Conference on Physical Education, Paris

50 Years of W.I. Cricket with Tony Cozier, 1978

As Chairman of the National Sports Council with staff, Guyana, 1978

normally got back in about 25 minutes which was very reasonable. The one handicap about L.A. was the time difference of three hours. It made my sleep patterns very erratic. If for example, I finished track and field and then moved on to boxing, I would not get home until after midnight which was 3.00 a.m. Eastern Caribbean time. I would then have to decide whether to sleep for two hours and book a wake up call, or do the edits then, so I could then get two hours' sleep, wake up 45 minutes before transmission time with my reports and voice clips ready, to file back to the Caribbean. Sometimes I did that and other times I was simply too tired and I would quickly make the decision to wake up an hour before and try to get the work done. Sometimes I was running very tightly against the clock. It was not as difficult for the written press but for radio the time difference worked against you.

The 1984 games saw a reversal of the boycott where the West boycotted the 1980 Olympics in Moscow because of Afghanistan. This time it was the East, with the exception of Romania, who boycotted the L.A Olympics. So like Moscow, L.A would also be questioned as a true reflection of the performance of the best. You really had to forget all of that and just judge what was in front of you, see how well the games were run.

From my point of view the weather was excellent, the games were well run and they had a very impressive opening ceremony with the former decathlon athlete Rafer Johnson opening the proceedings by lighting the flame. The attendance was out of this world, and although Caribbean athletes did not do that well, I still enjoyed the basketball at the Forum where the Lakers play, the cycling, swimming, and track and field. The 1984 Olympics will be a games remembered for the dominance of Carl Lewis who won the 100m, 200m, the long jump and a gold in the relay equalling Jessie Owens' accomplishments in 1936. Bert Cameron was recognised as we went to L.A. as the world number one and had a good chance of winning gold for Jamaica and the Caribbean but pulled out with muscle trouble in the semis and had to withdraw altogether in the finals.

Don Quarrie did lead a Jamaican 4x100 to the silver medal and was consistent getting a bronze on two occasions. Elvyn Ashford won the women's 100 metres and Briscoe Brooks won the 200. We also saw an American athlete that the world was going to know about later, Florence Griffith, "Flo-Jo" as she was to become known. Four years later in 1988 we could not have imagined the times she was recording, or the way she was running compared with what we saw in 1984. There was a lot of innuendo and suggestion but she was never found guilty of taking any illegal substances and I think the jury will always be out on whether she was clean or not, and I suppose the debate will go on forever.

One of the things that did strike me was the politics of the games in terms of Grenada. Grenada had just come back into the fold of democracy and the Americans had done just about everything to get Grenada membership in the IOC, speeding up the papers for their participation. In those days you needed to have five national bodies of Olympic sports all accredited and up to date to participate. Grenadian boxer Bunny Wilson, fighting an African opponent was losing the bout on points, but in the third round started to produce a tremendous combination of punches which knocked his opponent out. It was a sensational win. I was elated, the Grenadians were over the moon, and the entire delegation and all the Caribbean journalists and athletes were watching. What was shocking at the press conference that followed was that for the first ten to fifteen minutes the American journalists did not ask one question about the bout or his fight record or training regime. The questions were all about the American rescue or invasion of Grenada, what democracy was going to do for Grenada and so on.

Irritated I stood up and managed to get the floor and protested that no one had asked Wilson about the fact that he had just won an Olympic fight. That brought a hush, and then there were a few questions about the victory and what it would do for the sport in Grenada and for him. I was really taken aback by the very narrowness of the questions put to Bunny Wilson, but I suppose it was the agenda of the news editors as Grenada had been very much in the news.

Broadcasting on All India Radio, 1983

Visiting the US Olympic Committee Office

Covering W.I. tour of New Zealand, 1980

With Hugh Crosskill and Tony Cozier, as part of the JBC team for W.I vs. N.Z Test at Sabina Park, 1985

ABC broadcast team in Australia, 1995. From left to right: Keith Stackpole, Jim Maxwell, Alan Marks, the author, Tim Lane, Norman O'Neil, Neville Oliver

Chapter 21
The OECS Years

I spent the first few months of my tenure at the OECS Sports Desk trying to assess the task ahead. Though it was September 1st when I commenced the work, I was aware that observers were expecting results. In the early days some had taken the position that perhaps an OECS born person should have been given the job and I was perceptive of those sensibilities. There was a Michael Findlay, Irving Shillingford or St Lucia administrator Laurie Auguste who could have done just as a good a job, but for whatever reason I was headhunted and selected. I was on the receiving end of some resentment but I did not allow it to bother me because the proof of the pudding is in the eating. Within months my detractors were conceding that I was doing a good job because they were seeing action. I remember Winston Springer Sr. who was working with Radio Antilles at the time, and who is now a government spokesman, saying to me at Jimmie's Restaurant one day, "I want to tell you something straight. When you were appointed I was very much against it; I thought somebody from the OECS should have been appointed, but I want you to know I have eaten those words and I must compliment you on what you've done." I understood where he was coming from and thanked him for his honesty.

When I came to St Lucia, the late Romanus Lansiquot was the Sports Minister and he was very welcoming and supportive, but more importantly so was his Permanent Secretary Mrs Aldith Isaac. I did not get the same warmth and welcome from the Sports Officer, Andrew Magloire who perhaps still recalling the failed efforts of Caricom, and was very wary.

At the first meeting I had with the Sports Association, President of the Athletic Association, Ali Black said pointedly, "Mr. Perreira, what are you going to do for us?" I did not have a specific answer to give but I said, "Mr Black, my name is Joseph but I'm not the father of Christ but I sincerely promise to give a hundred and ten percent." It was gratifying two months later when we ran the first OECS half marathon with Ken Boyea and East Caribbean Flour Mills as the sponsors, that he was impressed. I was happy with the outcome of the event and I did feel the pressure prior to it being run. I had to believe that if I was patient and committed that I could produce results.

Those early months at the job in 1984 gave me a chance to start to plan 1985 even before the year was finished. In addition to the half marathon I was able to coordinate a tennis event working closely with Johnny Easter and the St Lucia Tennis Association and an OECS Open event was staged at the Cunard La Toc courts with Trinidad, Barbados and the USVI participating with the OECS family. The third and final event was the first ever Basketball Championships and Dominica, which had a progressive and energetic basketball association was chosen as the venue. Dominica which was originally a Leeward Island was in the middle of the island chain and therefore the associations of the Windwards and Leewards did not have to battle with a large travel cost.

In conjunction with Dr. Vaughn Lewis and the late Gus Compton the event was held in early December of that year to accommodate general elections in the Spice Island. Working closely with Sports Director Cecil Greenidge and government officials, the funding was approved for the Grenada National Team to participate just days after their nation had cast their ballots. The finalists were Dominica and Antigua and a huge crowd of over 3,000 people was on hand to witness the first jump ball and this historical event. Between Havis Shillingford, the Sports Officer and the basketball officials it was arranged for Prime Minister Eugenia Charles to be in attendance. She was not known to be a great follower of sport, but when she saw the large turnout it became clear to her that the decision in Monsterrat the previous year to start the OECS Sports Desk was a wise one, and had the potential of impacting the standard of sport and the lives of OECS constituents.

In 1985 we grew from three to six events and each and every year at the desk there was an addition of four or five events. The challenge in trying to cater for the many disciplines that existed in the OECS was coordinating through the various Ministers of Sport, the respective sports officers and the very important National Sports Associations, who had to be fully involved. Though we were separated by bodies of water I could not simply decide at the Sports Desk that this was going to happen. I had to take into consideration where it could happen, the sponsorship and the degree to which the countries were willing to participate. As the sporting events grew, travel logistics became crucial. If an event was held in the Windward Islands one year, the sensible thing to do was to host it in the Leewards the following year so that the responsibility of travel would be shared between the groups of islands.

I think the region was ready for a take off and I was lucky in that respect. There were in fact two Caricom sports officers who covered the Windwards and Leewards but I do not believe they were as successful as they were hoping to be. The impact on the OECS territories had been mainly made up of visits and meetings but little came about in terms of action. To be fair to the Caricom sports officers, they had to wait until July for the Council of Ministers and the Ministers of Sport to meet in Georgetown to approve their work programme. This obviously had a negative impact on what they were trying to achieve as many months of programming were held up by this bureaucracy, as I am sure similar programmes were also subject to final but late approval.

People wanted to see action and development, and that was the key to success, from both the competitors' point of view and the spectators'. I had a good relationship with the press who would have been very negative if they saw that nothing was happening and I was conscious that they would simply have written off the Sports Desk.

The OECS region, because of our colonial allegiance with the British did not enjoy the infrastructure development that was an integral part of French and Dutch colonial policy, so we had to make do with whatever infrastructure was there. There were countries that could not host certain events because the infrastructure simply was not there. I was careful to identify when that was the case so there was no suggestion of slight or favour and kept Dr. Lewis fully briefed.

One of my first orders of business was to shrink the distances between the member territories. The cost of travel was fairly pricey even at that time and prohibitive for a struggling volleyball, netball or boxing association. With the permission of Dr. Lewis, I approached the head of LIAT Arthur Foster and the P.R.O Kathleen Pinder, and proposed a partnership between the airline and the Sports Desk. The Sports Desk agreed to maintain a season that ran concurrent with the low travel season from the middle of April to mid-July and then early September to the end of year, in exchange for a fifty percent rebate for OECS teams. It seemed a win-win situation, a team of 15 players and personnel equating 7 or 8 full fares, was better than no seats filled at all, and the agreement was finalised in a document weeks later. It was a major breakthrough because it allowed a fuller, more meaningful participation of the various territories. This was just one of many breakthroughs that the Sports Desk would enjoy.

The technical fund administered by the Winera Boxing Plant in Vieux Fort which was not just for St Lucia, allowed the Sports Desk to provide resource people for the region. In addition to OECS officials, I recruited the expertise of Trinidad, Guyana and Barbados officials to come in and help run tournaments and officiate. It was clear to me that we could not treat the OECS as a calabash. The add-on benefit of that outlook was that it also helped us to be able to attract sponsorship from outside the OECS, for example the LIAT arrangement and later with United Insurance, Texaco, Cable and Wireless, Nemwil and Shell who sponsored wicket keeping and fast bowling clinics.

What proved to be a long and fruitful relationship with United Insurance that continues today, started quite by chance. I had heard a call by Kenny Hobson for boys under 19 to turn up at the Queen's Park Cricket Ground in Grenada on Radio Grenada and I called the head of the association and asked him what this was about. He replied that there was no secondary school cricket in Grenada, and that it was the only way they could pull together a team. I thought that this might be a situation repeated across the OECS so I went to see United Insurance and spoke with Tommy Pearce. I argued that if the nursery was not producing, players would not come through the Windward and Leeward ranks and that eventually West Indies cricket would suffer. Pearce liked the concept, his father had also been involved in Barbados and W.I. cricket, as a Barbados player and former manager of the W.I team, so cricket was very much part of the Pearces' world. But he was also a businessman and saw the opportunity for tying United Insurance with the product. Lo and behold we got United to sponsor cricket in every OECS island starting with a sum of about seven or eight thousand dollars. That sponsorship also extended to St Kitts though there was no United presence there so United's outlook was broad and visionary.

The sponsorship drive became as central to the Sports Desk portfolio as the actual arranging of training and events. I became finely attuned to potential for funding and was always ready to turn chance into opportunity. I recall seeing a huge, impressive building in Basseterre on one of my visits, which it turned out was the head quarters of the ECCB. I resolved to go see Dwight Venner, now Sir Dwight, and asked whether he had ever thought of aligning the bank with a sport in the sub region. The event we discussed was netball which had developed traditional friendships when it was played in the Windwards and Leewards that had endured, and it was another opportunity to involve more women in the sports programme. We agreed to pursue netball at the under 23 level so it would be a nursery for the national teams that played in the Caribbean Championships. The sponsorship was substantial; if I remember correctly it was 65,000 dollars which included a 5,000 dollar sum given to the Sports Desk for administration purposes.

By this time Dr. Lewis and the OECS had allowed me to create a separate Sports Desk fund to be disbursed by me and managed by the accounts department. I was also able at a heads of government meeting in St Lucia to get each government to agree to give 5,000 dollars towards the Sports Desk fund so that we had a working capital of 40,000 dollars. That allowed me to travel on the LIAT rebate so I could move around fairly cheaply and I could get a lot done on my trips. That seed money, along with the Winera Technical Fund gave the Sports Desk a small budget that allowed it to carry out its mandate.

Texaco came on board as sponsors of the OECS Track and Field Championships. I do not know the exact cost but it was substantial and they paid for everything. We ran the Championships in Grenada with great success. The athletes were able to express themselves in a way they had not been able to before. We ran another event in St Kitts at Warner Park, and Antigua's ARG that were very successful and attracted the patronage of MacDonald Bailey, Herb McKenley, Hasely Crawford and Ben Johnson. We then tried it in St Lucia but it was not very successful because we did not get the Mindoo Philip Park which was not in the best shape. We then decided that we would go back to Grenada and it was more or less decided between the Sports Desk and the sponsor that we would establish the OECS Track and Field Championships in the south, in Grenada, and a base in the north in St Kitts and we would use those two countries because they had the infrastructure, the experience, and the hotels which were very important.

Sadly we lost the Texaco sponsorship. When St Vincent put in a bid to host to the various heads and sponsor, it fell short with accommodation. Mainland St Vincent does not have it; when you had teams of thirty multiplied by eight you could not accommodate that number in St Vincent's two or three hotels. Texaco was not satisfied with their visit to St Vincent, as reported by Kay Donovan who had worked closely with the Sports Desk, and general inflexibility in terms of whether we could go back to the original plan of Grenada and St Kitts unfortunately resulted in Texaco pulling out.

However, during that period Texaco further embraced the sub-region by supporting the best performers who made the OECS team to compete in the Barbados Texaco sponsored games. The OECS won those games so it was really a shot in the arm for athletics. Further to that, Texaco, with the exception of St Lucia, which had sponsorship from Minvielle and Chastanet, sponsored all the national championships of the sub-region. At the Sports Desk, however, it was clear that we were not going to improve athletics if we only turned up to compete in the regional Texaco Championships. Of key importance was growing sports from the lower level and so further assistance was needed. To run the national championships in terms of cost of venue, medals and overall costs, Texaco provided something in the vicinity of 8,000 dollars to all the track and field associations as their contribution to the development of athletics. It also aided the various countries because the ministries did not have to find that money anymore and it catered for all the talent coming out of the secondary schools to the national championships each and every year.

The private sector continued to be a major player in mobilising sub-regional sports. My association with cricket as a commentator helped open doors. Eastern Caribbean Flour Mills out of St Vincent supported the Sports Desk's efforts; then Head Ken Boyea and I had met through cricket in Montserrat. I worked very closely with Cable and Wireless with many events especially golf and volleyball. Most of the managers controlled their own budgets and it was not centralised then as it was later, so they were able on approach to negotiate independently. C&W turned into a major sponsor.

The half marathon came out of Trinidad funds. Nemwil, the insurance company sponsored the half marathon to the tune of 25,000 dollars and helped pay for and provide incentives in terms of prizes. We also worked with the Caribbean Football Union to develop a coaching programme where three persons qualified to go to England for training – Stewart Charles, the St Lucian player and coach qualified at a very good level in England with his F.A. coaching badge and was able to eventually go to Trinidad, at St Lucia's loss, to become national coach for a short period. He now coaches the W. Connection, a professional team out of Trinidad. This was collaboration between Jack Warner the CFU head and the desk, agreed on at a meeting in the BVI. Though we did not share views on a number of things, we put our politics aside and we got the job done.

Through discussions the Sports Desk was able to get the Australia High Commission to provide us with a netball coach. This Australian official spent three weeks in every member state working with selected coaches. The focus of that three month stay was the training of coaches, something crucial to the continued growth and development of the sport of netball and central to the philosophy emerging out of the Sports Desk.

When the Sports Desk was announced, everybody thought it would be a macho affair but I am happy to say we pushed for netball and had the OECS under 23 tournament and the OECS Club Championships which gave the best clubs in the sub-region a chance of meeting and deciding the best OECS netball club. We also arranged an OECS versus Trinidad meeting played in St Lucia. The matches were exciting and Trinidad won by just the smallest margin. To me it was not a disaster to have lost, Trinidad was pushed, the crowd was enjoying it and the players could proudly proclaim that they had played for the OECS. There were also OECS teams emerging from our Squash Championships and an OECS team qualified for the Caribbean Squash Tournament.

Golf started off similarly, with limited facilities. Antigua had a good facility at Cedar Valley, but Frigate Bay in St Kitts may be the best and we managed to put together an OECS team. With the Four Seasons Hotel in Nevis the reach of golf was expanded. Infrastructure slowly got better and we were able, with the help of St Lucian George Noon who coordinated the sponsorship, to get that OECS team into the Caribbean Championships. It was a major breakthrough; after attending the championships it was our turn to host. St Kitts had now become a designated venue and Ricky Skerrit agreed to be the Director of the tournament. We specially brought him to Barbados the year before St Kitts was to host to see how the Barbadians were running the Caribbean Golf Championships and I think he got a very good insight into the protocol, the advertising, the format etc. St Kitts did a wonderful job.

We were able also to have a presence at the Davis Cup. The International Tennis Federation decided that each major Caribbean country would have to play Davis Cup as an independent nation. Previously the region played under the banner of British Caribbean. This new ruling by the ITF was quickly taken up by Jamaica, Bahamas, Barbados and Trinidad but it meant no opportunity for the Leeward and Windward Island players under the new system. Working with OECS tennis officials, the ITF gave special permission for the OECS to play as a sub-region. We also had to host the cup and we did so in St Lucia, Antigua and St Kitts, a period which brought tennis to its zenith. The then President of the OECS Tennis Association Dennis Byron played a major role in the creation of an OECS tennis nation using his persuasion and diplomacy skills as a trained judge. There were many good things that came out as the programme expanded. It was teamwork among the desk, the ministers of sport, the directors of sport, the private sector, the public and the media.

During my tenure at the Sports Desk I paid great attention to the media. I felt that there was great value to making sure they were informed and involved and that they could contribute to the development of sport. I volunteered my time to what was then CBU. They had CANA, a daily radio programme, and whenever I could I would offer information to that regional body. I would also call the Voice of Barbados with whom I had a relationship and they gave OECS activities a lot of coverage. When I visited any OECS member state I made sure I spent an hour or two with the media. There was a challenge getting events into Nevis, Montserrat and the BVI but I was very happy to say that in spite of limited infrastructure availability we managed to get as many things possible into those nations and it was important that they were not marginalised.

The Sports Desk was a team of one; there was no money to employ an assistant but I had help from the regional sports directors. Mrs Monica Destang who worked for Dr Lewis, typed my mail but the work of Dr. Lewis obviously came first. In order to keep up with the volume of correspondence going out to ministries, national associations and sponsors, I paid out of my pocket to get drafts done privately; there were no emails and the fax was the major breakthrough. UNESCO had originally sponsored the desk, they paid my salary and the running of the desk but there were no funds to run any of the programmes. In fact, many years later I was told by a UNESCO official out of Jamaica, that Paris had not expected the desk to be up and running after a year, that it would be a waste of money.

I am very happy to have proved them wrong. Paris had a European view of sports administration that did not necessarily obtain in the Caribbean. They would come to me and ask what percentage of the national economy was donated to sport in the various countries, or what the national policy was. Well, some of these countries were trying to develop an agricultural policy, or were now trying to establish a tourism policy, so for them to ask for a policy on sport at that time was almost laughable. What I did was to focus more on the information that was relevant and positive and showed the growth and potential of Caribbean sports.

I was fortunate in a number of respects – I came at a time when bananas were doing well in the Windwards, and when the cost of travel to the Leewards and Windwards was still reasonable especially with the LIAT rebate agreement. Tourism was doing well in the sub region, there was buoyancy in the economy and the EC dollar remained stable. I think my background in cricket helped immensely for networking. I would get the opportunity to speak with a potential sponsor where others might not have got through the door. I was allowed a certain flexibility by the OECS and I made it count; I would come back from cricket jobs having made some connections.

One of the weaknesses of sport in the region, and it went beyond the OECS, was the fragile club structure. By 1985 - 1986 I was preaching that we needed to have a club structure that encouraged people in the communities to become involved. Essentially what needed to prevail to ensure continuity and efficiency was the creation of a non-playing executive, so that you had a non-playing treasurer, president, vice president, secretary, and committee members. The playing arm would be represented in the executive. But what obtained at the association level was captains and vice captains representing the various clubs. I knew it was not rocket science to create a structure with non-players; I did not have to reinvent the wheel because I had gone through that in 1969 when I became President of the Guyana Basketball Association. We worked a document where people could go into their communities and recruit people and they did and it worked.

The other weakness I felt was the absence of a facility which I had seen in Suriname in the late fifties which could be used as a youth facility – a bunkhouse where you could keep 30 or 40 people with double bunks. It would cut out the expense of staying in guesthouses and hotels for guest teams. Nobody in the OECS ever built it and I think it would still be relevant today. It is a simple solution – you bring in labour to provide the breakfast and wash up and that's it, a small cleaning staff and the overhead of running it would be very small. The Dutch did that extremely well. The facility could be used for any youth event whether in sports, agriculture or the arts and would be in demand throughout the year. I did make a breakthrough in St Lucia. The Courts manager agreed to lead this drive and I reported it to the then Minister of Sport Desmond Brathwaite and told him that this gentleman would run the project and work with the private sector to get the cement, the steel, the blocks, all he needs is the land. Unfortunately nothing became of it and an opportunity was missed.

I used to try to attend as many sporting events as I was invited to. It was one way to show very clearly that you were in touch with what was happening. That meant early mornings and long days. I could not live in St Lucia and say what was happening at the national level was not important. I had a duty to show up, to interact, talk to officials, say a few words if asked while never appearing to interfere. I had a few friends but I was a bit of a workaholic and I was out of St Lucia very often. I was on the road sometimes twice or three times a week. I felt my presence at the events in the region was important not only symbolically but also to avoid the mishaps that could occur from time to time like insufficient media coverage, to complications with technical things like the lights and the venue. The sponsors had to be assured of their media mileage also at the various tournaments.

A number of regional persons made a tremendous and vital contribution to the OECS sports programme by the coverage they provided on the major radio stations in the sub-region. Ray Roberts and Trevor Twaits from Grenada, Jack Matthews, Denis Seon and King Frank I of Antigua, Teddy Francis, Hervan Henry and Ryan O'Brian from St Lucia, Colin James, Glenford Prescott and Michael Findlay from St Vincent, Curtis Matthews and Havis Shillingford from Dominica, Keith Greaves and Rose Willock of Montserrat and Vaughn Southwell and Aubrey Rogers of St Kitts, while support was also provided by Von Radio of Nevis.

The various sports officers also played an important role in the administration and execution of the programme. Reg Samuel and Pat White of Antigua, Ossie Saravin and Havis Shillingford of Dominica, Alfanzo Bridgewater of St Kitts, Huston Payne from St Vincent, Cecil Greenidge from Grenada, Brian Penn of the BVI, Alkin Rogers from Anguilla and Darnley Boxilly and Fitzroy Buffonge of Montserrat.

In early 1986, I realized that there was an opportunity to attend the CAC Games in the Dominican Republic. Once I had insured that my OECS programme was no way affected I decided to attend. It seemed to me important to attend and support something which was happening in such close proximity to the OECS when I had been as far a field as LA for the Olympic Games and the Commonwealth Games in Canada.

The 1986 games took place in Santiago, the second city of the Dominican Republic from June 24th to July 5th and I flew in via Antigua on June 22nd in order to get my accreditation and to have a clearer idea of the dates and venues for this multi-sport championships. I was certainly looking forward to the track and field, football, boxing, basketball and cycling and had secured the commitment from Voice of America and the Voice of Barbados to provide daily reports for the respective radio services. After the opening ceremony which had the typical Latin American flair and colour, my first commitment was to attend the Barbados versus Dominican Republic football clash some 25 miles outside of the city. On the day in question I reported to the transportation section early and was informed that since I was the only English- speaking journalist wanting to attend the fixture they would provide a chauffeur driven car to take me to the stadium.

All seemed to be in order as we left on time and drove along a well-surfaced highway taking in large areas of the countryside before we got to the venue. Since the game was not that well attended I was able to get my driver to sit in the press area so that we could be in touch with each other for the return trip to Santiago. The home side defeated Barbados 2-0 in a game of missed opportunities for the Bajans, and I was somewhat disappointed with the result. We were only about ten minutes into our return when an awful incident changed all that I was looking forward to during the games. My driver, while overtaking a parked container vehicle found to his surprise a young lady of middle age making an attempt to cross the highway without first checking to see if there was any oncoming traffic. Our vehicle did not have a chance to stop in time and although brakes were applied she was hit by our vehicle still travelling at a fast rate. She was struck by the bonnet of the car, her body smashed the windscreen and hit the top of the vehicle before falling onto the trunk and unto the highway where she lay apparently lifeless. I immediately expected the assigned driver to stop but instead, despite my appeals in my broken Spanish, he kept on driving away from the scene. It was only when we reached the edge of the city that he tried to explain to me that if he had stopped, the community might have attacked him. I insisted that he report the incident to the transportation organizers and next morning I heard that although she was badly bruised and cut up with broken ribs and legs it was not life threatening.

For the next forty-eight hours I just could not get the incident and the horror of it out of my mind. My appetite disappeared, sleep deserted me and I was haunted with images of what took place along the highway. My ability to file reports was badly affected as I had never experienced such a nerve-wracking incident in my life. I was not enjoying the games at this stage and informed both Voice of America and the Voice of Barbados about what had taken place and decided to return to St. Lucia. All the previous sporting events I had attended in my life were happy and enjoyable memories, but that incident continued to give me the nightmares for a long time.

During my twelve years at the OECS Sports Desk, I was given an opportunity to visit the USA on two occasions. In all my travels during that period I looked for every opportunity to obtain or negotiate some form of assistance for the member states in terms of equipment and coaching.

The first such visit was in February of 1987, when the organization received an invitation from the US State Department for me to visit the USA on an educational tour. I was aware of these programmes as they were offered to teachers, trade union leaders, personnel in culture departments and librarians, etc. It was normal for these individuals to spend a week in four cities which had a relevant interest in their field of work that would easily have covered a period of thirty days. The programme was to be finalized in Washington DC and I decided that I was going to take the opportunity to seek as much assistance while in the USA. I was allowed to participate in the make up of the travel programme and was able to choose cities where sporting equipment was manufactured. In all I was able to cover thirteen US cities in the period and brought back a commitment from a volleyball and basketball company in Seattle, while in Denver I visited a small town called Sidney just outside of the major ski centre that produced boxing equipment. All the visits were pre-arranged and I was met on arrival at the various airports and taken to the places of interest. In the case of the boxing equipment producers, the management assembled the entire staff on the factory floor for me to explain how the equipment that they were producing and donating was going to benefit the islands I was representing.

While in New York, I met with the well known and well organized officials of the "People to People Program". This group had a good track record in providing Third World countries, coaches in various disciplines, and equipment. It was clear that the possibility of assistance was enormous but the demands on this institution were great and despite positive discussions in "the big apple" and follow up correspondence on my return to my desk at the Morne I must admit that I was not able to secure my goal.

I did, however, arrange for a volleyball coach to visit Dominica and he proved to be an excellent resource person working both with the Ministry of Sport and the Dominica Volleyball Association, which also benefited from an equipment gift and coaching material. I was fortunate in the cities I visited to have access to NBA special tickets which included dinner in most cases prior to the various games, and was privileged to see the Nicks, Washington Bullets, Seattle, LA and the Nets which were all a real life experience of professional sport run by a professional organizations to full houses. My one disappointment, if I can dare suggest, was not being able to attend a Bulls game and watch the Boston Celtics.

In all I was able to negotiate about US $20,000 worth of equipment from the two suppliers which was sent on my return to St Lucia; arrangements were made for duty free entry and distributed equally among the member states.

In 1989 I was part of an historical sporting event in Canada with Tony Cozier and Erskine King that was to have a personal impact on my life. The event was a cricket match that brought together the West Indies in contest against an international side, in aid of the United Way charity at the impressive Toronto Sky Dome. And it was during this time that I became reacquainted with a friend from Guyana, who would later become my wife. I had known Bernadette Roberts well through the group we interacted socially with in Georgetown and had always remembered her as a woman full of life with a strong, independent mind. She herself had married and started her family and had become an avid hockey mum. I had moved on from Guyana but had kept in touch with my acquaintances there and learned over the years that she had divorced and had moved to Canada.

I met up with Bernadette again while in Toronto for the match and invited her to the event. We remained in touch and on two occasions I returned to that Canadian city to mainly see her and visit the rest of my family. I was always of the view that any man deciding to offer marriage to a woman must at that point be in a position to offer some basic things. I was permitted by the John Compton administration to have St Lucian citizenship and a passport which made acquiring land and the building of a home simple. My job with the OECS was going well and I was respected in my field and able to travel the breadth of the region. Although I was experiencing great satisfaction from my professional life, I did feel the need for companionship and a fuller life of sharing. Bernadette's own children had all come of age and had started their own lives, and taking all into consideration we felt that at our age marriage was the natural step.

We were married far away from the region where we were both born, on the 11th of August 1990 in Scarborough, Toronto to suit both of our families who lived there. Our nuptial day was threatened by a moment of panic when the appointed priest failed to show. Happily, another priest, who was waiting on the bride and bridegroom he was to marry, was able to step in and perform the ceremony to the relief of all.

Bernadette was very happy to move to St Lucia with me where we began our married life at an apartment at Villa Apartments on the Morne. In the meantime I had taken steps to acquire the land in Bonne Terre and to commence the building of my first house. The marriage was very successful for the first year and a half but I then started to realise that the problems of Bernadette's first marriage haunted ours. The extensive travel demands of my job and her difficulty with trust took its toll on our relationship. During this time I leant heavily on my brother Desmond and neighbour Gene Lawrence for counselling and advice, but with no apparent improvement in sight I raised the difficult question about our marriage with her. We agreed that it was not working and undertook divorce proceedings; I made sure a financial settlement was made to her approval. It was not an easy time for me, but my work absorbed my energies.

Haiti, I'm Sorry

I did not just borrow this line from that award winning David Rudder song. In every sense whenever I hear or read something on this independent Caribbean nation I am overwhelmed by a feeling of guilt and the building of hope for its people in the area of sport and recreation. In January of 1990 I was approached by the CARICOM Secretariat in Georgetown to join a CARICOM team visit Haiti which shortly after the return of democracy had indicated an interest in having closer ties with the English speaking Caribbean. The delegation was mandated to examine and report on a number of areas of Haitian life; it was led by the well known Barbadian and CARICOM diplomat, Orlando Marville and made up of a number of CARICOM nationals including the late Lloyd Best of Trinidad and Tobago.

The head of our delegation Ambassador Marville held a lengthy discussion with his CARICOM team on the opening day, setting out the objectives of the visit and outlining the terms of the final report to CARICOM. I was attached to two members of the Haitian Ministry of Sport and the two young officials were clearly enthusiastic about the visit of their English speaking neighbours. For a period of four days they drove me to every possible sporting installation in Haiti, which in the main were defunct. I was also able to meet with the Haiti Olympic Committee whose focus was gaining admission to sporting events well-established in the CARICOM region. I did have an opportunity to visit the National Stadium which was small and needed major refurbishment but this was not a project that I felt CARICOM itself could have undertaken since it would have incurred substantial cost.

Two weeks after returning from Haiti I completed my report and provided it to CARICOM Secretary General Edwin Carrington. A few days later he requested that I provide a short report on eight projects that CARICOM could implement immediately to further demonstrate CARICOM interest in helping this French speaking nation. My recommendations included the repairing of the national swimming centre which needed fairly minimal work to restore pumps, filters and some degree of masonry work: the putting back in playing order the national gymnasium, which was once used by the occupying Haitian army and had had major roof damage which led to the deterioration of the flooring. I felt however, that this project was within the scope of CARICOM and in collaboration with friendly countries it would be relatively easy to put back in playing order.

During my visit I noted that Haitian women were little involved in national sporting life. I recommended that, in conjunction with the Caribbean Netball Association, and using Patois speaking coaches from Dominica and St Lucia, there was an opportunity to develop a discipline where Haitian women could join the Caribbean netball family with a minimum financial commitment needed for the infrastructure. I further recommended that Olympic stars Hasley Crawford and Don Quarrie be taken to Jamaica for a weekend motivational visit where they could meet Haitian national athletes and coaches and interact with a special group of young sprinters. I also suggested the use of large car parks for the playing of basketball and volleyball as another method of providing instant playing facilities with little expenditure. Jamaica and the Dominican Republic, because of their proximity, could have spearheaded, on behalf of CARCIOM, a number of competitive initiatives to stimulate international competitions and the coaching of coaches.

I am sure that Secretary General Carrington meant well but this and other recommendations had to go forward to the Heads of Government meeting and that was the last I heard about the initiative. The recent earthquake tragedy in Haiti is further reminder of our neglected commitment. I am in no doubt that the international community and CARICOM will play an important role in trying to re-establish the major facilities of that nation in education, health, tourism, housing etcetera. Although FIFA and the IOC have clearly indicated that they are prepared to help the national structures and national sportsmen and women, CARICOM will have to take on a pivotal role.

With W.I. team in Bombay during the 1983 W.I. Tour

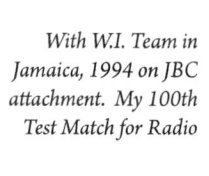

With W.I. Team in Jamaica, 1994 on JBC attachment. My 100th Test Match for Radio

Chapter 22
A Life Changing Event

I had been in the habit, during my years at the OECS, of saving up all of my holiday time for the very end of the year when I would pursue my first love of broadcasting. In 1995, the West Indies team was touring Australia. Fazeer Mohammed had commentated for the test matches and I was invited by the CBU to continue with the One Day Internationals as Fazeer was returning home to attend another event. I travelled to what by then had become familiar stomping ground, looking forward to an exciting season and to catching up with old friends. The schedule was quite punishing and so though I am usually very social, I had decided on Old Year's Night of 1995 not to accompany my friends and hosts John, a lawyer and Carol Magrudder, a Trinidad born trained nurse. They had plans to attend a Grenadian fete but as I had an ODI the following day at the Sydney Cricket Ground commencing at 2 p.m., I decided against it. After John and Carol departed their Sydney home, I watched a documentary on Australia as a colonial country which focussed on how this vast land was developed. I microwaved my Old Year's Night dinner which Carol had kindly prepared and with a glass of wine I looked forward to the New Year and working at the SCG the next day which was projected to be a sell out in the match between West Indies and Australia.

I was vaguely aware when they got in at about four a.m. on New Year's Day and I remember getting up to go to the bathroom about an hour later before drifting back to sleep. At about five thirty, I woke up wanting a coffee but as I made an effort to rise I became aware that the left side of my body was feeling very strange. I thought for a minute that I had had a cramp, that perhaps I had slept badly, but it became apparent it was something more, I had lost all movement on my left side. I struggled up, managed to get to the kitchen, made myself a cup of coffee was still trying to assess what was happening with my body. The sensation went away, and I had free movement again, but the incident worried me. When Carol got up, I told her and she advised that we should go and get a doctor. Had I known then, I would have taken an aspirin and it might have just saved the day, but neither of us knew quite what was happening. The feeling came back and went away again in the time it took to get ready. I got into the bath, had a shower, got dressed with free movement, walked down the driveway and got into her car. It was the first morning of 1996 and the only doctor we could find was Jewish. I suppose all the Catholics had been out all night. Sitting at this doctor's desk the feeling came back. I was trying to explain what had happened and he was taking notes. That was the last moment of me being what I knew myself to be.

By about 7 o'clock I was admitted into hospital. I had no insurance to show, but the game of cricket came to my rescue again, because Carol explained that I was in Australia broadcasting for ABC at the Sydney Cricket Ground and the door was opened. I was admitted as casualty and by 7.30 was settled in the hospital ward. My movements were less and less free and I could not turn my hand to look at the time anymore. I was slowly witnessing my life careening towards its worst ever shape.

In spite of my dismay, I was aware of how fortunate I was. The attention was great; had this happened three weeks later I would have been in another country where perhaps the care might not have been so good. Within a matter of hours I was hooked up to a machine which started to thin the blood and it was the start of a seven week stint in hospital in two different facilities. It really took the strongest mind and the best of will power to fight that. For the majority of time in the first hospital, St Vincent Hospital, they were trying to assess the extent of the damage.

I was not getting any real signs of recovery, they were simply trying to verify the damage, whether my heart or brain were affected and to what extent. I was able to communicate, but I had a slight slur in my speech. I remember deciding to do my own diagnostic and I checked my memory. I was lying in bed one night and I said to myself, Joseph, remember something way back when. I willed myself to recall something from my past and funnily enough I thought of cricket. I recalled that the highest opening partnership at the regional level on record was at Bourda between then British Guiana and Barbados in 1950 with Lesley White reaching 260 and Glendon Gibbs scoring 216 in an opening stand of 390, and this small exercise told me my memory was okay.

Within a few days of my being admitted, word had started to get out, not only in Australia but in the Caribbean. Jim Maxwell, my fellow Australian commentator had said nothing during the match on New Year's Day as he had not heard a first hand report of my illness, but did mention it two days later during the broadcast, indicating that I had had to be hospitalised for a stroke. Hugh Crosskill at the BBC somehow got the hospital number and he called me to express his regrets. The hospital staff advised me of the incoming call and asked if I would like to take it. When I agreed, I had to be lifted from my bed and wheeled to a telephone down the corridor. Crosskill asked if I would be up to an interview to which I agreed, and he began to roll the tape. I struggled through that interview, it was not me. I had lost confidence and I was in the worst shape of my life. But the interview was aired on the BBC and it brought hundreds of people into the know and the calls began to come in. My energy levels were extremely low but I tried to be as available as I could. Once people knew about my condition it brought a warm supportive response that is almost impossible to describe.

I got calls from Ministers of governments, the President of the West Indies Board Peter Short and St Lucia's then Minister of Sport Stephenson King. The Royal St Lucia Police Force sent me faxed greetings. I had faxes coming in from left, right and centre and the hospital was overwhelmed. Pat Rousseau who was then a cricket board official called and said he and some friends in Jamaica were behind me and were not going to forget that I was there, and he offered me their every support. Three days later he called and advised that he would need a bank account number for me. I was moved by the gesture.

I had an old friend who I had stayed in contact with, Mary Francis from my days in England and she and a small network of friends from Australia helped organise this. I gave the account number to Pat Rousseau and the next call I had was to say that US $18,000 was coming from the Jamaica private sector. The news was overwhelming. I had no insurance as I found out, because although the OECS insurance division had sent a fax which indicated I was covered and they allowed the course of treatment to proceed, it turned out that the coverage did not extend to Australia. The bed was $500 Australian a day, and that did not include the visits by specialists, the x-rays, the medication, the blood samples going to the lab, and all sorts of things like that. So the money was very reassuring.

I had a small support group in Australia made up of Carol and John, Mary Francis, Judy McIntyre who would bring her mother's bread pudding, Lloyd Ferreira and my cousin Richard Texeira who drove thirteen hours from Melbourne to come and see me after hearing of my illness on the radio which was indeed highly appreciated.

I have the distinct recollection of the day when I realised the strength of my friendships and how they could bridge distances. It was about three days after I had been admitted and a tall man was approaching me with a bunch of flowers. I had been convinced that he was coming to the wrong bed. When he pulled up short alongside me and said, "Are you 'Reds' Perreira?" I could not have been more perplexed. I said that yes indeed I was and he handed over the flowers saying they were from Leslie Clarke, my dear friend and neighbour from St Lucia. Soon after this, Jones Madeira who I had known from 610 Radio in Trinidad and who had also worked in Guyana both in radio and at the CARICOM Secretariat, called and kindly couriered about two weeks' of the Trinidad Guardian newspaper and a T-shirt that said the "Trinidad Guardian". This gesture certainly helped my spirits and instantly brought me in touch with the region.

The world was indeed turning out to be a very small place. I was visited by the wife of the gentleman who had brought me the flowers, and it turned out that young Rhory McNamara, son of friends from St Lucia, was a friend of these people. They continued to visit with me and to come and collect all my clothes and wash them while I was in hospital. Rhory who had been travelling in Australia also came to see me so I actually had a touch of the Caribbean during my convalescence. Many people from the cricket fraternity came to see me, and the highlight was the West Indies cricket team, and the manager Wesley Hall coming to the hospital. I think then the staff got more interested in the West Indies team than the patient. The visit was really uplifting and it was marvellous to see this big group around my bed; my energy was not very good so it was not a long visit. The rest of the staff ended up getting more autographs than they ever imagined and people came from all parts of the hospital to witness the spectacle of this sought after team around my bed.

When the visitors were not around, these were the darkest moments of my life. Had it not been for my brother Desmond, I do not know how I would have managed. He played a very important role in keeping my spirits up, calling me from Toronto almost every two days just to give me a little bit of encouragement. My family had decided not to tell my mother, who was still alive then, what had happened until they had a better understanding of the prognosis. When I was out of the woods and moved to Prince Henry Hospital for rehabilitation, they got together and told her.

Prince Henry was an old hospital converted into a rehabilitation centre and a lot of people there were amputees or had brain damage, so I saw it all. In my diminished condition I was better off than many and maybe saved the life of one person with whom I shared the ward, who was suffocating on his vomit. I couldn't reach the bell to get the attendant and had to fall from the bed to the floor to ring for assistance. The attendants were able to resuscitate him and luckily I did not do any damage to myself.

I was also helped immeasurably by another Guyanese living in Sydney, Lloyd Ferreira. He had been quite a good football player and had played for a team of mine back in Guyana and we had remained good friends. I remember that we once walked 69 miles together from Georgetown to New Amsterdam as friends. Lloyd had played football for the BGCC team that I had coached and was a person who was full of adventure; he rode from London to India by BSA motorcycle along with his brother Cuthbert who resides in Sydney and Ivor Defreitas who now resides in St Lucia. He was living in Sydney after spending some time in the USA and he would come to the hospital to help me go through my exercise regime, especially on the weekends when the gym was closed. We would get permission to get the keys and use the handrail and the various machines in the gym. Lloyd would have to travel an hour to get to the hospital that I was moved to for my rehabilitation. And he did this most weekends with a generous heart. Lloyd would come and spend that time with me, and though sometimes he might benefit from a visitor who would give him a ride back into Sydney, most times he would catch the bus. He showed friendship above and beyond.

I was also assisted by an acquaintance Derek Leon from Trinidad who worked in the pharmaceutical industry. When the hospital began to permit me day outings to help me rehabilitate and accustom myself to being social, he had offered to take me out for a change of scene. When he could not make it, he arranged for some lovely people, who were complete strangers to me but big cricket fans, to come and get me for the day. There I was in my Sunday best in a wheelchair waiting for this stranger to arrive and I saw this tall gentleman approach me with his son. They picked me up, helped me into the car and folded up the wheelchair which they put into the back of their car, then drove me to their home and gave me lunch. Fortunately it was a one level home and I did not have to contend with stairs. I had a specially built fork for my left hand which I have kept to this day. I stayed with them until 3 or 4 when my energy level began to wane and they drove me home. The excursion gave me an opportunity to see a change of scenery, cars and buildings that I could not see from the hospital which was on the edge of a golf course. I remember envying the golfers walking, swinging their clubs and I resolved one day to walk again.

Though convinced I would again walk, I had all but abandoned hopes of being able to broadcast again and I tried to reconcile myself to this fact, grateful to be alive. I looked forward to the day that I would return to my home in St Lucia and set about dealing with the disappointment that my work life would come to an end. During this time even the smallest step forward was an accomplishment. Though initially frustrated with my progress, I began to appreciate the ability to make small gains with my mobility and as time went on my hopes and aspirations got better.

Lloyd Ferreira assisted me in this respect and helped me start to re-engage with my work life from my hospital bed in Australia. I had been concerned that it was January and that the OECS programme would not be able to go forward if I did not start laying the groundwork from then, though I was ahead of the game because I had always advanced the following year's programme by about 80% by the end of November of the previous year. Lloyd devised a letterhead, arranged for the use of the fax at the hospital and would take my dictation, go home and type the letters and then send them out. When I eventually got back to the Sports Desk it was not a total close down situation. A colleague at the OECS, a Trinidadian Deirdre Jesame, was my point of contact and she helped to relay the information to the many hosting associations in the sub-region, sponsors and the various ministries.

The doctors encouraged me in this respect and advised that as soon as I could take charge of my life and get back to work the better it would be for my rehabilitation. While spending the last week at Prince Henry my two Australian colleagues and commentators Jim Maxwell and Neville Oliver paid me a visit that lasted for almost two hours. They had driven all the way from Sydney and had brought me some Sydney newspapers and cricket magazines. It was great to see Jim and Neville in my hospital room but if I could have turned the clock back these were the two Aussies I had initially planned to share the commentary box with during the entire tour.

I came back via Los Angeles. Because I was to cross several time zones on this trip, I had to work out with my chemist prior to leaving Australia, the times to take my blood thinner medication, warafin. It was sensitive issue as it was imperative that the medication was taken at the appropriate times to avoid allowing the blood to get too thin or thick. Air New Zealand was extremely accommodating and luckily for me the flight was not full from Sydney to L.A. and they provided me with three seats for my comfort which I used to lay out.

An old friend of mine, Malcolm Young, a lawyer, agreed to put me up for the one day layover. To make me feel comfortable he had arranged for another friend Jackie Gordon who is a doctor, with her husband Edward to come down from Bakersfield to spend the night at his home. We went out to have a meal together and the next morning I flew down to New York which was a lot colder. Another in this network of great friends again came out to support me. Frank Dechalus was in Trinidad attending carnival but had called his son and insisted he meet me at Kennedy Airport, take me home and make sure I was well fed and comfortable.

When I arrived at Kennedy there he was. It was very cold, and he drove me up to Union in upstate New York to have dinner and rest for the next leg of my journey. Ken Corsbie drove for almost three hours that night to say hello. He was then living in Long Island which was quite a distance and though he could not stay for long, this visit from a friend from way back in the days of basketball and my brief involvement in the theatre, was most moving.

I flew next morning from New York to Barbados to make my connection which was LIAT. Once we landed I stayed back until everybody got off the plane because I was moving rather slowly. When I came to the door of the plane, there at the bottom was Tony Cozier with a wheelchair; I could not control my emotions. It was a powerful reunion. He assisted me through the airport to customs and immigration and he wanted to take me to Kensington because there was a game on there and people at the ground wanted me to come. At this I was overwhelmed but I knew that I would not be able to handle it. We made our goodbyes at the airport and I caught my LIAT flight, arrived at Vigie, now George Charles Airport and came off in a wheelchair to at last be home. I was met by my neighbours Melvin and Analee Henry who took me to my Bonne Terre home.

My sister Joan and her husband Bertie had offered to come from Toronto to help me through the first early weeks but I felt I could manage on my own. I found I had an incredible support network in St Lucia. Gene and Katherine Lawrence had prepared cooked meals nicely packaged in my freezer so that I would not go hungry – all I had to do was warm them up. And friends rallied to coordinate a system of car pooling to get me to my appointments and to do my errands. I had, to of course, see Dr. Ken Louisy immediately. I had had my doctor in Australia fax him my files so he knew what I was on. I was taking warfarin but it required very close monitoring as my blood could vary from day to day so it meant regular blood tests and assessments to know whether to go down on the dose or increase it. I went back to work about ten days after getting back; it was important for me to take charge of my life again. Soon I was answering the telephone, making calls, reading correspondence, sending mail, taking charge of the Sports Desk once more.

The car pooling was all organised by these incredible friends. Diedre Jesame who lived in my neighbourhood as well as Katherine Lawrence and Ivor Defreitas and a number of people were part of the car pool that took me to work and to hospital and the rehab centre. I worked with the physiotherapist there, Eyonthe Husbands as best as I could. Dr. Louisy also made regular house calls to check on my progress and when he concluded his visits he always left me more confident. On days when I was not going to hospital or running errands, I was fairly tired by one o'clock and I found it difficult to manage even with all of this wonderful support. It became apparent that I needed my sister Joan and Bertie to come after all. When I called them and asked that they come as quickly as they could there was no hesitation. I was not dying but I realised that I could not manage on my own. They came and spent two months.

During my convalescence I received a lot of mail expressing support and encouragement from virtual strangers. One of the most touching events of all this was receiving a letter from an inmate from the prison in St Vincent wishing me very well. During a visit to St Vincent whilst attending an OECS event, I offered to speak to the first offenders at the penitentiary. It was arranged for me to enter the prison and about fifty persons of various ages attended. Here again the wonderful game of cricket did help even before I arrived as many of the inmates followed the game on radio. My theme was fairly simple to them, that every day in this institution was a wasted day in their lives and when returning to society they were not to give up. I used my own boyhood struggles as an example in speaking to them.

I had tried to be as active as I could as my health improved but I had lost the ability to swim – my left side was too weak. My brother sent me a jacket so I could float and I used to go down to the yacht club and float around and try to get stronger exercising my left arm and leg in particular using the resistance of the water. I must give a lot of credit to Elaine Clement, a British VSO volunteer who had come and stayed in St Lucia because of marriage. I managed to find that she was available and she came to my home three times a week to help me to get my hands stronger which were very painful; my fingers had started to open but I could not move my shoulder or scratch the back of my head. Slowly but surely through the physical therapy and the emotional support she gave I was able to improve. I was again able to swim. I remember the day I went to Club St Lucia, took off the jacket and swam the length of the pool.

In May of 1996 St Vincent was hosting a One Day International between the West Indies and New Zealand, and the management at Radio St Vincent insisted I come and join the panel; I was not sure that I could but accepted the invitation. I remember as clearly as ever I went on the air and Ambrose was bowling, Michael Findlay had been giving comments and when he had finished he introduced me. In that moment it was as if my world had stopped. I momentarily had a doubt in my mind whether I could start to pick up the commentary and then, just out it came – "Ambrose from the commentary box end comes in to bowl to Crowe…" During the visit to St Vincent for this match I was warmly accommodated at the home of the Balcombe family at Indian Bay. Such was the hospitality of the family that they had arranged for a young Vincentian doctor who I knew from Grenada to come over the morning of the game and check my blood pressure. They had a beautiful, large home on the beachfront and the view of the Grenadine Islands was indeed inspiring and brought home to me how fortunate I was despite the hurdles I still faced, when I remember that morning of January 1st 1996 in Australia.

I really appreciated the efforts of the Vincentians to bring me back into broadcasting because it was a kind of therapy. Shortly after Voice of Barbados' David Ellis invited me to join a commentary panel for the same New Zealand tour. Working with Tony Cozier, Bryan Waddell, "Prof" Edwards and Franklyn Stephenson was most helpful to me. I was not in the best shape but it was in fact a re-establishment of my life, a therapy indicating that maybe I could get back to live a fairly normal life.

I only got EC $7000 from insurance for the bills I had accumulated in my months hospitalised in Australia. The money I got from Pat Rousseau from the various Jamaican private sector companies I used to pay the last of the first hospital bill off totally so I left in good shape. I had started to pay back the second hospital which would send me invoices. In 1996 December 15th I resigned from the OECS Sports Desk. I had given twelve years and my rehabilitation was to be my new vocation. I remember saying to myself that I had come without a trumpeter and I was leaving without a trumpeter; I left very quietly. I wrote to advise the hospital of this and one day the invoices just stopped coming.

Chapter 23
A Year in My Old Stomping Grounds

I recovered significantly from my illness with the help of so many around me including my physician Dr. Ken Louisy who was marvellous as he treated me with the regard of a friend as well as patient. My sister Joan and her husband Bertie had to return to Canada and there was some question among my intimates of my coping living alone. For me that was not really a problem; I was having more of a psychological battle. At times, to use the colloquial, I felt like I was losing it, like my mind was not strong and I was consumed by negative thoughts about my ability to resume my professional life. I understood what kept me going, and that was listening to radio, communicating with people, listening to music, and working for the Voice of Barbados. Paul Mayers and his team at VOB kept me active, calling me often and requesting my reaction to various developments that were happening in the world of sport. Still, I felt that it was not enough. I was working from home, on the radio and the telephone and I felt like I needed a change of scene, to immerse myself even more into a working environment. It was a matter of re-establishing my confidence to achieve the things I knew I had been capable of before my stroke.

I decided to head to Barbados. I had no difficulty as I had achieved immigrant status and was there so often in my OECS days it was as though I had never left. I had always had a warm welcome at the VOB and Barbados thanks to cricket which is almost a lodge and a religion. I took the very bold step to go to spend a year or so there. The decision took some planning. I had to rent my house, which I had always cherished very dearly. Claude Guillaume, the architect who designed it, and Gene Lawrence who built it, really gave me a wonderful home – the loft is extremely special because it housed my music, computer, television and books, a retreat that was not easy to part from. I worked with a real estate agent Biddy McNamara, and got the house rented. The OECS had brought me from Barbados and they had an outstanding commitment to get me back so I used that card, so to speak.

In my first weeks back in Barbados I lived out by the airport and eventually found a flat in Forde Road which is very central to Accra Beach, Bridgetown, Garrison Savannah, the airport and just about everything I could want, and I was very happy there. The work was challenging. I did a lot of the talk shows and the Saturday cricket where we went from ground to ground. Still I did feel that because of my background and experience with twelve years at the OECS that I might have been involved a little more in some small part of sport development in Barbados. There were many committees on the National Sports Council that I could have served on but that did not quite happen. Toward the end of my stay in Barbados, I went to Cave Hill to cover a game involving many personalities, and Prime Minister Owen Arthur did ask me what I was interested in doing, but at this point, I had to be honest with myself as I had already made the decision to return to St Lucia and did not want to start something that I could not follow through. Had such an offer come when I had arrived it might have been a different story, but that is fate.

I enjoyed my work with VOB and tried to lift the level of our cricket and sports news coverage. The experienced Erskine King had moved on from the River Road station and the department now included Annette Beckett who had a very good take on sport in Barbados and later became president of the Barbados Netball Association and a member of the world body. A number of good ideas regarding the coverage of sport went by the wayside simply because there was not at least the conviction to try.

David Ellis and I did not quite see eye to eye, primarily I think because David is not a sports person at heart. His decisions were driven by the profitability of the programming whereas I was concerned with the pureness of coverage and worked to enhance the reputation of the station. I had great respect for his intellect and his knowledge of current affairs but I was a person of practical application and our methods did not always fall in sync.

I have always been well treated in Barbados by government and cricket officials, national associations and my fellow press colleagues, but I come from a drop-in society where I did not have to call a friend on a Sunday morning to say I was going to pass around. It is different in Barbados, and I missed that feeling that I could get in my car and go over to a friend's without calling. I respected that that was the Barbados style, and I always had a welcome at Tony Cozier's house, but I could not live on the man's doorstep. Often I felt quite isolated.

While in Barbados I consulted psychologist Dr. Mahy and we had sessions from time to time that were positive, and Dr Jordan looked after my health in terms of ensuring that I was okay physically. But perhaps the best therapy I received in my year there came from the most unlikely source. The owners of Bubba's Sports Bar George and Habib Elias really took to me. I had met them when they opened, and from time to time I would go by. Because I lived very close to the bar which was in the Rockley area, I found myself going to watch the NBA, European soccer, the English divisions and there would sometimes be boxing or a major international sporting event on television.

The owners and staff embraced me and I was allowed to sit and use the manager's table. Without my knowledge, the staff had been told never to accept money from me. I suppose they had known that I was recovering from my stroke and thought I had made a contribution and should be looked after, but they really made me feel at home. I spent many happy hours, socialising and meeting people and following my favourite sporting events. Over the years I have stayed in touch and got to know both of their wives very well.

My decision to make the move I think was a good one. I am not too sure if I had stayed alone in my Bonne Terre home that I might not have succumbed to a depression. I think I proved to myself that I was still capable, could produce radio shows, and interact with the public. After almost a year, I went back to attend a function in St Lucia and stayed with long time friends Gill and Ivor Defraites in Grande Riviere. I decided to take a drive up to my house to have a look at how it was getting on and found the gate open and the occupants out. I drove up the driveway got out of the car and went on to the balcony and all of a sudden I was jolted. All the plants I had left had died, and when I looked in through the glass door it looked like a kindergarten, all the furniture was against the wall. In that moment it came to me that I wanted to be back in St Lucia and back in the familiar comfort of my home.

When I went back to Barbados I thought about it and decided that it was time to return to St Lucia. I wrote to the then Prime Minister Kenny Anthony to advise him of my plans and let him know I was available. He was happy that I had chosen to make St Lucia my home again and I got the impression that he was hoping I could be involved in St Lucia's sporting development, but it was not a view that was widely shared. I did not push or ask why; I just was sensible enough to understand that while his position was unsupported nothing would materialise.

I was extremely happy to come back to St Lucia and came back a stronger person mentally and in spirit.

I married Zandra De Florimonte on June 9th 2001 in a lovely ceremony at Bay Gardens that brought our friends and family together; my brother Desmond and his wife Joan came from Toronto. Zandra was from Georgetown and her father was an outstanding journalist in Guyana. I am sure he was happy to see that his daughter had followed in his footsteps and had joined the world of radio to become an on-air personality in the sports department. One of her assignments was to be the producer during matches at Bourda and she had gained even further respect and regard of cricket authorities when she was allowed to score at the first class and regional level.

It was through the world of radio and cricket that our relationship developed and at the time I was again living alone in my Bonne Terre home and feeling the need to share a life and companionship. Zandra was happy to accept my proposal of marriage, but she was younger than I and I insisted that she visit the very different St Lucia to see if she thought she could make a life here with me. She did so and was willing to move to St Lucia. The marriage has been an extremely happy experience solidified by our genuine love for each other and a shared passion for cricket and sports in general. Our main concentration as a team is to give our daughter Kimberly the best life.

With the OECS Golf Team, Jamaica

OECS Tennis Tournament, Grenada, 1990

Chapter 24
The St. Lucia Tourist Board Years

On a visit to Guyana I was invited to breakfast by Edwin Carrington who encouraged me to apply for a position as sports coordinator for CARICOM. It was flattering to be considered but I had felt my own time had passed for that kind of high level job. After I came back to St Lucia I became involved again in local sporting arrangements. I kept my work going with VOB which was fairly constant, commenting on regional and international events three or four times a day, so I was fairly active. But an opportunity that brought me a lot of pleasure came my way – I got a call from then chairman of the Tourist Board Desmond Skeete, who suggested a meeting with himself and Hilary Modeste, then director. They offered me a position as sports consultant and I knew this was going to be a good fit. I hit if off with both of them; they seemed to me forward-thinking and possessed of imagination, people who wanted to lift the level. The situation was ideal. It allowed me to use some of my energy in the direction that they wanted to go in and the work stimulated me. I could still perform my VOB role. The move identified very clearly that the Tourist Board was serious about sports tourism and so our efforts on many fronts was to carry out their vision. I began my work with the Tourist Board on September 15th, 2002. The World Cup was just five years away so there was a lot of early discussion about how to place St Lucia to host this event.

In 2002 I went to England to promote the Beausejour Grounds, and of the sixteen counties, I visited thirteen in the matter of just over a week. It was an effort to introduce ourselves and our world class facility, to induce them to consider St Lucia for pre-season training in February and March. It was a very bold initiative by the St Lucia Tourist Board, and I was able to meet people in the very highest echelons of the English county clubs. At the very least we had put ourselves in the market place and had made an effort to compete. A lot came out of the progressive thinking of Desmond Skeete and Hilary Modeste.

During our time in England we were also able to convene a meeting with the English Test and County Board at a restaurant close to Lord's Cricket Ground. Desmond Skeete, Hilary Modeste and I attended. An idea was proposed to the English authorities that their two champions of the knock out competitions in England come to St Lucia for a playoff best of three series. Our hope was that the winning counties would have brought about two hundred supporters each which would have impacted positively on our hotel occupancy. We left with an assurance that what we proposed would be discussed at an executive meeting due in early 2003.

During my visit to the counties, Desmond and Hilary were doing the travel market and a dialogue started about a World Double Wicket competition at Beausejour in collaboration with an English company whose responsibility it would be to get the players contracted. It was another forward thinking idea and we spent a lot of time trying to educate the public about what the double wicket was all about. The event was scheduled for April 4-6th 2003, but was not as successful as perhaps it could have been. I think one of the errors that were made was the pricing of admission tickets. If they had charged a more reasonable price we would have had two and three times more spectators, but I think the English company misread the double wicket market.

The other disappointing thing was that it did not attract the kind of worldwide television audience that they were hoping for. India did not participate because the Indian Board had decided to concentrate on the tours that were coming and wanted their players to take a break. When the double wicket tournament came it clashed with the Indian arrangements and not getting some of the top Indian players affected the hopes of television coverage. If you get television in India, it goes right throughout the sub continent to Sri Lanka, Pakistan and that would have met the Tourist Board objective to promote St Lucia not just as a cricket venue, but also as a destination for people to come on holiday or to get married. However, the event did attract some of the best players in the world: Shahid Afridi and Wasim Akram, Adam Hollioake and Andy Flintoff, Mahela Jayawardene and Aravinda de Silva, Jacob Oram and Daniel Vettori, Chris Gayle and Carl Hooper, Steve Elworthy and Alan Donald, Alistair Campbell and Guy Whittall, John Davison and Greg Blewett. The World Double Wicket event was won by the experienced New Zealand pair of Daniel Vettori and Jacob Oram who beat Sri Lanka's Mahela Jayawardene and Aravinda de Silva.

It was a good effort though; often the small islands complained when a similar event would happen in Trinidad or Jamaica that it did not happen enough in the OECS. Well it was happening here. It was thinking outside of the box and although it was not a total success it was a fine effort.

I was in South Africa in 2003 when it was announced that West Indies would host the 2007 World Cup. It was in fact my second visit; I had covered the ill-fated 1988 tour by the West Indies which had the high drama of the W.I. touring party led by Brian Lara with Carl Hooper as his deputy. They had taken the decision after arriving in South Africa for the team to return to London, requesting a meeting with the hierarchy of the West Indies Board on a number of issues. The impasse had thrown the tour to South Africa in major doubt and West Indies Board officials who initially had fired both Lara and Hooper as captain and vice captain, recanted the decision after the said outstanding issues were resolved. The action of the players seemed to have dampened interest in the test series and South Africa were never really that threatened by the men who almost seemed reluctant to play. Nelson Mandela, the South African president, had sent a letter via former S.A. player and captain, the highly respected Ali Bacher, to the West Indian players while they waited for their negotiations to start with West Indies Board. Bacher was made to wait in the foyer for over two hours before the West Indian players received him. Mandela never attended one of the international matches, and this was in itself a statement.

One of the great, overwhelming experiences I had in South Africa was being invited to present trophies and address the audience at the closing of a football tournament in a township just outside of East London. The officials of the area had used the football event as a means of stopping the ongoing fighting between various groups in the township and had in fact reduced the level of violence substantially. When I joined the large gathering at the small town hall I had some difficulty deciding what to say to the various teams and officials. Just before going to the podium I decided to speak about my own life as an example of not giving up against hurdles and obstacles. I told the young audience that I was not born with a gold spoon and did not come from a rich background and although I faced issues of stammering and education I had persisted. My message to the group was simply not to quit in the endeavour to improve oneself.

The announcement about World Cup was a major achievement, and a major decision by the ICC. The West Indies had made a substantial contribution to World Cup tournaments winning in '75, again in '79 and lost in India in the '83 final. It was fair that it was now our turn to host the event. The West Indies Board mobilised a lot of their executive members to go to South Africa at some expense I would think, to view the World Cup and to look at all aspects of hosting, not just the cricket but the question of security – the words "ambush marketing" became a new catch phrase. There was ticketing, merchandising, player and official transportation – every aspect of World Cup was under examination so that when they came back they could report on it and use their experience at S.A 2003 as a guideline. The one clear point at that time was that the West Indies were scattered venues from Jamaica all the way down to Guyana on the South American mainland so that in itself straightaway was a challenge. When you are dealing with independent countries with their own immigration requirements etc. and travel logistics – moving players, press, media, ICC officials and umpires and spectators, this was something that had to be worked out.

To deal with this Desmond and Hilary, showing the initiative and vision I so admired, proposed the plan of pre-clearing the 2003 visiting Australian and West Indies team, sponsors, board officials and television crew before they got to St Lucia. The pilot programme was an attempt to prepare St Lucia to deal with the demands of World Cup, to make travel into St Lucia easier, hassle free, with little time spent in the crowded VIP lounge, and ensure player comfort. It was decided that the Tourist Board in conjunction with the Immigration Department would send an officer from Immigration to Jamaica. I suggested I go along to contribute my knowledge of the board and officials and players to round out the team. It worked very well. I made the contact with the various managers, the ICC people, the umpires and television crew, and we pre-cleared over a hundred people, so when they arrived at Hewannorra International Airport in St Lucia they virtually walked off the flight and were in their respective buses in eight minutes. Since customs and immigration had worked out a system where the passports would have an indicator that showed they had been pre-checked, the process worked well. That kind of innovation up to today has kept going. The players really appreciated it. Only St Lucia has ever done it and we got a lot of kudos for providing this facility.

Desmond had played an important role in St Lucia's bid for the World Cup, and after the bid was approved at a special meeting in Jamaica, he played a very constructive role in the plans and preparations for hosting. I think at this point one of the advantages was that St

Lucia already had a ground while the majority of the other hosting countries and those who eventually won the bid had to build new grounds. Sabina Park in Jamaica had to be refurbished and Kensington Oval in Barbados totally redone. One must give Honourable Mario Michel credit for the foresight. A couple of years previously England were coming to the West Indies and St Lucia was given a four day game at the Mindoo Philip Park. Of course the local association was keen to provide some cricket for the public but after looking at the short term and long term impact and the initial expense, Mario Michel turned down the opportunity to host saying that a lot of money would be spent simply putting Mindoo Phillip into shape to host the game but the ground was not viable in the long term. St Lucia had to bite the bullet and build an international facility. The public was a little disappointed with the decision but it was in the best interest of the island.

Sadly on the eve of England's arrival in 2004, Desmond met a very tragic end. I had gone to Grenada on April 22nd to make the pre-clearing arrangements for the England and West Indies teams and other officials and I had come back on the night of April 23rd. I called him that evening to tell him that I was back along with the immigration officer and that the trip had been a success. When I called he was having dinner with some friends and we agreed to meet at George Charles Airport the next morning. I got up that morning bright and early and got to the airport where Trevor Philip, the president of the Cricket Association, asked if I had anything to tell him. I was perplexed and said no, and he asked me to have a seat, and delivered the devastating news that Desmond had died that morning. The shock hit me that a man I had spoken to a matter of hours ago was not with us anymore, but I knew he would have been very happy to see some of the ideas that we had worked on coming into being. The players and officials walked from the airport tarmac onto the coach and out of the airport in just five minutes. The news of Desmond's death went through the cricket fraternity, not just in St Lucia, I would think throughout the Caribbean and the international scene. Somehow we managed to keep our heads knowing Desmond would want us to stick to the game plan.

We had great success with the "Helen of the West" Netball Festival. We secured sponsorship and the best clubs of St Lucia played against the best clubs of Trinidad, Barbados, Antigua and St Vincent. The participating clubs could win 3,000 US dollars for first place, 2,000 for second, and 1,000 for third. It was sports tourism in action as the visiting teams, as well as having an opportunity to compete against the best teams in the region, paid their way, booked accommodation, and spent money on their food and shopping.

The Viv Richards Golf Tournament was played the day before the One Day International. Whenever a major one day or test match was played, I got Sir Viv to agree to lend his name to the tournament which he did free of charge. The event turned out to be a winner because we got the commentators and former test players and umpires to come out to play, and those who liked both golf and cricket participated and met people that they would not have had a chance to meet normally. The potential was not really developed; another Caribbean country would have received strong support from their Tourist Board and from the golf club involved. It is the sort of thing you want to shout about from the mountain top: Come and play in the

Sir Vivian Richards Open. It was not a question of spending a lot of money. It would have been easy enough to use our London, New York and Toronto tourism offices to sensitise people. I did not get that support. The owners of the golf club need to change their fees if they are to attract more St Lucians and Caribbean citizens to the sport of golf; for example, a Caribbean person living in St Kitts only pays 500 EC dollars for membership. This of course will not cover tournament and cart fees.

I had a major problem with Permanent Secretary Henry Mangal when we attracted Gulliver travel here. The internationally known Gulliver Travel Group that would take rugby teams to New Zealand, Australia and South Africa, had an interest in St Lucia. They came down on a fact finding tour, to see the facilities, check the hotels, and to research the various activities that young people could do while here. I arranged a meeting with PS Mangal because in a sense the facilities belonged to the government. There was a clear discussion on cost: Gulliver would pay for the umpires, maintenance of pitches and provide lunch for both their players and the opposition. Everything seemed to have been settled at the meeting. However, a few weeks later, Gulliver received a letter from the PS saying that the cost of using Beausejour would be in the vicinity of 2,000 EC dollars. This had not been part of the negotiations. You just do not tell a school that you have sold a package to St Lucia that it is going to cost an extra two thousand dollars. That kind of costing would have to have been known up front so that the total package could have been presented and the school could fundraise. It was never mentioned during the visit here. Initially these schools had gone to Barbados and we had made a breakthrough in attracting them to St Lucia. It had taken a lot of dialogue and persuasion. Other than the economic benefits to our own sports development, the exposure of our young St Lucian cricketers had its own value.

A case in point was Dalton Polius who scored a hundred and seventy batting against an English school for Castries Comprehensive. The Yorkshire School was so impressed they offered him a scholarship on the spot. I contacted his parents to confirm they were interested; they said yes. We got his transcripts and sent them to the school in England and Ernest Hilaire assisted with the visa. Dalton was able to attend the school, and did extremely well which eventually led to him to being the captain of the Windwards under 19 competition team in Jamaica and was voted the outstanding all rounder. He is about to take up a contract with a Yorkshire club, all because of his personal ability and sports tourism.

I think Desmond's passing had a bearing on my activity at the Tourist Board. Those who followed did not have the same kind of vision and imagination, or the willingness to take chances. I was disappointed that subsequent Tourist Board directors did not share my vision. It seemed to me common sense to have a unit or a sub-committee comprised of the Tourist Board, Sports Inc, Ministry of Sport and Ministry of Tourism to promote the activities of sports tourism. That type of coordination exists successfully in Grenada and Barbados.

Another thwarted effort was my attempt to launch a cricket festival. The Sir Garfield Sobers tournament is played annually in Barbados in July, and St Lucia could have created something in August in the memory of St Lucia's cricket icon Mindoo Philip and I am certain that his wife would have given the event her blessing. A lot of the Barbadian schools who stayed home to play in the Sir Garfield Sobers Tournament could have been attracted to take part along with the senior secondary schools from Trinidad and later the UK. It was a missed opportunity to create another sports tourism event.

One year I managed to get St Michael's schools in Barbados to come, and through Deryck Murray we managed to get a Trinidad school to participate. The Cricket Association split the island in two, a schools north and a schools south and there was in fact a small pilot that could have been enlarged but it never came to pass.

Unfortunately I did not have a budget to promote it. In order to finally be provided with a budget I was asked to make a presentation to the Tourist Board. With the kind assistance of Aquila Luncheon who was head of the statistical department, a power point presentation was made. The feedback was very positive and there was a promise of a small budget which never materialised. I understood the need to promote St Lucia Jazz, Carnival and the ARC but sports tourism never really got the financial support that was necessary to take St Lucia to a higher level. In the final analysis I would have to say that the various chairmen of the boards and the ministry responsible for tourism failed to provide enough support. As neglected a sector as it was, it still managed to bring in over a million EC dollars through our direct contact with travel groups in the UK.

An indoor facility would be a boon to the sports tourism efforts. Without one it is difficult to move sports tourism further. No college or organised club is going to come to play volleyball or basketball on an asphalt surface – it would just be too dangerous. The facility would need to hold at least 5,000 people. There would be a benefit locally to give the disciplines somewhere to run their championships where they can have a decent seat, cover from the rain, and toilet facilities, a place to take the family, with drink and food facilities. It does cost money but these things need to be supported. St Lucia swimming enjoyed major strides with the building of the 25m swimming pool. It has been a revolution. The programme is churning out swimmers and there is a competition among schools. A 50 metre pool would lift the level even more, but when I first came to St Lucia in September of '84 the swimming association headed by David Peterkin conducted their training in the sea. It is a fine example how without the facilities you can help move the process along.

I had tried to get things done against the odds: I went once to a brunch and met Allen Chastanet who was then had a senior position at Air Jamaica. He had remarked that the Chinese built stadium in Vieux Fort was finished and I replied that it positioned us to host quality track events. He then made the offer that if the St Lucia Athletic Association were interested, he could provide 25 airline tickets for people to come, the best in the region and perhaps the US and UK. I could not answer for the Athletic Association but said that I would pass on the offer. When I relayed the news to the Tourist Board and shared the offer in writing with the Athletic Association I got a reply saying, "Thank you but no thank you", and requesting that in the future I not discuss athletics with anyone without first clearing with them. That gave me a clear idea about how I had to go about my work around these problems.

When the Gros Islet Athletic Club was planning 5 and 10 K races, I measured from the outside of Sandals Halcyon to Sandals Grande and just by accident, discovered that from Sandals to Sandals the distance was exactly 10 K. I realised that if I had written to the Athletic Association with a proposal to approach Sandals I would probably have gotten no where and St Lucia would not have benefited, so I went to Kashmi Ali who was the regional director of Sandals and who was very receptive to the idea of a Sandals to Sandals 10K. I proposed he write a letter suggesting the sponsorship of a Sandals 10K event and in no way mentioning my involvement, and it happened. Had I written the letter it probably would not have transpired.

I think the Showtime boxing event in 2007 by Allen Chastanet, by then the Minister of Tourism was a strong effort to see the long-term picture. It was reminiscent of the type of forward thinking Desmond Skeete had always displayed. I cannot say if it was an economic success, that will be determined in time, but the exposure was immense, as millions of people watch Showtime all over the world. I was happy that St Lucians were mainly involved in setting up the event. St Lucia showed their ability to produce a venue suitable for a world title fight in the future. It should have led to a title fight; unfortunately when the second promotion was being thought of a year after, one of the welterweight champions got hurt and that affected the promise by the promoters and Mr Chastanet to produce a world title fight but St Lucia had made a bold effort to compete with the rest of the world.

Boxing in St Lucia got a shot in the arm from it – facilities improved, and equipment was secured. If this is to ever be tried again based on economic factors I think it should be a Pro-Am boxing card with the St Lucian amateurs being allowed to display their skills and later to be followed by the professionals, using different judges and referees. Such a mix is allowed by the International Amateur Boxing Association and would make the event even more meaningful.

Two years prior to my departure I presented the idea of a golf tournament as part of the official Atlantic Rally for Cruisers (ARC) programme. This would have meant that the participants would have had an opportunity to make use of a major 18-hole facility at Cap Estate. Providing those entering knew well in advance, it could have been easily subscribed by the ARC participants and owners and the local golf community. It would have also brought economic benefits to the golf club. Unfortunately it remained just an idea.

I got to the point where I did not enjoy just going through the motions, I was not getting job satisfaction, something I always had in my other roles. I had to be true to myself – I could have stayed and continued collecting a pay cheque but my conscience would not allow me. With the passing of Desmond Skeete, and Hilary Modeste moving on to join a major hotel in Antigua and later the Antigua Tourist Board in London, I did not get the same type of support I had enjoyed earlier. I must admit that after making the decision I was relieved, and a lot of the stress went out of my life, but it was a disappointing period overall.

Chapter 25
Amateur Boxing Years

It was early June of 2004 when I received a call from George Alfred, vice president of the St Lucia Amateur Boxing Association, requesting a meeting with a delegation at my office at the St Lucia Tourist Board. I had an interest in the discipline, both amateur and professional, which dated back to the early 1950s when a British boxer of Guyanese descent, Randolph Turpin, surprised the world by beating Sugar Ray Robinson for the World Middleweight Crown. I had also closely followed the progress of Yoland Pompey of Trinidad when he fought, unsuccessfully, to take the Light Heavyweight title from the ageless Archie Moore. The delegation from the ABA which also included David Christopher and Teresa Alcee, had come to find out whether I would be interested in running for president of the St Lucia ABA as they were not happy with the attention from their president Alfred Emannuel and the lack of activity for the sport in St Lucia.

Having grown up in Charlestown at the corner of Russell and House Street, the Alboystown YMCA was just a few minutes away by foot. As the National Amateur Championships approached it was the equivalent of the Gleason Gym in the U.S.A, as boxers in all divisions with different styles would fill the downstairs hall with shadow boxing, skipping, punch bag work and sparing. When I joined the Guyana Broadcasting Service the station concentrated on live coverage of boxing and a large number of boxing cards were covered. I did the blow by blow account with colleague Alan Mann, the inter-round expert. The American Armed Forces Radio further stimulated a boxing mad country with live commentary from Madison Square Garden each Friday night. My involvement with OECS boxing gave me good insight to the problems and challenges facing most associations.

I advised that I would be interested in serving and wrote a short letter of interest. The AGM was scheduled in about two weeks and they promised to contact me about the outcome of the elections. However, three days later I was informed by the Secretary Teresa Alcee, that the president Alfred Emannuel had resigned by faxed letter and that the executive had to deal with the upcoming Caribbean championships which were scheduled for Trinidad in July 2004. The elections were held as scheduled and I was voted in as the new president with George Alfred as first vice, David Christopher as second vice, Teresa Alcee as secretary and Ian Herman as treasurer. Because of the uncertainty and prolonged inactivity of the association only two boxers were active. The new executive was devoted to getting them to Trinidad to demonstrate a clear commitment to both the boxers and the public and to show that the association was trying to move forward. Light heavyweight Darius Cetoute and Patrick Wilson a middleweight, were to represent us; Sagicor provided two tickets, I paid for one and Leslie Clarke assisted with the finance needed for the three-man delegation under George Alfred to participate.

While this event was about to take place in Port-of-Spain, the new executive turned its attention to the task of rebuilding from the ground up. The gym at Vigie had been vandalized and everything stolen; only the metal frame of the ring remained. The equipment, toilets and even the wash basin were missing, making the gym an empty shell with the grill door hanging wide open. The task seemed enormous as the new association had no files or correspondence; the bank account was empty and affiliation dues to the regional and world body were outstanding. The Ministry of Sport further informed us that there was no written copy of a constitution in their keeping and the new executive faced a daunting task. However, thanks to the private sector, major strides were made towards re-establishing the sport of amateur boxing. Shelly Black of Windward and Leeward Brewery had had a long standing interest in the sport and agreed to refurbish the gym completely. His company had previously provided an international ring in order to bring St Lucia up to date with the required ring standard.

The gym was re-equipped with the auxiliary facilities while Sunbilt management generously agreed to put the ring back in shape with the necessary plywood, turnbuckles, ropes, canvas and sponge. Slowly but surely the gym reopened, and boxers started to appear out of the woodwork. A boxing coach of Guyanese background, Conrad Fredricks worked single-handedly with the association to establish a gym at the Ciceron Secondary School. It is a credit to Principal Isaacs who advanced the initial idea, and the initiative brought an immediate and positive response from the association.

With the help of Chris Renwick and his company who provided transportation, we started a road show programme with the available boxers, including some of the new school talent. The first in the series was held at the Beausejour Cricket Ground, thanks to the kind initiative of the chairman of Sports Inc. Claudis Francis. The boxing card was of a fair standard in front of an appreciative crowd, and with the help of the media, the nation was informed that amateur boxing was slowly getting onto its feet again.

Similar exhibitions were held in Babonneau, Choiseul, La Clery, Soufriere and the Derek Walcott Square in Castries, which further stimulated the interest of the public and private sector, Ministry of Sport and the media. This interest was of key importance to the development of the association. The association had to find a corps of officials to serve as referees and judges. An international IABA referee/judge James Beckles of Trinidad was brought in to carry out the necessary training, at the Cara Hotel. The year ended with a small and simple function at the Vigie Gym where the executive made an effort to show its appreciation to the boxers and major sponsors.

The US Virgin Islands was awarded the bid for the 2005 Caribbean Boxing Championships which brought more financial pressure on the association. Because of the tragedy of September 11th, all boxers and officials had to travel to Barbados to apply for visas. It was a party of seven boxers and three officials to make the journey to St Thomas. The airfares and payment for visas were an extra financial burden on the team and there was an additional hundred dollar US fee levied. However, thanks to the Bank of St Lucia who provided five thousand EC dollars, along with two thousand dollars from the Bank of Nova Scotia, and a small amount from the National Lottery, we were able to meet our financial commitments. The team was managed by first vice president George Alfred and the delegation headed by me. We had also secured the services of the experienced Guyanese coach Carl Franklin who was trained in Hungary and was recommended by the Guyana Olympic Committee. He did an excellent job preparing the boxers for St Thomas. The young St Lucia team did extremely well, and competing mainly in the novice and cadet classes returned to Castries with a number of silver and bronze medals.

In 2005 an attempt was made by the association to upgrade the standard of coaching. Working with the British High Commission in Castries, the ABA was able to secure the expertise of Alan Sanigar, an English coach who had worked in Africa and Asia. We organised a two week programme for ten coaches at the Bay Gardens Inn each evening. The association felt that this was an investment necessary for the future, as without coaches who mainly were former boxers, the sport could not move forward. Unfortunately, many who were trained did not follow through. The UK boxing coach, accompanied by coach Conrad Fredericks, also visited the schools and an effort was made to include the Massade Boys Training Centre.

Trinidad was again the venue for the 2006 Caribbean Championships as the alternative country could not host the event. It was good for the sport of amateur boxing that Trinidad volunteered at short notice to stage the championships. Again with the help of the private sector which was approached to finance one individual boxer and the help of the Ministry of Sport who was no doubt impressed by the work of the association, we were able to participate. The team again performed well under former champion Guy Lawrence as coach and returned with a gold medal in the Novice Heavyweight division thanks to an outstanding effort by Jason Auguste, along with a number of silver and bronze medalists.

The association was facing a problem with boxing equipment since none was available in St Lucia. The previous president, from what we were told by other OECS delegations, had failed to collect equipment that was ear-marked for St Lucia during the PanAm Games in Santo Domingo. However, the shortage of equipment was overcome by the grace of God in every sense, as a letter sent by the executive to Catholic Archbishop Kelvin Felix in St Lucia was successful in raising some five thousand US dollars in support. A similar request to the Church of Jesus Christ of the Latter Day Saints also brought much needed equipment. This was a major shot in the arm for the association and for the sport. Efforts were further made to expand boxing in the Secondary Schools as George Charles and Vide Bouteille entered the programme, and equipment was given to the community of Choiseul which worked with the Youth and Sports Council to establish a gym in that area.

The world governing body (IABA) sent out invitations to all financial members to attend its congress in Santa Domingo and the St Lucia ABA holds a great amount of gratitude to Charles Devaux and Ferrands Food Products Limited who graciously agreed to pay all our outstanding dues prior to the congress, making us eligible for all programmes of IABA. The congress saw Dr. Wu of Taiwan challenging the long standing world body president Professor Chowderley of Pakistan, and lobbying for votes of delegates as they arrived at the international airport. Dr. Wu's election campaign officials offered to provide first class hotel accommodation as I came out of immigration and customs with members of the organizing committee also at the airport.

On a matter of principle, although I was in support of Dr. Wu, I decided to be transported to the official hotel. Barbadian president Joyce Bowen played a major role in coordinating the

Caribbean votes and with the support of twenty English speaking Caribbean delegates, the Taiwanese doctor won by four votes, although prior to the voting the feeling was he would have won by a much wider margin as there was clear evidence that Professor Chowderley had run the organization into trouble with the International Olympic Committee because of undemocratic decisions and lack of transparency. The evening prior to the elections, the votes of delegates were virtually being bought by the outgoing executive and in fact I was offered financial reward to support them. I am pleased to say that I cast my vote for Dr. Wu without any consideration for what was offered. Lamentably a number of the promises made in Dr. Wu's manifesto did not come to fruition and the Caribbean nations who had played a major role in his election felt let down. The associations did benefit from an electronic scoring system and new equipment but the commitment to provide each association with five thousand US dollars and a new boxing ring never materialised.

    Amateur boxing in the region had a major set back in 2007 when the Caribbean Championships slated to be held in St Maarten were suddenly cancelled. Though they had confirmed their hosting arrangements, when a large contingent from St Lucia with manager Ian Herman, the ABA treasurer, arrived in St Maarten, they found out that the government had not provided the financing to look after the accommodation for the countries taking part. The championships were cancelled. Thanks to the quick action of Herman, the St Lucia team was able to move to a small guest house and flights were acquired back via Antigua with the association insuring that the boxers were comfortable and looked after during this 48 hour period of drama.

    The secretary of the Caribbean body Kathy Harper-Hall must be given a great deal of credit for her efforts in trying to assist the delegations that had arrived and had attempted to check in at the official hotel of the championships only to be turned away. This cancellation was a major disappointment to all the countries that had arrived in St Maarten. Only Dominica had received the news at the airport just before they departed. The disaster cost the St Lucia association over sixteen thousand EC dollars.

    The boxers were no doubt very disappointed but instead we organised a number of road shows, including a major one at the Rodney Bay Marina which drew hundreds of supporters and spectators who were competitors from the international yacht race across the Atlantic to St Lucia (ARC). My last responsibility prior to stepping down in December 2008 was to see our young boxers participate in the first ever Caribbean Youth Championships in Trinidad. The twin island republic's ABA must be congratulated for the staging of this important nursery of a championship and St Lucia was able to return with three silver medals and four bronze medals.

    Another opportunity was in the offer for regional competition in St Lucia with the resumption of the OECS Boxing Tournament which had not been held for the previous five years. The executive was confident that St Lucia could have staged, but had to have the assurance of sponsorship to cover the cost of hotel accommodation for the boxers from Dominica, St Vincent, Grenada and officials from the region. Antigua Barbuda and St Kitts Nevis were invited but unfortunately did not respond. Thanks to the Ministry of Sport and to the Minister himself, Lennard Montoute, sixteen thousand dollars was made available for the event while the Bank of Nova Scotia also made a contribution of two thousand dollars. The executive also took a decision on principle that the St Lucia team of boxers and their coaches would be housed at the official hotel of the championships, Palm Haven, a co-sponsor, and this decision worked well in achieving team spirit and discipline.

St Lucia won three titles but lost out to Dominica and Grenada in terms of overall points. Looking back I certainly felt that Travis Maynard our bantamweight got a bad decision and had our heavyweight Jason Auguste not come down with a shoulder injury and was fit to box, we would have secured enough points to have taken the overall title. What was important to me was that the championships were well run. Palm Haven turned out to be an excellent little village with their staff going out of their way to assist the delegations. The medical checks and weigh in were done on property along with the draw of the competition, and this meant boxers and officials had very few problems in participating in this procedure. The association appreciated the assistance of Dr. Ken Louisy, former ABA president and Dr. Martin Didier of Tapion Hospital with the medical checks, and Peter Barnard kindly provided an international quality scale.

Although the Vigie Multi-Purpose Complex might have attracted more spectators, because of the uncertainty of the weather the Dame Pearlette Louisy primary school auditorium, with the permission of the Ministry of Education, was used as the venue. It turned out to be an excellent choice as it was cool and spacious and the boxers participating were made comfortable in two dressing rooms.

We were able to get the secretary of the Caribbean Amateur Boxing Association to attend as tournament director with referees and judges coming from Bermuda, Trinidad and Tobago, Guyana and Dominica along with the St Lucian referees and judges. The Caribbean ABA secretary Harper-Hall was very impressed with the large turnout of well trained and well attired St Lucian officials and made a point of stating this.

Because St Lucia had helped to restart the championships, Grenada, under president Ralph James, accepted the challenge to host in 2008. In preparation for the visit to St George's the St Lucia ABA took the ambitious decision to create a live-in camp at Marisule two weeks prior to departure. This meant extra pressure on our finances with the executive taking the responsibility of ensuring that all arrangements were in place so the camp could run smoothly and meaningfully. This allowed the coaches two training sessions a day with the boxers, with breakfast arranged at Bay Gardens Inn at 7 a.m., which allowed the boxers enough time to prepare themselves for school or work. The evening and morning sessions were all held at the gym in the Boys Scouts building in Gros Islet, and dinner provided by the Palm Haven Hotel was served at 8 p.m. Vice-president George Alfred coordinated the dinner arrangements and since I lived close by in Bonne Terre, my responsibility was to make sure that breakfast was ready at Bay Gardens Inn to be served on time.

This exercise did prove to be somewhat costly but ensured a high level of fitness that was not achieved before, as morning road running which is not a natural habit yet in St Lucia, was implemented. The whole exercise helped the team building programme with Courts providing a large screen television to allow the coaches to show the latest world amateur championship bouts and a scale was provided at the camp so that the coaches could monitor the weights of the boxers closely. The actual championships in Grenada saw St Lucia being edged out by Grenada for the title, as the host country was able to enter a boxer in each division. However, St Lucia did return with three gold medals, three silvers and two bronze. The St Lucian delegation also included referee-judges Julie Bonnet and Robert Joseph.

In order to create a major national training facility where one of these rings could be erected full time, the association was provided with an old banana plant building in Chassin, Babonneau. The building which had obvious potential no doubt had to be renovated in terms of the roof and flooring and the association was well on its way in achieving these aims when the change of government saw the new minister of agriculture ear-marking the building to become an agricultural station.

With the hosting of Showtime in 2007 the St Lucia ABA was presented with a brand new Everlast ring by the promoters along with the equipment, and this meant that St Lucia had gained its third international ring but begged the question of a suitable venue to create a national training centre as the Vigie Guinness Gym which has made a great contribution to boxing in St Lucia over the years was simply inadequate in size.

On the eve of the burial of Prime Minister Sir John Compton in September 2007, I was contacted by an Englishman Bernard Clarke, who was here for the funeral. He was particularly interested in boxing and engaged me in his efforts to determine how best to support the development of the sport. He had suggested supporting a St Lucian boxer to attend the 2012 Olympics but had little idea of the procedures involved. I asked him for some time to consider and promised to keep in contact with him after he left. I gave it some consideration and decided that the best contribution he could make would be to donate a portable ring. This was not without complication, however. I was able to secure the support of the Geest shipping line, who agreed to transport the ring without cost, and an agreement with the St Lucia Air and Sea Ports Authority (SLASPA) which waived the duty costs. Minveille and Chastanet, the shipping agents also agreed to drop their fees and it was in this way that the Sir John Compton Memorial Ring came to St Lucia. The ring was immediately put to use in the OECS Championships and for a tournament against Barbados and duly announced in the name of Sir John.

During my tenure as president I did not have the best relationship with the P.S of Sport Henry Mangal. Although I made numerous attempts to seek an appointment one was never granted. I was perplexed by his non-communication as I felt that as president of a national body I needed to bring him up to date with our plans and share information so that we could move forward in cohesion. Though invited, he never attended any of our exhibitions or tournaments and only on one occasion did he attend an event which was the opening of the gym in Marchand. By contrast, his own minister, the Honourable Mario Michel made it a point to attend each and every event that the boxing association put on. I was invited as president of the St Lucia ABA to accompany then Prime Minister Kenny Anthony to Cuba in 2006 to meet with Fidel Castro and ascertain possible Cuban assistance. I did have the pleasure of meeting the Cuban leader when the St Lucia delegation paid an official visit to him. I was honoured to be introduced by Prime Minister Anthony and simply thought it would be a protocol dictated shaking of hands and move on. However, through the interpreter President Castro engaged me with a question of why Caribbean people like cricket so much. At this point I was face to face with a world revolutionary icon and my mind ran at a thousand knots an hour remembering when I first heard of the overthrow of Fulgencio Batista, the American blockade and the Bay of Pigs etcetera. However, I quickly managed to grab hold of my thoughts and through his interpreter I explained that cricket was brought into the Caribbean by the British colonial power and West Indians not only learnt the game very well but were able to beat England in 1950 at the time when West Indian leaders and intellectuals were thinking and discussing among themselves the whole question of independence. Then it flashed through my mind that our love for cricket was similar to the Cuban love for baseball.

After being informed by Prime Minister Anthony the Cuban commandant quickly arranged a meeting with the Cuban Ministry of Sport (INDER) to discuss possible assistance from Cuba for boxing in St Lucia. On my return I attempted to secure an urgent meeting with the P.S so that I could apprise him of what transpired in Cuba as discussed with Attorney General Petrus Compton. His response through his secretary, was that I should meet with an officer of his ministry, Victor Reid. I felt that this decision was neither practical nor cooperative and was disappointed with his attitude.

I did not have the smoothest relationship with the secretary of the St Lucia NOC Alfred Emmanuel either. This probably related to my arrival in St Lucia to work at the OECS in 1984, when I was told he had been in opposition to my appointment. In some quarters it was felt that the late St Lucian Laurie Auguste, sports administrator should have been considered. In simple terms, he argued, my navel string was not cut here. When I tried to make a contribution by starting the Gros Islet Athletics Club, an affiliation with the St Lucia AA was denied, although a constitution had been provided and several successful events such as the Courts Women's 5K and the Cara Men's 10K, along with a track and field meet at the Mindoo Philip Park had been executed. When we pursued our affiliation status we were granted tenuous observer status and could attend meetings based on the discretion of the Chairman.

Gros Islet Athletics was more than just track and field as the club had started to work with the basketballers and netballers of the area. The courts were repainted and the backboards were fixed and a number of matches were arranged; in fact the basketball team of Gros Islet played in a Castries competition. The work of the club in Gros Islet would have been more successful if we had the cooperation and assistance of the ministry officials and other community leaders assigned to that district, but this never happened and we were left on our own to mobilize the community. Without affiliation to the St Lucia AA, it was difficult to build a club membership and despite our activities we were given a cold shoulder by the authorities.

The relationship between myself as ABA President and Mr. Emmanuel was not helped when I replaced him as president of the boxing association. In fact, he had resigned after hearing that a delegation of the executive had sought my agreement to join the association. Perhaps our positive development was embarrassing to him as the association made further strides. In my four years as head of the St Lucia ABA I was surprised and taken aback that the National Federations (NF) never met with the NOC executive en bloc to discuss matters of mutual interest and development.

The meetings that I did attend related to the changing of the NOC constitution, the signing on to WADA and an information session to advise of a visit to St Lucia by the president of the IOC and the head of PASCO. Other Olympic associations in the region normally would meet their National Federations once a month or at least once a quarter. The lack of meetings virtually gave secretary general Emmanuel almost complete control over the association and the majority of decisions seemed to be made unilaterally. If he did not particularly like the association in question, its executive would have to work very hard to gain any assistance. Often a meeting with the technical committee of the NOC meant a meeting with only the secretary general which could not lead to a transparent situation in terms of what information might go further to the president and other members of the NOC executive.

In the final analysis I would have to lay blame on the office of the president Mr. Richard Peterkin and not necessarily the secretary general whose aggressive personality did not sit well with many of the NFs. Richard, I have always found to be a decent and very capable administrator who was highly respected throughout the region and the international NOC family, and the honour given to him by the IOC was most fitting. I however felt that on the home front he needed to ensure that his organization was operating in a fully democratic way at all times. I do not think that the St Lucia NFs benefited in the same way as the NFs of Grenada, Dominica, St Vincent, Antigua, St Kitts Nevis and the BVI in terms of programmes that may have been available.

Thanks to the initial work of the Kenny Anthony Administration and the follow-up action by Minister of Sport Lennard Montoute, a Cuban boxing coach was acquired which was a great help towards developing boxing in St Lucia. The association only had a few days notice of the arrival of Renaldo Telledo and had to quickly ensure that a number of secondary schools were brought into the schools programme, so that the Cuban coach would have several schools and students to service along with the senior boxers. I spent the first three weeks of his stay in St Lucia personally picking him up each and every morning and taking him to the various secondary schools to ensure that he met the Physical Education officer and the principal of each school. This action proved to be very successful as the programme was up and running immediately and the Cuban official had direct links to the schools which allowed him to carry out his sessions. When Renaldo arrived in St Lucia he knew very few English words but with dictionary in hand I was extremely impressed how quickly his English improved which allowed him to communicate with school authorities, boxers and coaches and the executive.

After four years as the head of the St Lucia ABA I felt that I had given it a hundred and ten percent, that a platform was established towards re-establishing the sport in the minds of St Lucians, the Olympic Committee and the Ministry of Sport. During this time my wife Zandra and daughter Kim were more than understanding as I was out almost every afternoon between five and seven and felt guilty as I got back in time for dinner and the evening news. Luckily Zandra was interested enough to attend the majority of our tournaments and exhibitions and this made my role and my absence from home much easier.

Chapter 26
World Cup Homecoming

I remember when the World Cup was officially launched by the W.I. organising committee; it was promoted as 'the best World Cup ever' which was a bold claim. In my humble opinion, and I had been to every one save the one held in India, Pakistan and Sri Lanka when I was sick, it turned out to be 'the worst World Cup ever'. I am not being nasty or anti-West Indian, but it could have been handled better. I think the ICC were over-demanding; a lot of West Indian personnel made errors. I was surprised that the World Cup was held so early, during our tourism high season, when the hotels are normally filled and the whole benefit was to give the economy and the industry a boost but it certainly was not going to give any added benefit.

My own involvement was as member of the St Lucia World Cup Committee and I was very happy to have been invited. I was put on a sub-committee led by Trevor Philip, former St Lucia Cricket Association president, to explore how St Lucia could benefit by hosting the event. It was then broken down into smaller committees, and I sat with Julian Charles and Brian Calixte, both well known cricket personalities, and we got together and came up with practical ideas based on the numbers we had been told were coming. We expected a large influx from the UK so I felt we could have had a programme where people could have volunteered their skills while here. For example, if someone coming was involved in sports medicine, or as a football or netball coach, whatever their sports–related ability, we could have coordinated through our Tourist Board in London at little cost, and then offered the programmes to our local sporting associations. I tried very hard to coordinate with the relevant authorities but it did not get any further. The other idea we had was a national festival.

While there were a number of days of cricket activity at the stadium, there were many with none and I suggested we host a netball or football festival, run a boxing tournament, and play a bit of rugby involving the national associations. It would have been an opportunity to showcase across the disciplines. It was also an opportunity for tourists to become involved, forming teams or joining the activities. I'm afraid however, that it didn't get past the presentation stage.

I had thought when I was in South Africa, that if someone had said bring a gift for South Africa, a tennis racket, a football, etc. I would have, and given it to the relevant associations who would distribute it to the clubs or institutions in need. I thought this was a good programme for St Lucia, one that we could have advertised: 'Coming for World Cup? Bring a gift!' It would have needed some coordination but the Ministry of Sport could have been the coordinating body; that did not happen either. I was frustrated; I felt that I had tried creatively to come up with workable plans that did not need big budgets but only conviction and the ability to see outside the box. Regrettably I could not convince the authorities.

The World Cup itself turned out to be very enjoyable for me overall. I had no role in St Lucia during it and I was invited by the VOB to be part of a breakfast show. Vic Fernandes, GM of VOB and an excellent broadcaster, and a young Trinidad lawyer Veoma Ali and I gave news, current affairs, cricket and music and we used the telephone to call around the Caribbean and interview. It was well planned and my role was to provide the cricket interviews and cricket related information along with VOB sports editor Paul Mayers. VOB provided me with a flat and a small car and I drove from my temporary St George's residence, owned by the Pilgrims. It meant getting up every morning at 5 a.m. and reporting to the station on River Road in Bridgetown. The programme format also allowed me to travel to the various venues, and I went everywhere except Jamaica. I was able to go to Antigua and talk with Sir Vivian Richards, and the PM of Antigua, and collected a lot of information that was pumped back into the programme. The same collection of interviews with various personalities applied to the other countries when I visited Trinidad, Grenada, Guyana and St Lucia. This included doing live reports from the various venues into the programme which ran Sunday to Sunday, so it was demanding. In Trinidad I witnessed the almost unbelievable knock out of India by Bangladesh. I saw Indians crying at the reality of not getting to the World Cup. It was like Brazil being knocked out of the Football World Cup. The programme provided me a great opportunity to enjoy the proceedings as well as cover the event.

Sadly the overall success of the event was compromised and I think that the ICC must absorb some of the blame for the failure of the World Cup Cricket. The ICC generated long lists of what we could not do, bring our whistles, food, music and I think this stripped the event of our uniquely West Indian flavour, one that would have been a further drawing card for spectators. I remember doing an interview with the Grenada Chamber of Commerce head who said had the ICC spent more time suggesting what we could have done and less time on what we could not do, we would have been in a much better position.

The cost of tickets was extremely high on the street. In the various venues there was one exciting match and the rest would not attract the same people at those prices. In St Kitts for example, you had a major game between Australia and South Africa and the rest was Australia –Holland, Holland-Scotland, Scotland-South Africa. The same applied to the matches in St Lucia where England and New Zealand were the two top countries along with Canada and Kenya. Of course it was a financial failure because not many people would attend the minor matches at those prices. The double blow was that the large influx of supporters did not materialise. India and Pakistan were projected to be major attractions with a large number of Indians and Pakistanis living in North America, but when they got knocked out of the tournament - Ireland defeating Pakistan in Jamaica and Bangladesh upsetting India in Trinidad – it seemed as if Murphy's law had applied. Some of those factors were major.

I had also felt that any type of opening ceremony should have gone to Trinidad. When you think of culture you think of the steelband and the pageantry of carnival, but perhaps because of logistics it went to Jamaica. Another mistake was the decision that Sabina Park would not suffice and the Jamaica Government built a new stadium in Trelawny where the opening ceremony was held, which must have cost millions. I could understand a ground being built in Western Jamaica to support first class cricket but I do not think it should have been an international standard venue. The ceremony could have been held in the National Stadium or Sabina Park.

I give St Lucia, St Kitts Nevis and Guyana credit for building realistic stadiums. Trinidad born architect Claude Guillaume built St Lucia's and gave assistance to Guyana and St Kitts. He had a more practical sense of the needs of the stadium. However, the Chinese built stadiums were so grand that there were rooms built that have never been used or occupied. Perhaps it is in the nature of the Chinese to build these grand facilities but when I think of the costs of maintaining them after the World Cup it brings more pressure on the local Ministry of Sport and the local economy. I do not think enough creative ideas have been explored to make those stadiums maintain themselves.

I was also taken aback by the number of people travelling up and down the Caribbean on World Cup business, and it seemed to me a large amount of people not producing very much. There was a case of an official based in Jamaica who was to deliver a certain plan. Thousands of dollars were spent in visits, discussions at the various venues and the plan was never delivered.

The disastrous final with the rains in Barbados, was the culmination of the World Cup disappointment. Match referee Jeff Crowe, I think got it wrong and chose too many overs to be bowled. The whole event ended in darkness and all the lovely work by Peter Minshall happened in the dark. It was not a great final as World Cup finals go. On the morning of that game I saw people with tickets, particularly Indians, standing outside of the Kensington Oval, begging people to buy them at half price. All the countries were hit with accommodation cancellations after India was out. Myself and Tony Becca, the Jamaican journalist, had been sitting next to each other in the press centre. As we drove away from Kensington, there was a relief that the whole experience was over.

From a St Lucian cricket development standpoint along with the potential sports tourism infrastructure gain, another major disappointment of hosting the World Cup in St Lucia was the unfulfilled legacy programme: six grounds were to be upgraded to almost first class quality. These grounds would have had a small pavilion, running water, toilet and bath facilities, bringing St Lucia in line with what is needed for better cricket development and sports tourism in the region.

When this was announced by the St Lucia World Cup office it was welcomed by the St Lucian nation as a whole as even those who were not great cricket fans were savvy enough to know that such a facility would benefit school, club and national association along with providing the St Lucia Tourist Board with a strong cricketing card to promote the island as a destination where cricket facilities of good order were available. When the St Lucian government received St Lucia's financial allocation there was still hope that this would be carried out, but disappointingly this legacy project has not been implemented.

Credit, however, must be given the governments in the overall administration of the tournament because they bent over backwards to be accommodating. For example, the Sunset Legislation which permitted easy movement among countries was inspired, and took a lot of work to get it framed in a way that was acceptable to all. It was marvellous to travel the region and feel like a citizen of the region – you may have been born in the parish of St Lucia or the parish of Jamaica but you were of one space and it was a proud feeling.

I certainly felt that the subject of hosting of World Cup in the region was a sacred cow and that any independent thought or criticism would have been seen as an effort to undermine the World Cup authorities. No doubt the CEOs faced a difficult task in dealing with the ICC, but if we the Caribbean journalists had been bold enough to raise all the issues that impacted negatively on this great Caribbean opportunity, we may not have been popular at the time, but our questions might have been helpful in rectifying some of the mistakes made.

Chapter 27
Endings

The Caribbean Media Corporation (CMC) had obtained the radio rights to broadcast matches being organized by the West Indies Cricket Board at the regional and international level. Prior to this, the field of broadcasting was very competitive and of a high standard among regional stations as station managers and programme directors made every attempt to attract the best regional voices, and where necessary to contract an international voice. My initial reaction was positive as I felt that CMC's involvement was going to maintain the standards which were already set and respected by radio counterparts in Australia, England, New Zealand, India and South Africa. A meeting was arranged in Barbados for radio commentators prior to the start of the 2000 Zimbabwe series in the West Indies with the CMC top brass addressing the gathering. The panel included: Michael White, Julius Gittens and Lance Whittaker who all explained the new style and the specifics that went along with the branding that was to be implemented and called 'Cricket Plus'.

As we departed Barbados for Trinidad many of the commentators (now to be called "presenters") may have been somewhat apprehensive about how the new format would work out in reality with the live action of a test match or an ODI. Among the new guidelines were stipulations that the presenters were to constantly remind listeners of 'Cricket Plus' e-mail, promote the KODAK moment, read incoming e-mails and advertise the lunchtime guest and personality for the tea-time break. There were also a number of giveaways and competitions that took place during the day's play and with all this new content and format I felt that the broadcasting of the cricket itself had become secondary.

It was two series later that my role was changed from presenting to doing the talk shows during the breaks. This meant that my days for doing ball by ball commentary were virtually at an end if this was not going to be changed. Individuals working for CMC had to sign a contract making his or herself available to the senior producer without a specific role designated. It was only after I agreed to be part of the CMC team that my role was assigned and so I had no contractual basis on which to challenge this change of situation. In life I was always a team player and I recognized the right of CMC to choose who they had felt more capable of doing the ball by ball presentation. I felt I was not above the new role and found it easy and enjoyable to carry out as over the years I had developed good and respectful relationships with players, former players and administrators.

Some of my senior respected colleagues however, thought that it was wrong for CMC to have asked me to carry out such a role. Although I proceeded to be innovative and was able to bring various personalities to our radio audience both regional and international, I certainly saw myself as a ball by ball commentator first, with skills capable of adapting to other roles. I decided to take a stand when India toured the West Indies in 2002 when Carl Hooper was appointed captain for the series. The opening test was in Guyana and I had received the usual contract which did not stipulate what role I would be carrying out during the Bourda test but took the opportunity to inquire of Michael White whether I was down to do any ball by ball. The answer was in the negative and although it would have been nice to be involved in the opening test, my conscience could not allow me to go on accepting this new role that CMC had carved out for me so I informed CMC.

I understood the need for exposing new talent but in some cases young commentators were thrown in at the deep end both at the regional and international level without any preparation. There was no one within the CMC structure who had a background of cricket broadcasting, although I say with great respect that Lance Whittaker as the sports editor and senior producer had built an outstanding reputation as a track and field and football specialist at the highest level. I knew Lance when I worked in Jamaica and his focus was not on cricket broadcasting. Julius Gittens had a very good background in current affairs and had worked for the CBU for many years in that area while Michael White to my knowledge was a late night DJ on JBC before he arrived in Barbados. The young commentators needed to be listened to and at the end of any assignment assisted in a constructive way about styles and techniques that would further improve their skills and confidence.

It was not easy for me to walk away from the world of test cricket as far as CMC was concerned but I felt I had to be honest with myself and to those who respected my work. It was ironic that in 2003 I was invited by the South African Broadcasting Corporation to join their team when that country held the World Cup, and I have continued to broadcast regional matches where CMC was not involved in countries like Grenada, St Lucia, St Vincent, Barbados and St Kitts. I am still a more than average listener and follower of the game and hold no grudge against the young men who broadcast the game today and would be most willing to pass on whatever I have learnt over the years.

Following the Bejing Olympic Games there was the demise of CMC as the rights holder for radio broadcast and I knew Barbados-based group, Line and Length had replaced CMC. Since assuming this role they have certainly made the cricket available to all stations almost free of charge which is no doubt greatly appreciated by the regional managers in this period of economic downturn and uncertainty. CMC's approach was totally different and if stations wanted the international series, for example, WI versus Australia, WI versus England, they had to buy the entire cricket package that Cricket Plus was putting out, a commitment which was simply beyond the financial capabilities of many of the stations. If Line and Length is going to continue to hold the rights for the regional and home series they must make every attempt to carry out their responsibilities professionally and aim for the very high standards prior to 1999 when the broadcasting of cricket was at a very high level.

The mantle has now been passed to Fazeer Mohammed and Simon Crosskill who are very capable of maintaining those standards that I grew to know before broadcasting my first ball. It was British Guiana versus Trinidad at Rose Hall Berbice in 1961, and I have finally finished with the great pleasure of having broadcast 145 test matches, the majority in the company of Tony Cozier. I have to extend my sincere gratitude to all the regional stations and the CBU for the privilege.

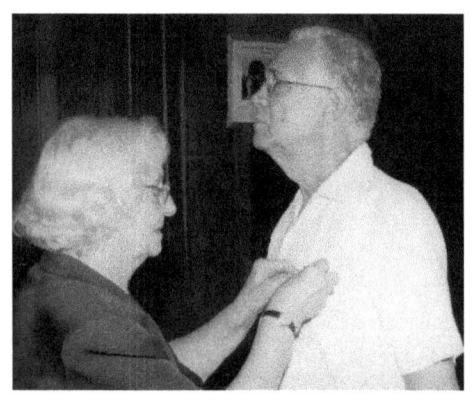

*Receiving my Arrow of Achievement Award from
President Janet Jagan, 1997, Guyana*

Chapter 28
Reflections

As I look back on my active life I must recognize how fortunate I was to be able to see some of the very best perform at the highest level and at some of the most celebrated cricket venues in the world, not to mention the opportunities to meet inspirational personalities along the way. In one sense I would have liked to have had a more finished education, but then I question that if I in fact had finished secondary school with enough passes to go on further whether I might not have chosen a different direction and ended up working in an institution in the region or in North America. If being more formally educated would have in fact changed the life and career I pursued, I would not choose it.

Who among the true cricket lovers could not relish the sight of having seen and had the privilege of meeting: Stollmeyer, Rae, Weekes, Worrell, Walcott, Gomez, R. Christiani, Hunte, Sobers, Kanhai, Collie Smith, Butcher, Nurse, Lloyd, Gomes, C. Davis, D.L Murray, Alexander, Hendricks, Dujon, Kallicharran, Rowe, Richardson, Fredericks, Grennidge, Haynes, Lara, Gibbs, Ramadhin, Valentine, Hall, Gilchrist, Holding, Roberts, Marshall, Croft, Garner, Ambrose and Walsh.

The English players included: Hutton, Compton, May, Graveney, Bailey, Cowdrey, Evans, Barrington, Laker, Statham, Trueman, Johnny Wardle, Boycott, Gower, Gooch, Knott, Taylor, Snow, Botham, Underwood, Willis, Thorpe.

The Australians like the West Indians were a delight to watch: McDonald, Morris, Harvey, Miller, Benaud, Davidson, Linwall, Langley, Johnston, Simpson, Lawry, I. Chappell, G. Chappell, Marsh, Walters, Lillee, Thomson, Mallet, Walker, Boon, M. Waugh, S. Waugh, Pointing, Gilchrist, McGrath, Lee, Aldeman, Lawson.

India like the West Indies got Test status late but quickly produced a number of outstanding players: Mankad, Hazare, Umrigar, Phadkar, Gupte, V.L Manjrekar, Borde, Ramchand, Roy, Apte, Sardesi, Durani, Bedi, Venkat, Prasanna. Chandrasekhar, Gavaskar, Viswanauth, M. Amarnath, Kapil Dev, Vengsarkar, Shastri, Tendulkar, Sehwag, Dravid, Srinath, Kumble, Ganguly.

Pakistan who only became a nation after 1947 produced Hanif, Imtiaz, Fazal, Saeed, Majid,

Zaheer, Asif, Mushtaq, Wasim, Intikhab, Sarfaz, Imran, Bari, Miandad, Inzamam-ul-Haq, Waqar Younis.

New Zealand: Turner, Congdon, B. Taylor, Burgess, Wadsworth, H. Howart, Hastings, Wright, Coney, R. Hadlee, M. Crowe, I. Smith, D. Vettore, S. Bond.

South Africa: Donald, Kirsten, Cronje, Kallis, Rhodes, Pollock, Boucher, Wessels, Ntini.

Because of my sense of early history I took every opportunity possible as I made my way up the ladder of commentary and moved around the Caribbean to seek out and talk to those early pioneers of West Indies cricket - men who had played in the unfamiliar, unforgiving, cold conditions of England and had travelled many long miles to take on the mighty Australia. In Guyana itself M.P Fernandes, C.V Wight, F.I Decaires L. Birkett, C.R Browne: in Trinidad there was P. Achong, D. Sealy, V. Stollmeyer C. A Roach, and when my journey continued to Barbados I had the further pleasure to spend time with H. Griffith, E.L.G Hoad, E.A.V Williams, while visits to Jamaica provided the opportunity to meet the great George Headley, Ivan Barrow and Ken 'Bam Bam' Weekes.

In every instance, these men were approachable and inspired me with their humility in light of such great achievement; their pioneering spirit and the strength of their characters was clear. To me it was like turning back the clock and revisiting a very important early era in West Indies cricket.

International sport should be played with passion and commitment and cricket is no different. However, it is equally important that the game is played in the right spirit and provide the right example to the many young aspiring cricketers who attend international matches. There are times in the heat of battle when tempers can flare and ugly incidents can occur and that has happened at times with all of our cricket teams. I certainly feel that Australia over the years has forgotten this sacred reverence and a win-at-all-cost attitude has become vital and important. The same cannot be said of the teams led by Ian Johnston, Richie Benaud, Ian and Greg Chappell, Bobby Simpson and Mark Taylor as they behaved in a different manner even when competing fiercely. However, Australian sides in the last decade and a half captained by Steve Waugh and Ricky Ponting did not maintain the high standards set by their predecessors. All international teams whether English, Indian, New Zealander, Pakistani or South African have generally carried themselves with dignity and respect for their opponents on the field of play. The champion team of the day has a responsibility for maintaining high standards of sportsmanship.

I think the difference can be traced to leadership and what the captain will allow. Waugh and Ponting allowed loutish behaviour on the field in the name of a strategy of "mental disintegration" or playing it hard at all times. Sledging and claiming illegal catches should never be part of a team's strategy and great teams have won without it. Thankfully the good West Indies teams led by Goddard, Alexander, Worrell, Sobers, Lloyd, Richards and Richardson, never embraced mental disintegration and as Geoffrey Boycott has repeatedly said in his TV broadcasts "the great West Indian teams never sledged a team they just got on with the job of winning". A fitting example that was well documented for all to revisit and read was that of the '60/'61 tour by the West Indies to Australia, with both captains Frank Worrell and Richie Benaud establishing the highest degree of leadership and sportsmanship that has not been followed. The catch claimed by Steve Waugh to dismiss Lara at Kensington in 1995 and the run out of Sherwin Campbell at the same venue in 1999 cast a very poor light on the leadership and spirit of that Australian team. I will never forget the sledging that was reported by our players over the years and led to the West Indies captain Brian Lara at 2005 at Adelaide leaving the non-striker's end to appeal to his opposite number to stop the barrage of verbals that his fellow Trinidadian Darren Ganga was receiving.

The need to win by the Australians was not only a question of skill of bat and ball but a psychological aggressiveness that was totally unnecessary. For example, a top order West Indian batsman simply playing a defensive shot to cover with no intentions of attempting a run would virtually have to get out of the way of a thunderous return to the Australian wicket keeper only inches away from him. For further support of my position I will further ask fair and independent cricket followers to research the behaviour of Australia in India in a losing series and the quite recent undisciplined display by the home team when India toured Australia and the statement from the former Indian captain Anil Kumble. Not for one minute am I claiming that only the Aussies are responsible for maintaining the true spirit of the game, as we have all been sinners at some stage. I certainly feel that Tony Greig went beyond that line and tore up the unwritten convention when he threw down the stumps of Alvin Kallicharran after Kallicharran had played the last ball of the day defensively with no intention of running only to be given out. This had to be an indictment against the spirit of the game concept and the umpire was just as much at fault for allowing the appeal to stand. The main difference was that Greig and past and future English teams did not have sledging and loutish behaviour as a deliberate part of their tactics in test matches. Recently we saw this behaviour of the Australians reappear during the West Indies test match at Perth in 2009 when wicket keeper Brad Haddin created an incident involving West Indies spinner Suliman Benn and escaped without any real censure.

I am happy that I have been able to write what genuinely was on my mind about a number of issues and I would like to express thanks to Katherine Atkinson for being extremely patient at times when I was searching for the right expression. I would like to suggest that anyone who may attempt the writing of their memoirs begin the process some twenty years prior to the actual start. When the final draft was completed I did feel a sense of relief, satisfaction and accomplishment with some surprise that I had told the story of my life in the way I did. When I started this with Katherine in July of 2009 I had no idea of a clear path that the book would take and I could easily have made the mistake of writing only about cricket.

My future focus will be on my family and to assist people and organisations in any way I can on matters of sport. My health will no doubt be a key factor but as I put together the final page I am like the soldier who was wounded in the war but is happy to have life, even though I face challenges each day. I will never run again, I walk with a limp, cramps reoccur every night and I experience a hissing in my ear that will never go away; I must, however, bear in mind the words of my Trinidad born doctor Attlee Clarke in Australia who said, "Let walking be your best friend." I've taken that advice to heart, both literally and symbolically. I get up each morning with the rising of the sun and embrace what the day will bring, with my friends and family close to my heart, no matter where they might be.

APPENDIX I
The Reds Perreira Sports Foundation

I was preoccupied with thoughts about how to give back to Guyana, the country of my birth, in a meaningful way for the majority of 2003. I had kept in touch with sporting officials and developments after I had left for Barbados in 1980 and had returned to visit about three times a year. During this period I did what I could to assist, encourage and motivate but the feeling that I had not done enough just kept haunting me. No one achieves anything by oneself and my experiences in Guyana helped to prepare me for my launch into the Caribbean. I discussed the idea of the foundation thoroughly in mid 1983 with my old friend and colleague Vic Insanally; our friendship dates back to the early 60s in London when he lived at Shepherd's Bush and I at Notting Hill Gate; we were both on the central line. Some research revealed that such a body had to be legally formed and constituted.

The next step was to meet with Miles Fitzpatrick, a well respected lawyer in the Guyanese community, and after a meeting at his Kingston office the process had commenced. Vic Insanally, Chris Fernandes, Hugh Chomodeley, Gem Fletcher, Joe Singh, and Dickie Fields all agreed to become directors and after going through the legal application process the Reds Perreira Sport Foundation Incorporated became a reality. I contributed ten thousand US dollars in order to kick start the funding with the hope that this non-profit organization would be able to attract contributions from the Guyanese private sector communities and regional organizations based on performance.

The Foundation was launched on December 5th 2004 with the kind cooperation of the Guyana Olympic Committee at Olympic House at Peter Rose and Church Street, and attended by all the major national associations. The purpose of the Foundation was explained and its mandate to work in conjunction with national associations to provide training and equipment for officials, coaches and individuals on a shared basis was outlined. The launching was well organized by Vic with excellent press coverage and it was now up to the national associations to come up with programmes that were realistically possible. The following initial objectives were achieved:

A batting clinic for under 19 selection was conducted by Gordon Greenidge
The coaching of Football club coaches by FIFA qualified instructor Alvin Corneal.
Seminar for senior club captains by former WI vice captain Deryck Murray.
A one month attachment of a Barbadian netball coach to national body.
Trinidad golf pro Bernard Benny did a three week stint at the Luisanguan course for thirty young golfers.
Kenmore Bynoe, a qualified Barbadian volleyball official, worked with Guyanese counterparts to improve game control and skills.
Former WI "A" wicket keeper Mike Worrell held a clinic for a dozen young keepers chosen by the Guyana Board.
Barbadian tennis coach Sydney Lopez visited for a one week period working with coaches and young players chosen by the GTA.
An international field hockey umpire from Trinidad upgraded skills of local umpires.
US trained Grenadian basketball coach Naka Joseph carried out a two week coaching programme for club coaches.
Netball equipment including bibs, balls, whistles and stop watches provided to national associations.
Tennis Association received three cases of balls for national youth programme.
A cricket commentators' workshop was conducted.
Boxing equipment for a gym in need was handed over to NOC.
Five quality rugby balls were donated to the rugby union.
Dinanath Ramnarine conducted a Spin Clinic.
Annette Beckett, Barbados Netball President helped to improve administration.
Wicket keeping gloves were provided for promising talent in Guyana.

A fast bowling clinic was conducted by Reon King and Collin Steward.

A course for public relations officers of national sporting associations in conjunction with the Guyana Olympic Association was held.

In order to sensitize the Guyanese sporting public, especially the younger generation, a number of events were organized by the Foundation called "Evening of Nostalgia" at the Pegasus Hotel with the public admitted free of charge. The following sport legends participated:

- Sir Everton Weekes and Sir Clyde Walcott
- Lance Gibbs and Wesley Hall
- Ian Bishop and Michael Holding
- Basil Butcher and Deryck Murray
- George De Peana and Ian Mc Donald
- Sir Vivian Richards, Roger Harper and Tony Cozier

The personalities who made themselves available free of charge in a sense were able to turn the clock back more than 50 years on some occasions as they discussed their outstanding sporting careers. The "Evening of Nostalgia" which was most appreciated by the Guyanese public and the media would have liked to have attracted more world greats but was subject to the availability of such personalities and the question of cost. Such a programme could not have been possible without the kind and excellent cooperation of the Pegasus Hotel and their management and staff. The main conference room was provided free of charge and special rates were given by Cara Hotel. Nights of nostalgia could be easily produced in Trinidad and Tobago, Barbados, Antigua and Barbuda, and Jamaica with all their rich sporting personalities.

In looking back I am sorry to record that even more could have been achieved if responses were forthcoming; for example, several attempts were made to get 1976 Olympic 100 metre champion Hasley Crawford to visit Guyana as he has never touched Guyanese soil in all his outstanding days. The proposal was for him to work with coaches who specialized in the shorter distances 100, 200 and 400. I personally knew Hasley well as I had met him way back in Scotland in 1970 when he won the bronze medal at the Commonwealth Games, and saw him regularly at the Queen's Park Oval during cricket.

Unfortunately I just could not get the go ahead from the Guyana AA as to a date for the visit which could have also included a motivating talk to hundreds of young athletes from the school system. This could have happened over a three day period that would have cost the local body hardly a cent as the Foundation would have looked after air travel and hotel. Another attempt was made to improve field events among women in Guyana through the services of qualified IAAF coach, Barbadian Jennifer Swanson-Jones. She was a teacher and had agreed to give her holiday period for the visit to Guyana, but again there was no response from the athletic body and the whole idea came to a halt.

I was not discouraged by the two failed efforts. I contacted Mark McCoy who is of Guyanese parentage but had run for Canada and won the Olympic 110 metre hurdles gold. North American Airlines was prepared to fly him to Georgetown but when the idea was presented to the AA, I was informed that there were no hurdles in Guyana. I did suggest straight away that a request be made to the IAAF and if that was not successful a local firm that specialized in carpentry could easily produce enough at the right height so that the clinic could have been held. This was a great opportunity missed as Mark had indicated to me when we met in Toronto, that he would have enjoyed carrying out this exercise in the birth place of this mother and father. There was some good history for hurdles in Guyana as Laurie Tait was able to represent Britain in this event. To this day the event is yet to be brought back to life.

A major effort was also made to provide the horse racing fraternity with a Jamaican resource person Chris Armond who had worked in the racing industry in Trinidad and Barbados. This individual was prepared to come to Guyana and spend four days visiting the many tracks, looking at the question of safety, the training of jockeys and suggesting a betting system that would have benefited both a national racing authority and the government. A proposal to improve boxing in Buxton never brought a response from the authorities and the money that was ear-marked for this project has never been spent.

I would like to thank the associations who responded positively and shared in partnership on the various programmes. The Foundation secretary Conrad Plummer, the former Guyana field hockey player must also be complimented for his contribution, though at times he must have found me demanding.

The Foundation was eventually closed but I would have like to have seen more action taken by the city council authorities and the regional fathers to name streets and avenues in Guyana after outstanding sports men and women in order to send a clear message to the youth of the country. There are streets that carry names from our colonial past that have no relevance to present day Guyana. I have always personally felt that the Blairmont Cricket Ground should have been renamed after the late West Indies opening batsman Roy Fredericks and through permission of Rohan Kanhai, this great icon, the house where he was born should have been maintained by the Guyanese Heritage Society through the assistance of Berbice Contractors as a national treasure for school children and interested citizens to visit on an organized basis.

It was great to see the naming of the Lance Gibbs Street and the renaming of New Garden Street the Shivnarine Chanderpaul Drive, but so much more could have been achieved at little cost. Guyana has produced some outstanding performers in track, boxing, weight lifting, table tennis, hockey, body building, rugby, cycling, shooting and volleyball, as well as umpires, judges and long serving sports administrators. The Providence Ground for example, could easily carry the name of Lance Gibbs and Colin Croft for the respective ends as the Barbadians have done so correctly with the Marshall and Garner end at Kensington. All these simple gestures send the right message especially to our very young nation.

APPENDIX II
For the Love of the Game; Commentators Who Made a Difference

A large number of Caribbean persons over the years and before my time as a commentator made tremendous contributions in broadcasting the game which at a time when we had no television, was followed closely on radio throughout the region. In the early days in particular most of the commentators may not have been paid for their work and did it for the love of the game. I think I will be failing if this book did not record some of those names that helped to build the great game of cricket which at one period we so elegantly dominated.

St Kitts Nevis – Fitzroy Bryant, Paul Southwell, Ray John, Charles Wilkin, Ricky Skerrit, and Dwyer Astaphan, Frankie Claxton, Aubrey Rogers

Montserrat – Franklyn Michael, Franklyn Greenaway, Keith "Stone" Greaves

Antigua – Billy Ryan, Royston Samuels, Tim Hector, Joe Bahri, Pat White and King Frank I

Trinidad – Maurice Corbin, Michael Lang, Bernard Patin, Ken Ablack, Ken Gordon, Raffie Knowles, Lance Murray, Dick Murray, Tony Williams, Alvin Corneal and Dave Lamy

St Lucia – Vance Pilgrim, Stephen Mc Namara, Gordon Stewart, Hervan Henry and Ryan O' Brian

Guyana – Kenny Wishart, Harry Creshall, Herman Decaries, Peter Bailey, Clyde Walcott, Brian Sadler, Claude Veira, Stanley Moore, Rockey Mann and Frank Bettancourt

Dominica – Jeff Charles, Havis Shillingford, and Ossie Lewis

Jamaica – Roy Lawrence, Peter Bailey, Vin Lumsden, Jackie Hendricks, Hugh Crosskill and Lindy Delapena, Maurice Foster

Grenada – Carol Bristol, Richard Mc Intyre, Harold Pysadee and Ray Roberts

St Vincent – Alex Hughes, Lennox John, Harley Williams, and Winston Baptiste

Barbados – Tony Cozier, Harold Kidney, Colin Belamy, Gerry Richards, Shell Harris, Peter Short, Algie Symmonds, Don Norville, Eskine King

These names are not written in stone, or in alphabetic order or in the times when they served. It is a genuine effort to do justice to those who especially in the early days painted the word picture of the game. If I have omitted any, it was not done with any malice or disrespect, but I mainly concentrated on ball by ball commentators and did not include the comments personalities. It however does not include or cover the present ball by ball commentators now working with the various local and regional organisations.

It is also important that we record some of the international voices that became very much part of our lives, men who painted their own word picture of this great game from afar.

England – Arthur Gilligan, Rex Alston, John Arlott, E. W. Swanston, Henry Blowfelt, Chris Martin Jenkins, Jonathan Agnew.
Australia – Johnny Moyes, Michael Charlton, Alan McGilvery, Norman May, Jim Maxwell, Tim Layne, Nevil Oliver, Dennis Committee, Smokey Dawson, Peter Mears.
India – Berry Sabatichari, Suresh Suriya, Dickie Rutnigar, Harsha Bhogle.
New Zealand – Ian Galaway, Alan Richards, Bryan Waddle
South Africa – Charles Fortune, Gerald Decock, Neil Manthorp, Michael Abrams.

APPENDIX III
Those Who Might Have Played

Although I have a vivid memory of seeing Jamaica play British Guiana at Bourda in 1947 on the Saturday of that game, and saw two days of the 1948 England/West Indies test when the schools were given a special half day, my first real memory of inter-colonial cricket was between Jamaica and British Guiana at Sabina Park via the daily Chronicle newspapers. By that time some cricket god got to me and I started, I suppose, during the 1950 WI tour of England to make a special effort to remember players who were good enough but never went on to play for the West Indies. The first two names that entered my memory bank was that of CB Williams, the Barbados leg spinner who bowled impressively with fairly cold fingers during that tour but could not get into the final eleven because of the success of Ramadhin and Valentine and Kenny Trestail who scored over one thousand (1000) runs during the tour but because of the strong WI middle order made up of Weekes, Worrell and Walcott, it was impossible for him to break in.

My first real attendance at a four day inter-colonial game at Bourda was between British Guiana and Barbados in 1951 his turned out to be a high scoring game with a record opening partnership between Leslie Wight and Glendon Gibbs of BG posting three hundred and ninety (390) which was a WI first class record until broken by Chris Gayle and Leon Garrick, both getting double centuries and both gaining one cap each for the West Indies – Wight in 1953 against India and Gibbs at Sabina Park against Australia in 1955. It was in that same year that I added the name of Norman Wight, the British Guiana off spinner who was over looked by the WI selectors, when Norman Marshall of Barbados played his solitary test match against Australia at Bourda. Wight was a talented all round sportsman who played football, hockey and rugby also at the national level, and although a bigger spinner of the ball than Marshall, his batting ability was not as good as the lanky Barbadian. Even before that on seeing Jamaica perform the name of Stanley Goodridge, the tall Jamaican fast bowler who give both Wight and Gibbs a great deal of trouble with his control and pace was later included in my list of those who may have played as his fellow fast bowler Roy Miller was given the WI cap against India in 1953. Commencing from 1949 against India West Indies batting was at a high point with Rae and Stollmeyer, Weekes, Worrell and Walcott, with Christiani and Gomez for good measure, yet when Rupert Tang Choon displayed his batting skills at the regional level, you quickly realized that he played like many, at the wrong time.

In 1956, when I journeyed by a coastal vessel to watch the WI trials at the Queen's Park Oval in Trinidad, it was quite a cricket education as I was able to see players who seemed talented but were not lucky enough to gain selection to the 1957 West Indies side that toured England. I referred to Alec Reid, the brilliant wicket keeper from Dominica and Frank Mason, the burly fast bowler from St Vincent. As I grew older and saw more regional cricket and talked to wiser older heads who I trusted and respected and who had seen the best of our colonial cricketers, I then really began to understand the talent that may have existed. I had seen with my own eyes, the skill and artistry of Nevil Bonito of Jamaica, and heard about the brilliant Barbadian Johnny Lucas, while those who followed the game in the Leeward and Windwards will speak with great respect for Leo Gore, Sydney Walling, Eddie Gilbert, Hubert Anthonyson along with John Da Silva, Ian Neverson, Garnet Brisbane, Evelyn Gresham and Theo Redhead.

I actually saw Redhead and Gresham play along with the Kittitian Len Harris at Bourda and was impressed with their all round ability. Pat Legall, the fast bowling partner of Charlie Stears was named in a squad for the West Indies Patistan test in Port-of-Spain but the selectors went for Jaswick Taylor who had success on his home soil.

I am sure that my colleagues Tony Cozier and Tony Becca can produce a number of other players who might have made the cut and gone on to play at the highest level. On deciding on the following names I would like to suggest that they may have done well also if in their era the shorter version of the game was played, (ODI and 20/20). Some of the players named may have toured but did not win an official cap:

Jamaica	Barbados	Trinidad & Tobago	Windwards	Guyana	Leewards
Stanley Goodridge	Carl Mullins	Kenny Trestrail	Alec Reid	Peter Bailey	Hubert Anthonyson
Nevil Boneito	C.B Williams	Oliver Demming	Evelyn Gresham	Norman Wight	Sydney Walling
Cecil Lawson	Johnny Lucas	Rupert Tang Choon	Theo Redhead	Pat Legall	Leo Gore
Renford Pinnock	Stephen Farmer	Prince Bartholmew	John Da Silva	Edwin Mohammed	Eddie Gilbert
Delroy Morgan	Rawle Brancker	Richard de Souza	Frank Mason	Philbert Blair	Len Harris
Sammy Morgan	Emerson Trotman	Alvin Corneal	Ian Neverson	Winston English	Jim Allen
Mark Neita	Franklyn Stephenson	Pascal Roberts	Garnet Brisbane	Rex Ramnarace	Alford Coriette
Aaron Daley	Hartley Alleyne	Buxton Peters	Mindoo Philip	Geoff Murray	Rawlston Otto
	Nolan Clarke	Randy Leon	Joe Gibbs	Rex Collymore	Victor Eddy
	Alfred Taylor	Theo Cuffy	Lockhart Sebastien	Andrew Lyte	Luther Kelly
	Donald Weekes	Tony Lewis	Kaleb Laurent	Andrew Jackman	George Ferris
	Roddy Estwick	Kelvin Williams	Casper Davis	Timur Mohammed	Danny Livingston
	Mike Worrell	Samuel Badree	Darnley Joseph	Keith Cameron	Anthony Merrick
	Winston Reid		Thomas Kentish	Sidney Matthews	
			Stanley Hinds	Sonny Eden	
			Ignatius Cadette	Lyden Joseph	
				Leslyn Lambert	
				Arnold Gibbons	

From all reports and to the surprise of many two names could be also included that could have played for the West Indies if an opportunity was possible in various forms of the game. I refer to Alma Hunte – batsman, and Charles Dolphin – fast bowler from Bermuda.

APPENDIX IV
Captain Hooper's Demise

There have been many ways that test captains have found out that they have lost the leadership of the national cricket side. For example, left handed opener Bill Lawry found out that he was to be replaced as Australia's Captain shortly after he returned from a disastrous tour of South Africa as he was driving through the city of Perth in Western Australia listening to his radio. Chris Cowdrey having being chosen to lead England in a home series was unfortunately injured in his debut test and was never recalled or involved. Jimmy Adams, after a disappointing tour of Australia, was not retained in the next West Indies home series, but was informed by chairman of the selectors, Michael Findlay, after the word had possibly gotten out via the press, that he was not going to be retained as captain or player. Kim Hughes on the other hand decided to end his role of captaincy when he called a press conference at the Brisbane Grounds to announce his retirement accompanied by a flood of tears.

I was once told that Allan Rae was initially chosen to lead the West Indies to England for the 1957 tour. After the West Indies trial of Port of Spain in 1956 the team was selected and given to Sir Errol De Santos, the head of the West Indies Board, who quickly informed the selectors that he had made a promise to John Goddard that he would lead the 1957 side to England. The selectors were then forced to name the new touring party, with Goddard as captain and Allan Rae out of the side totally. I must, however, confess that I have never been able to verify the story.

With Carl Hooper it was somewhat different, as after leading the West Indies in the 2003 World Cup in South Africa there seemed to have been an organized move to replace him as captain. The West Indies had not gotten through to the "super six" in South Africa through no fault of Hooper or the team, as rain had washed out their game against Bangladesh, and New Zealand had refused to travel to Nairobi to play Kenya for security reasons, so the African nation was in fact awarded the points. Despite these circumstances, the failure to make the "super six" was attributed to the captaincy of Hooper and his fitness. The rumours around the Caribbean were that his knees had gone though he had had an operation to correct the problem; this was compounded by speculations that he had put on some weight which was affecting his cricket overall.

Chairman of the selectors Sir Vivian Richards was keen to re-name Hooper who had started his leadership role well against India in the West Indies, had beaten India in a one day India series and achieved the same result in Zimbabwe. On a personal level his second marriage seemed to have had a positive impact on his lifestyle and he had become much more settled as a person. Co-selector Joey Carew was backing Brian Lara as the new West Indies captain while Gordon Greenidge seem to be on the side of his chairman. In order to verify Hooper's fitness and form, Sir Vivian Richards travelled up to Albion in Eastern Guyana to attend the Guyana versus Jamaica regional game and was able to observe first hand Hooper's fitness and free movement as he put together a classy hundred and bowled a substantial number of overs.

I was having late bite when play resumed after lunch and was in the company of the chairman of the selectors, who himself was finishing his lunch when his cell phone rang. It was the President of the West Indies Board Wesley Hall informing Richards that the Board, on a recommendation of Carew and Greenidge, had replaced Hooper as captain and that Brian Lara was to be appointed. The telephone conversation continued for a short while and after its conclusion this great Caribbean icon was visibly upset, taking a large white handkerchief out of his back pocket to dry his face. Since we were in close proximity at the back of the player's pavilion he went on to explain that he was very hurt and felt that as the chairman of the selectors who had come to Albion to see Hooper first hand he should have at least been allowed an opportunity to report to his fellow selectors and to the president of the board before and decision was made. He felt however that Carew was able to convince Greenidge to support Lara and the deed was done. I had seen the great West Indian batsman upset before when given lbw before in Delhi after Kapil Dev had only grunted an appeal.

Hooper was named in the squad of players when the announcement was made but was naturally unhappy with what was taking place and Sir Vivian made every effort to keep him in West Indies cricket. Carl Hooper and Chris Gayle had come to St. Lucia to represent the West Indies in the world double wicket tournament and while Hooper was paying a visit to my home my phone rang. It was the "master blaster" himself asking to speak to Carl about playing under Brian Lara. I handed Carl the handset and gave him privacy needed on my balcony, but despite a long thirty minute-conversation it ended with Hooper informing the Chairman that he could not play under Lara in the circumstances and that was the end of his international career.

APPENDIX V
Letters of Testimonial

1. The friendship of Reds and myself goes back to our days at primary school – St. Mary's R.C. which was also known as "Brickdam" because of its location – how time has flown! He is one who can tell how my athletic career got started. Reds' contribution to sports in general and cricket in particular – his commentaries during the games, have been second to none. His efforts to support sports through his Foundation, also deserves the highest commendation.

'Living My Dreams' in which he documents his outstanding contribution to sports in general, will, I am sure, serve to inspire young sportsmen and women and also remind past sportsmen and women of their contributions to their respective sports.

I am sure this book will be most informative and interesting.

Finally, the formation of his Foundation and his effort to present the programme in which he featured past sportsmen and women (and I thank him for including me in one of the presentations) has made a commendable contribution to the history of sport in the Caribbean.

George De Peana, Former PanAm & Olympic Athlete and Trade Unionist, December 16th, 2009

2. When we recommended the appointment of Reds Perreira to the post of OECS Sports Coordinator, he already had an extensive reputation as a sports commentator and advisor in the Caribbean region as a whole. He immediately moved to establish a viable programme for the area, and easily got the approval for it of our Ministers responsible for Sports. In turn we quickly perceived that Reds saw the various kinds of sporting activities not simply as just that, but more importantly as avenues for encouraging the sub-region's young people in various spheres, to understand the long-term value of developing proper and deliberate approaches and attitudes to personal discipline, organisation and continual self-development.

Soon, in Reds' tenure, the OECS mode of collective regional organisation for sports came to be acknowledged as relevant to the CARICOM sphere, and the OECS was able to enter into a profitable relationship with that wider regional arena. He brought the talents of sporting personalities and organisers from the Region to us, helping to maximize our efforts. And by the time he left the OECS, we all acknowledged that he had done, for us, a job which few could match, particularly given the limited financial resources available to our institution.

But many of us too, were impressed by Reds' irrepressible optimism about what it was possible to do. That aspect of his personality went a long way to making him persuasive to others, and to encouraging them to go beyond the call of duty in assisting the OECS. He left a definitive mark on the OECS as one of the original core of employees responsible for starting up the various activities for which we had responsibility, and for that I, and many others, have remained very grateful.

Vaughn A. Lewis, Director General, OECS, 1982-1995, 27th October 2009

3. Joseph 'Reds' Perreira, the ultimate journalist, cricket commentator, sports administrator, family man and sincere friend all wrapped up in that one bundle which makes him the resourceful, versatile and efficient person that he has always been since I met him over thirty years ago.

Reds loves a challenge, and he has been known to make a significant difference to every role that he has taken on, despite the challenges with which they come. His level of creativity and tact, coupled with his yearning always to get things done, places him in the category of those special types of leaders who almost always meet their personal objectives and those of the organisations they serve.

He is a Caribbean person at heart, one who has lived across the Caribbean and served the Caribbean with distinction. As he sets out to meet this personal goal of writing his memoir, therefore, I am sure that every line, every page and every chapter will reflect his 'Caribbeanism'.

Kathy Harper-Hall, Caribbean Netball Official, September 2009

4. For over 50 years Reds Perreira, as he is affectionately known, has given yeoman service to the development of cricket and other sports in the region.

Joseph 'Reds' Perreira continues to be one of the leading sports broadcasters and cricket commentators, who had not only brought the games to the people of the region, but his distinct voice has captured the attention of many throughout the world and has contributed significantly to the promotion of interest in West Indies cricket and indeed the islands of the Caribbean.

This Caribbean icon, illustrious cricket commentator, and ardent advocate for the development of sports has served the region with distinction over the years both in the private and public sector at all levels. He has a big heart and has made tremendous sacrifices to see the development of cricket in the region.

Throughout the many years that I have known Reds Perreira, I have found him to be very open. He has consistently demonstrated a deep concern and interest in West Indies cricket without bias for any particular island. I have also admired his keen interest in the development of young crickets in the region particularly those from the smaller OECS sub region.

Keith Mitchell, Former Windward Islands Player, Former Prime Minister, Grenada

5. Reds is a man of many words!!

Just ask him about life in Guyana when he was growing up there. Or better yet, ask him to tell you about the great moments in West Indian cricket that he witnessed as a radio commentator. You would soon know that these stories and anecdotes had to be preserved for our benefit and pleasure.

I got to know Reds when designing his house here in Saint Lucia and was able to draw on his extensive knowledge about the layout of cricket grounds all over the world when designing the Beausejour Cricket Ground.

It was therefore with delight and great expectation that I received the news from Reds that he was working on his memoirs – to tell us about his boy-days in Guyana, growing up in a Portuguese/Guyanese cultural milieu and overcoming his difficulties with a serious stammer to eventually become a renowned cricket radio commentator full of knowledge about world cricket, West Indian affairs and indeed sports in general.

This should be a work that will inform and inspire.

Claude Guillaume, Architect

6. I met Joseph 'Reds' Perreira during my first visit to Guyana for a Shell Shield cricket match in early March 1970 and we have been friends since then. We shared common interests. He was a passionate sports enthusiast, who was just about starting out as a regional cricket broadcaster. I was Chief

Sports Officer in a newly established Sports Department in the Ministry of Community Development in St Vincent, captain of the Combined Islands Cricket Team and a freelance journalist. With so many common interests we became great friends over the years. I remember as if it were yesterday, the many trips we made in the early days to different sites of interests in Georgetown as pillion rider on Reds' small Honda motorbike.

Over the years my admiration for Reds grew as he overcame many challenges to become one of the leading cricket broadcasters and sports administrators in the region. He gave many years of dedicated and committed service to the development of sports as the OECS Sports Coordinator at the St Lucia-based Organisation of Eastern Caribbean States (OECS) Secretariat, the economic grouping of the territories of the Leeward and Windward Islands. In fact since his retirement, no one in the post has been able to match Reds' drive and passion. The result has been that much to detriment of sports in the sub region, a number of the programmes which he inaugurated, and which became part and parcel of the OECS sports calendar, are no longer organised. The people of the OECS, especially the sportsmen and sportswomen, owe Joseph 'Reds' Perreira a great debt of gratitude.

Reds and his family now enjoy the luxury of a fulfilling retirement in his adopted home, St Lucia, but sports runs deep in his life blood and he still takes every opportunity that comes his way to ensure the continued development of sports and the sportspeople in the OECS.

I am confident that readers will find this book to be an amazing tale of the strength of character of a great West Indian whose friendship I have always treasured. I thank you Reds for being my friend.

T. Michael Findlay, Former West Indies Player, 20th September 2009

7. Reds Perreira's dulcet tones and gentle manner have long been an appreciated part of the cricketing scene. Readers may not realise that, like Huckleberry Finn, his story starts with a river or that he left school without satisfying any examiners or that he stuttered in his boyhood but they know they could depend on him. They sense that he has survived a few bumpers and an occasional duck and once in a while even a poor umpiring decision. They know that he cares and that he is accurate and fair, and they like him for it. They trust him, too. After all he has been around a long time, has seen life in all its colours...

Reds is a wonderful and distinctive commentator. Whenever he comes on the airwaves he brings with him a richness that awakens the ghosts of history and a chuckle that tells of flying fish, rum, dancing and steel bands. Humour and humanity have been his hallmarks; sanctimony is not to his taste. His love of the game and relish for life can be sensed in his words as they put cynicism to flight, keep dullness in its place. He brightens the box and the call.

But Reds' contribution is not restricted to matters of bat and ball. Cricket has not so much defined him as released him. Mindful of his own struggles, he spends much of his spare time visiting reformatories, urging the inmates not to waste their lives, telling them, that hope is intact so long as the spirit remains unbroken. Boys listen because he talks quietly and from experience. He knows their yearning because it was his own. Nowadays he organises conferences and day by day does his utmost to guide youth towards the healthy life. He reaches out to those in trouble, tells them to stop taking risks, that no runs can be scored in the pavilion. It is not fashionable work but it is important.

On and off the field Reds has made a superb contribution. He has reached 70 in style, and seems to have quite a few more runs in him."

Peter Roebuck, former Somerset captain and cricket writer

8. Dear Reds,

Let me congratulate you on your decision to write a biography about your life and experiences not only as a sports commentator but more importantly as the O.E.C.S Sports Coordinator.

In your role as a sports commentator, your clear and incisive analysis of different events and in particular your grasp of the nuances of West Indies Cricket, enriched and brought joy to those of us who worshipped at the shrine of West Indies Cricket

In Antigua and Barbuda's case you made us proud by the way in which you lionised our cricketers from a small island, namely, Sir Vivian Richards, Andy Roberts, Richie Richardson, Curtley Ambrose, etc and helped to place them in the pantheon of great West Indian Cricket.

But what gave me the most pleasure is the role I played in helping to secure your appointment as the O.E.C.S Sports Coordinator. You grasped the opportunity and lifted O.E.C.S sports and its organization to outstanding heights. You set a great example which will be difficult to emulate.

We all owe you much thanks and gratitude for what you achieved on behalf of the O.E.C.S, its leaders and also its sportsmen and women.

Hon. Lester B. Bird, Fmr. Prime Minister, Leader of the Opposition
Antigua and Barbuda, November 12, 2009

9. Joseph "Reds" Pereira is the type of guy you hear about before you meet him. For over 35 years his sports commentator's voice has been so popular across the Caribbean region, that even if you hadn't met him in person, you were bound to know of him, or at least be able to recognise his voice. I was lucky to meet both the voice and the man over 25 years ago and have been privileged to observe his love for the Caribbean sports in general and passion for West Indies cricket in particular ever since. It was this same passion that first drove him to raise the resources necessary to venture overseas from his native Guyana to join a cricket commentary team abroad in 1970. It wasn't long before Reds' voice became synonymous with radio coverage of the West Indies Cricket Team, no matter where. His Caribbean and worldwide travels and his repertoire of international friendships taught him the interconnectivity of the human race and the beauty and common values of "one" Caribbean.

Reds greatest achievements include his administrative dynamism as OECS Sports Coordinator from 1984 to 1996, based in St Lucia, where he has been resident ever since. Sports administrators and athletes across the sub region benefitted greatly from his infectious enthusiasm, "never say die" attitude, and the never ending energy and creativity that he invested in launching programmes designed to raise internal awareness, and external recognition of the OECS as a region of talent and achievement in sport.

Perhaps more so than most of his other friends, I had the opportunity to see Reds in operation internationally. This is because as West Indies team Manager I saw him frequently up close, both professionally and personally, all over the world during my four year service to the team from 2000 to 2004. My respect for Reds grew further during this period because I learnt that his sporting broadcast adventures abroad were mostly done at great financial and personal sacrifice, with his love for West Indies cricket at the forefront of his motives. Similarly, I believe his recognition of my personal qualities also expanded as he observed the challenges that I faced up to in our seemingly insurmountable quest to lift standards within our squad, both on and off the field.

Reds is a quintessential Caribbean man with a rare but genuine knowledge and love for the smaller islands of our region, and a strong belief in the rich sporting talent that can be found here. I am proud to be one of his longstanding friends.

Ricky Skerritt, Minister for Tourism, St. Kitts & Nevis
Former W.I. Cricket Manager, October 19th, 2009

10. Prior to his appointment as Sports Coordinator for (OECS) in 1984, Mr Joseph "Reds" Perriera was well known throughout the Caribbean and the world at large as a premier cricket sportscaster, having travelled to and reported on most of the Inter-Caribbean island games, as well as most International cricket matches always in close competition with Tony Cozier of Barbados.

However, once appointed to the post of Sports Coordinator he made it strikingly obvious, that he in fact had a keen interest in multiple sports disciplines.

As OECS Sports Coordinator based in St. Lucia, "Reds," as he was popularly known locally, immediately set about becoming involved in local netball tournaments in preparation for the 1985 Caribbean Netball Tournament, which was to be hosted in St. Lucia.

He actually attended practice sessions and gave input re strategic plays and moral support. He even sorted out overseas coaches with a view to improving the standard of play on the island.

I recall his vivid reports on the games as they were being played, accentuating the highlights with such colour that despite it being a radio broadcast, persons listening in were able to get accurate images of what was happening.

His interest in broadcasting was always imparted to other individuals in an effort to teach them the specifics of being a good sports broadcaster.

In discussing sports with the Ministry of Youth and Sports, Reds suggested that government take a look into the development of cricket in St. Lucia by looking past the Mindoo Phillip Park and instead turning its attention to establishing a new cricket ground of a standard which would allow St. Lucia to host not only local, but also regional and international games. This was accomplished with the building of the Beausejour National cricket stadium and his advice has borne good fruits.

Reds interest in developing the art of boxing, specifically among the youth, should not be overlooked. Even after retiring from office he has continued the participation of students in the sports, sourcing out coaches and the necessary equipment for training in many of the secondary schools.

In hindsight I do not know that Reds was ever an outstanding athlete and in fact delving into history, suggests that he probably was not. Yet he was able to demonstrate for many young people that participating in sporting events can occur through other lucrative and far reaching avenues like organizing and overseeing the development of sports of their interest. He seemed to understand clearly the rapidity with which an athlete's period in the limelight dissipated. His view was that athletes should recognize that their interest and participation in sports can be maintained long after the normal effects of time step in.

While he no longer occupies the position of OECS Sports Coordinator, Reds did establish an impressive launching pad with the correct directives, so that his successor would have guidance and continuity, enabling him or her to move smoothly forward in the improvement and development of sports in the region as the years go by.

Having had close interaction with Joseph "Reds" Perriera during my tenure in office as Permanent Secretary in the Ministry of Youth and Sports from the date of his appointment in September 1984, I have been privy to his wide scope of interests in sports and his devotion to promoting sports among our youth. His advice has always been well founded and his contribution to the development of sports can genuinely be documented, especially by the sporting benefactors.

Mrs. Aldith Isaac, Former Permanent Secretary
St Lucia Ministry of Sport

11. I am delighted to learn that Reds is writing his life story. It will be a remarkable Caribbean tale of difficult beginnings, adversity and long odds overcome, opportunities grasped, challenges met and dreams fulfilled – altogether a fascinating personal odyssey.

It will also certainly survey a wider panorama of regional sports than anyone else could possibly attempt. His accounts and anecdotes of events and personalities in all the sports and games you can name – from a totally engaged first-hand point of view – will be enough to make this story memorable and valuable.

Reds has been a friend of mine for nearly half a century. My sport was tennis and I recall his enthusiastic interest in the game all those decades ago when I was playing in the Brandon Trophy inter-regional tournaments and in the Davis Cup international matches. His knowledge of the game and the competing teams was astonishing, especially given the fact that this was just one of not many but all the sports he took an enthusiastic interest in regionally. He was always keen to help and encourage and publicise and promote our games and he was always great fun to have around as a raconteur and fan and friend when he was with us.

Of course, I knew Reds as a famous cricket broadcaster. He had applied himself with complete dedication to mastering what is a very difficult art and he succeeded in becoming one of the standout and most recognizable West Indian cricket commentators. He will always be remembered as a skilled and colourful media personality in the golden age of West Indian cricket. Tony Cozier and Reds Perreira represented West Indies cricket marvellously well in the journalistic field. They deserve our unstinted praise.

One of the many initiatives taken by Reds is his Sports Foundation in Guyana. In addition to assisting development in a number of sports, this Foundation has had the interesting idea of sponsoring Nights of Nostalgia when West Indian sporting heroes attend and exchange memories between themselves and the audience. In this way our sporting heritage is recalled and given new life. Those who have participated include Clyde Walcott, Everton Weekes, Viv Richards, Michael Holding, Lance Gibbs, Ian Bishop, Wes Hall and Tony Cozier. I remember attending one of these events with the great long distance runner George de Peana, Basil Butcher and Deryck Murray and thinking what an innovative and useful initiative this was – Reds, again, conjuring up and organizing events to raise the profile of sports and keep alive our interest in them and all they mean to us.

Perhaps it is as a cricket commentator that Reds gained his greatest public fame. But I believe his deepest and most remarkable contribution to all our West Indian lives lies in his life-long love and sponsorship of all sports across the regional board. Nobody equals him in this. He has demonstrated this love and pursued this sponsorship over the decades through his dedicated and indefatigable work of organization, publicity and development in all sports that needed help and encouragement throughout the region. I have never known anyone who loves all sport more than Reds, who believes more strongly that its encouragement and assistance is an essential part of nation-building. And I have never known anyone who has given more of himself whole-heartedly to the appreciation of West Indies sport and the greatness of all games.

Ian McDonald, Writer & Dramatist

12. Joseph "Reds" Perreira is a Caribbean person in the pure sense. He has committed his life to the development of sport in the region favoring no one and no country only tirelessly working to help all administrators and sports persons achieve their goals. The goal of regional integration needs more "soldiers" committed as Reds is to the dream of "one people, one nation."

"Reds" and I became friends and colleagues while I was working for the OECS in the 1990's based at the Economic Affairs Secretariat in Antigua. I looked on with amazement and a touch of envy at the energy and self-confidence Reds brought to his work, not to mention the success he had in ensuring that a wide variety of sports – tennis, table tennis, boxing, volleyball, swimming, soccer, and much more – were thriving throughout the sub region. Reds did all of this with a very small budget and virtually no staff but as is typical of the man he did not complain and did not shirk his tasks – he simply got on with the job. While I sat contemplating the challenges of assisting the sub-regional governments to deepen economic integration between themselves and with their CARICOM brothers I drew a lot of inspiration for my work from Red's indefatigable spirit and sense of optimism. That spirit shines brightly as Reds continues to keep all of us informed on the developments in WI cricket and while I have frankly lost all hope that the new generation of players and the WICB will ever find common ground, Reds' reports on these events accentuating the positive and minimizing the negative. If only the players and administrators possessed a similar commitment and passion for the game.

True to his nature Reds continues to be very active in retirement and in his adopted country of St.Lucia works in any way he can to support the development of sports and strengthen its links to tourism. He has also found the time to write and I am personally very pleased that he has told his "story" as it will be an excellent motivator for young people and many will appreciate the real value in my friend as I do. Our friendship continues to grow.

Meredith A McIntyre, Deputy Division Chief
Caribbean Division, IMF, September 23, 2009

13. Reds Perriera is the quintessential Caribbean Man. He embodies the soul and sunshine of the region. His contributions to sports development and broadcasting are outstanding, but it is his cricket commentary that makes him truly special.

Reds brought to ball by ball commentary a freshness and a warmth that was as delightful as a bright Caribbean morning. His love, respect, and reverence for the game and its importance to the people of the region were the pillars upon which his commentary was built. He did not have the journalistic background of Cozier or the poetic flare of Arlott, but he crafted his own unique style, a wonderful mix of lively descriptions and thoughtful discussion punctuated with flights of great excitement.

His descriptions were done with intensity and passion because he knew and understood that from that privileged position behind the microphone he represented the eyes of the Caribbean people.

He brought the bowler in with variation and an eye for detail and a sense of timing that was brilliant: "Garner turns without stopping and begins his giant strides in, he's half way there, moves past Umpire Barker as he goes over the wicket to ….".

He described each stroke with a crisp sense of uncomplicated completeness and an obvious enjoyment of the moment, made that much more special by excellent use of the crowd reaction. "Richards…off the back foot, hits that to the left of cover… … …and down to the boundary for four". He was very good at expanding the moment, buying time to allow the crowd to convey the true excitement: "Haynes is forward and drives through mid off… …..this could go a long way out towards the long off boundary…...Gower is chasing but will not get there… … as it goes into the boundary for four".

And his sense of timing was best conveyed when he, uniquely, described the action from the fielder's perspective: "Harper comes in from the cover boundary, attacks the ball, knocks it down, keeps it in front of him …...and then drives Dujon away from the stumps with the return."

He had the dexterity of mind to give listeners a quick "news flash" style update of other sporting headlines and cricket scores but still brought us "back at Kensington…." for the next ball. The same skill enabled him to cleverly work in scorecards and bowling figures into the running commentary without ever interrupting the flow: "the work of Marshall ten- two- twenty seven- two ….as Walsh begins to move in".

His ability to solicit the best from his comments personalities and interview subjects came from a genuine curiosity on behalf of the listener rather than any self serving pontifications about the game. He never imposed his own thoughts but with a simple conversational style led his interviewee into providing valuable technical analysis, informed opinions and nostalgic flashbacks.

Reds respected the natural rhythm of the game, appreciated that Cricket is a game of pauses, of light and shade. His sense of timing was always in harmony with the action on the field. He used short phrases to effectively paint word pictures so that something as simple as a quick single brought "rotation of the strike".

And Reds' commentary always exuded a sense of pride.
Joe Bahri, Former Antigua, Leeward & West Indies commentator

14. I only know Joseph "Reds" Perreira as "Reds" from way back when we were both sports activists in Guyana. I was a basketball and athletics enthusiast and Reds was an ardent activist of all sports. I saw him go to England on his own meagre resources, and somehow was allowed to observe training sessions of 1st Division football clubs. I saw him go to Suriname and study their basketball and football training methods, and I saw him become president of the Guyana Basketball Association. I saw him coach the top club of the grassroots "yachting shoe" football league and also two senior clubs – and be actually laughed at by some members of the elite Guyana Football Club because he actively coached from the sidelines. I saw him laughed at by the crowd at the big annual cycling and athletic meets in the Georgetown Cricket Club when he participated in the walking race and was almost lapped. I saw him transcend his humble up-river beginnings and become "sports reporter" at the fledgling Guyana Broadcasting Service then the Government's sports adviser. I saw him transform himself from a stammerer to one of the Caribbean's most active and respected universal sports commentators with cricket his forte and single-handedly run the sports desk of the OECS (the Caribbean's "small islands").

"Reds" was never an outstanding athlete, but I see him now as the one-man Reds Perreira Foundation that organizes coaching clinics in his Guyana. I see him still advising, still commenting, still reporting throughout his beloved Caribbean. I see him now being stopped by strangers in restaurants and on streets to discuss and argue who should have opened the batting for the West Indian or for England and who is a better spin bowler, x or y or z. I see him as the complete Caribbean sports icon…

…and I hear him now with one of the most enduring story-jokes in my repertoire about how Bajans give directions - told to me by my true true brother, "Reds".

…and I see him now writing a book of his colourful life, and I'm shamed and inspired to get the book I've been promising myself to write for the past five years.

So it go.. *Ken Corsbie, September 18, 2009*

15. I first met Joseph 'Reds' Perreira in the early 1970s during my initial assignment with the CARIFTA/CARICOM Secretariat in Georgetown. At that time, I was Chief of Economics and Statistics and later Director of the Trade and Integration Division of the Secretariat. This was well before the advent of television in Guyana: Reds was therefore heard primarily on the radio as a newscaster and commentator. More that being 'heard' however, he was 'seen' as an organiser, facilitator, and advocate for sports at all levels; from the urban street to the village and the nation at large.

As an avid cricketer myself up to University level, and subsequently fan of most major sports, primarily cricket, it was almost natural that I followed and admired Reds' work in Guyana and the Region.

I was extremely pleased when later I learned that he had joined the Organisation of Eastern Caribbean States (OECS) as Sports Organiser, where he was to serve the Region for many years. In bringing his many innovations to sport he tended always to focus on its role as a builder of character and a hedge against negative influences, which challenge many of our youth, especially those who are not exposed to sport.

His relations with CARICOM was to strengthen when later, as Secretary-General, I invited him in late 2004 to help rejuvenate the Secretariat's Sports Desk. This was to lead to the institution of the CARICOM 10K road race in July 2005, now a standard feature preceding the Annual Regular Meetings of the Conference of CARICOM Heads of Government.

I thank and salute Joseph 'Reds' Perreria, a man who lived for the thing he loved – sport, an icon of Caribbean sports development – a most critical area of human and social development for our region.

Edwin W. Carrington, Secretary General, Caribbean Community
Avid Sports Fan November 13, 2009

16. It is not often that life provides encounters with one so utterly selfless and without obvious fault as 'Reds' Perreira. Our contacts have been mostly in Guyana, and I was always proud that we shared the kinship of belonging. But what drew me closer to him was not so much that national identity, but the naturalness of his larger humanity. It was to ensure for Reds a role in Caribbean regional sport where he earned the respect of all he worked with and the affection of the sporting communities who were the beneficiaries of that work. Nowhere was this more apparent than in St Lucia which he took to his heart, and throughout the OECS countries to which he gave devoted service.

I am glad that Reds decided to set down his own account of his life, although I expect that his natural modesty will tend to attenuate his achievements. Even so, that account of a life of challenge lived with perseverance and with courage will be an inspiration to all who read it. That a young man of humble origins from the very rural – and very lovely – Pomeroon region of Guyana should have succeeded at home, regionally and in the world of sport beyond the Caribbean will be tonic to an aspiring generation. That he should have done so against the odds makes his account a testament to our human capacity to overcome, and our West Indian potential to strive beyond boundaries.

I hope that this book is widely read, even as Reds himself goes on for many years to inspire by his deeds the young people of today and tomorrow – on and off the field of sport.

'Sonny' Ramphal, Former Guyana Foreign Minister
Former Secretary General of the Commonwealth, November, 24 2009

17. Joseph 'Reds' Perreira was born in Guyana, he lived in Barbados for a while, and he now resides, with his charming wife, in St Lucia. Reds, however, is not a Guyanese, he is not a Barbadian and although he loves the place to his heart's content, he is not a St Lucian. In everything he does, especially in sport, be it as a fan, as an administrator, as a writer, or at his best when he is behind a microphone and talking and talking, he is, but for the fact of his birth, a Caribbean man.

I first met Reds in the early 1970s during the Sunshine Showdown world heavyweight title fight between Joe Frazier and George Foreman in Kingston, Jamaica, I met him the next time in Australia during the 1975/76 Test Series between Australia and the West Indies and since then, travelling the world together and so many times in the company of Tony Cozier of Barbados, we have been very very good friends.

Reds Perreira is a great cricket commentator. He is, however, and especially so to me, much more than that. He is a great Guyanese, a great Barbadian, a great St Lucian and even though he was not born in the West Indies but in South America, a great West Indian.

Over the years I have known Reds, I have never heard him say an unkind word about anyone – and definitely not against a sportsman or sportswoman. He is one of a kind.

Tony Becca, Former Jamaica Gleaner Sports Editor & West Indies Cricket Writer

18. I played in my first 'regional tournament' in 1962. It was at Rose Hall in Berbice against a powerful Guyana team and, at the time, it was of little significance that, also enjoying a 'first' was a budding commentator, Joesph 'Reds' Perreira.

During those few days, I was obviously preoccupied with the challenges posed by the oposition – Clyde Walcott, Rohan Kanhai, Basil Butcher, Joes Solomon, Charlie Stayers and Lance Gibbs among others – but there was still time to socialise with Reds and the others.

Thereafter, Reds turned up in the unlikeliest places; all the more surprising because, in those early days, media personnel hardly ventured 'away from home' to cover cricket matches, Reds has an insatiable appetite for sport, in general, and not only for major international events but also the domestic and regional games.

This commitment and dedication was, is the hallmark of Reds Perreira and his determination to attend and broadcast from even the most remote of venues earned him the respect and admiration of players, spectators and his peers. I was recently reminded that Reds and I also share a common birth date, 20th May, and as such coincidence only serves to cement the bonds of friendship. I wish Reds well with the publication of his life story.

Deryck Murray, Former W.I. Vice-captain

19. More than just being one of the distinctive voices of West Indies cricket during the greatest-ever period in our history, I personally owe 'Reds' an enormous debt of gratitude for inadvertently getting my own career in cricket commentary launched.

It was the 1992 regional first-class match at Queen's Park Oval between Trinidad and Tobago and arch-rivals Barbados, and desperately keen to get a foot into the commentary door, I accepted my sports editor's offer to be a comments personality (yes, a player with no first-class experience as a 'personality'!) as the ball-by-ball slots had already been filled by local stalwart Dave Lamy, Reds, and Barbadian Erskine King.

I enjoyed it immensely and was especially appreciative of the advice imparted by Reds on the general modus operandi of ball-by-ball commentary. This was offered in a fatherly sort of tone and certainly not with the air of superiority that might have been expected from someone with his vast experience. In fact, looking back on it, I remember thinking to myself that here I am, sitting alongside and sharing opinions with a man who has travelled the cricketing world and described live, some of our greatest cricketing moments, like the 1975 World Cup final triumph at Lords!

Unfortunately (fortunately for me though), Reds had to leave after day three to attend an OECS event and I was given the opportunity to fill his slot on the last day as a ball-by-ball commentator. Keeping his advice in mind and not wanting to be described as a pitiful limitation of Reds, I felt comfortable and confident in the role, due in no small part to his hands-on guidance over the preceding three days.

But that's not the end of the story, not by a long shot. More than five years later, I again benefited from his enforced absence, this time for an international assignment.

Reds and Barbadian commentator Andrew Mason were virtually on their way to Pakistan to provide commentary of the three Tests the West Indies were playing there at the end of 1997 when the veteran maestro was ruled out for health reasons, giving me the last minute chance to fill the breach.

So it was never planned, but the Creator had determined that Reds would be significantly connected to my own development in a profession he served with such distinction, enthusiasm, and most importantly, respect for the game.

His life story of overcoming adversity, making the most of opportunities and, very significantly, giving back to sport, not just cricket, in many different capacities inspired.

Fazeer Mohammed, Writer for Trinidad Express & W.I. Commentator, November, 2009

20. For those of us who cherish almost every aspect of sport, the memory of listening or viewing the various disciplines often leave us with some pleasant memories for a lifetime.

It was the year 1961, when I was sent on a work assignment in Guyana and in my quest to find a game of football, I made my way into the well known British Guiana Cricket Club (BGCC). Strange as it may seem, I was not expecting to see football, as the name of the club implied cricket. However, the sight of a friendly face with a genuine interest to find out what I needed, was my first meeting with Joseph Perreira, who ushered me to meet the rest of the guys when I sought permission to join his session.

Reds made an immediate impression, simply because of the courteous manner with which he welcomed me to his team. This was the commencement of the numerous years of my association with this amiable Guyanese sports expert, whose knowledge in almost every aspect of sport was far deeper than superficial. In some cases like cricket, football and track and field especially, Reds was the ultimate grandmaster of statistics, tactics and sports psychology, whereby his analysis was always built around sound understanding of the sport to which he referred.

His commentaries on West Indies Cricket often contributed to keeping the Caribbean fans awake in the wee hours of the morning when the battles between West Indies and Australia were brought into our homes. Reds was forever enjoying the matches, but more importantly, bringing vivid images of the game through the art of good communication. In a span of nearly fifty years, the other cricket commentators could only have been as competent, and Reds may well have edged them with the broadcasting of information and results of international sports which may have been taking place in various parts of the world at the same time.

While covering the Commonwealth Games in Edmonton, Canada in 1978, I saw the extraordinary repertoire of his absolute knowledge of all sports, and it was a learning experience to simply carry on a conversation with this sport fanatical Guyanese. Having lived in quite a few Caribbean countries, Reds was always an excellent host when any of his contemporaries visited, by his immediate desire to take you to lunch or drive you to the exciting spots in the country.

He was very close to the West Indies cricketers, many of whom he nurtured through their illustrious careers. No doubt, documenting his memoirs will be an enthralling experience in the life of one of the most truly Caribbean sporting experts. His lifelong achievements should easily find their way into the schoolbags of the students around the world. I am honoured to have known Joseph Reds Perreria and I am certain that there are many who share my feelings.

Alvin Corneal, FIFA Coaching Instructor & Sports Consultant
Former Trinidad Cricketer and Footballer

21. Like all young boys growing up in the Caribbean, Reds Perreira fantasized about playing cricket for the West Indies. He did not realize that dream but he became a champion off the field as a sports administrator. He dedicated his life to the development of sport, particularly in the Eastern Caribbean states where his work had a big impact on the lives of many young people.

I have admired Reds for a long time and have always been impressed by his work ethic, discipline and high level of motivation, as well as his courage, doggedness and ability to stay focused, essential qualities of successful people.

Reds loved to play sport but his real passion was to become a sports commentator, a field in which he eventually excelled. He was an 'old-time' radio cricket commentator who mastered the basics of his profession and brought great joy to millions of listeners. His strengths were his great powers of observation and his ability to talk about the action on the field in a way that created vivid imagery in the minds of his listeners.

Few know what a great and daunting challenge it was for Reds to become a sports commentator. As a child and young adult he had one of the worst stammers imaginable. That speech impediment played havoc with his self-confidence and at times must have caused serious doubts about his capacity to reach his goal. Reds never gave up and practised extremely hard. He gradually overcame the problem and years later when his flat mates heard him on the radio they could not believe it was the same person they knew in London.

Just a few years ago Reds had a debilitating illness that affected his speech, body movement and balance. Using the same type of will power and doggedness that he used to defeat his speech impediment he was able to overcome his serious illness.

Rafer Johnson the great Olympic decathlon champion once said: "What gave me the biggest thrill was the way I reacted when I was beaten – what I thought about when I was beaten and had to come back from defeat. To my mind, the greatest champions are the ones that react to defeat in a positive way." What I have admired most about Reds is the way he bounced back from his misfortunes and setbacks.

Rudi V. Webster MD, Former West Indies World Series Manager, September 26th, 2009

22. When I hear the name Reds Perreira my mind immediately pictures Joseph 'Reds' Perreira, the Guyanese born West Indian sports journalist, who is well known outside the West Indies as a famous cricket writer and commentator but equally well known in the West Indies for his association with many other sports including table tennis, football, netball and track and field.

Knowledgeable and enthusiastic but not afraid to offer new and critical insights, he has brought to his reporting on sport, a great clarity, honesty of view and a unique voice and style that are instantly recognisable. I remember his determination and courage to fight his way back from the unfortunate and debilitating illness that occurred in Australia while he was on tour there, covering West Indies test series. In our many conversations while he was still in hospital and after his return, he never once complained that he was unfortunate or reflected a negative position; a man of real courage.

I am pleased to be allowed to call him my friend and even more pleased to contribute this short message to his autobiography. Delivered in his unique style and guaranteed to be well written, it will be worth reading. Keep well my friend.

Patrick Rousseau, Former W.I. Board President, July 31st, 2009

23. Joseph 'Reds' Perreira was one of a small group of extremely talented persons who helped launch the Guyana Broadcasting Service (GBS) in October 1968. Guyana had been an independent country for just over two years and the institutions of independence were still being constructed. GBS had the task of trying to develop a national consciousness through radio broadcasting (there was no television) while competing with the entrenched Rediffusion owned, Radio Demerara. The task was not only to lure audiences from Radio Demerara but also to set a benchmark for the role that radio could play in helping to mould a new society and to promote participation in all aspects of its life.

Reds joined himself to this task with a unique commitment. Sport- and all sport- was his primary focus, and he traversed the country recording sporting events for broadcast. His work gave recognition to keen and dedicated people in sports all over the country. In turn, the recognition encouraged them to compete more and to improve their gamesmanship. He became best known internationally as a cricket commentator and none could doubt his knowledge of the game or his faculty for remembering individual and team scores, and more particularly, the performances of players – good and bad.

Sports in a young, newly independent Guyana benefited enormously from Reds' enthusiasm and commitment as a sports commentator, but it would be wrong to create the impression that, in those early days of nation-building, it was only in sport that he made a contribution to the part that broadcasting could play. GBS was called 'Action Radio' – it developed a reputation for being on the scene broadcasting live whenever a significant event occurred. Reds was very much a part of that action.

Two stories tell a tale about Reds. First Muhammad Ali was fighting George Foreman and the bout was being shown on television in Trinidad. Guyana had no television and therefore could not see the fight. Reds flew to Trinidad, watched the fight on TV and broadcast a blow-by-blow commentary live to an enthralled GBS audience in Guyana by telephone. Second, he had become so popular that 'Reds' was a national name. A soft drink company in Guyana, Weiting & Richter, produced a product called 'Juicee' but it did so in competition with another company, Rahaman's Soda Factory, that manufactured 'Red Spot'. Weiting & Richter desperately wanted the association with Reds' popularity. They offered him a lucrative advertising contract on condition that he would change his name to 'Juicee'. Fortunately, Reds opted to stay with the name he was always called, or the cricketing world may have known him as Guyana's 'Juicee' Perreira.

Sir Ronald Saunders KCMG, Former GM of GBS

24. When I left London in 1954 to take up my appointment with the Booker Group of Companies in Guyana as Athletics Organiser to the group, I had absolutely no illusion as to the great challenge I would have to face. I realised that people would be expecting me to wave a magic wand in order to produce champions. But this job was more than that...

I would often see the quartet – Laurence Taitt, Claire Mont Taitt, Ken Crosbie and another individual who was addressed as "Reds" Perreira. They would always be on the go at the Queen's College Auditorium. 'Reds' I noticed unlike the others was not so much a player, but an administrator... I eventually met him in a formal way at around 4.30 in the morning on the road to Atkinson Field. It was like this. I was involved in the promotion in one of the first road running events as part of the program I had introduced in Guyana – a road relay from Atkinson to Georgetown, a distance of 20 odd miles. My wife and I were driving up to the start of the race when out of the dark bushes on the West Coast Road a figure appeared waving frantically for us to stop. In the poor light, I managed to recognise the figure of none other than 'Reds' Perreira looking pale and very much worse for the wear. He had had a severe attack of indigestion; however, we were on our way.

This strange incident meeting 'Reds' in the dark told me one thing: this young man is genuinely interested in sport. I don't think any normal individual not interested in sport would have left his bed in the wee hours of the morning to see the start of a race, particularly when they had no transportation. I think 'Reds' would have walked to Atkinson, if I or any other person had not come along to give him a ride. It was only natural from that time onwards that 'Reds' Perreira and I became more acquainted, discussing all the various ideas for the development of athletics/sports not only in Bookers, but in Guyana generally...

My friendship with 'Reds' Perreira grew, and when I eventually left Guyana in 1963 after nine very productive years, I was not surprised to learn that 'Reds', after former WICB President Kenny Wishart became the first Chairman of Guyana's Sports Council, followed in his footsteps. I have no doubt that 'Reds' Perreira is now a household name among international cricket enthusiasts listening to the cricket commentary from all the major cricketing countries in the world. 'Reds' brought a new dimension to cricket commentary in that he thoroughly learnt the game; studied its history, so that when describing a test match for example, he had at his fingertips a wide variety of records. What I think is particularly fascinating, is the colour 'Reds' would introduce during commentaries, not only about the various achievements of cricketing individuals in the game (especially past), but in other sports such as track and field...

I wish 'Reds' every success in his book. He has become a great success in the work he has done, especially in charge of OECS Sports, and I doubt anyone could have done the job as thoroughly and with the vision of 'Reds' Perreira.

E. MacDonald Bailey, Former Olympic Sprinter

25. I am a big fan of yours since I was a kid growing up and listening to you on the radio commentating on cricket, football, boxing and other sports. I lost my sight at a young age in Guyana, and I can recall listening to you while I was in the hospital recovering from my unsuccessful operation.

I want to let you know how much comfort you have brought me, as a blind boy growing up, and even now. I can still recall how you would bring the game to life whenever you would come on for your commentary stint. I used to wonder how your time used to finish so fast, but it was when I grew up that I realised it was because I was enjoying it so much.

Subash Tribhuwan, March 8th, 2007

Milton Keynes UK
Ingram Content Group UK Ltd.
UKHW041503190724
26UKWH00084B/1423